ENGLISH PHONOLOGY

AMSTERDAM STUDIES IN THE THEORY AND HISTORY OF LINGUISTIC SCIENCE

General Editor
E. F. KONRAD KOERNER
(University of Ottawa)

Series IV - CURRENT ISSUES IN LINGUISTIC THEORY

Advisory Editorial Board

Henning Andersen (Los Angeles); Raimo Anttila (Los Angeles)
Thomas V. Gamkrelidze (Tbilisi); John E. Joseph (Hong Kong)
Hans-Heinrich Lieb (Berlin); Ernst Pulgram (Ann Arbor, Mich.)
E. Wyn Roberts (Vancouver, B.C.); Danny Steinberg (Tokyo)

Volume 99

John T. Jensen

English Phonology

ENGLISH PHONOLOGY

JOHN T. JENSEN
University of Ottawa

JOHN BENJAMINS PUBLISHING COMPANY
AMSTERDAM/PHILADELPHIA

1993

The paper used in this publication meets the minimum requirements of American National Standard for Information Sciences — Permanence of Paper for Printed Library Materials, ANSI Z39.48-1984.

Library of Congress Cataloging-in-Publication Data

Jensen, John T. (John Tillotson)
   English phonology / John T. Jensen.
      p.   cm. -- (Amsterdam studies in the theory and history of linguistic science. Series IV, Current issues in linguistic theory, ISSN 0304-0763; v. 99)
   Includes bibliographical references and index.
   1. English language-Phonology. I. Title. II. Series.
PE1133.J46   1993
421--dc20   93-36898
ISBN 90 272 3600 3 (Eur.) / 1-55619-551-6 (US) (Hb. alk. paper)   CIP
ISBN 90 272 3601 1 (Eur.) / 1-55619-555-9 (US) (Pb. alk. paper)

© Copyright 1993 - John T. Jensen.
No part of this book may be reproduced in any form, by print, photoprint, microfilm, or any other means, without written permission from the publisher.

John Benjamins Publishing Co. · P.O. Box 75577 · 1070 AN Amsterdam · Netherlands
John Benjamins North America · 821 Bethlehem Pike · Philadelphia, PA 19118 · USA

Contents

Preface ix

1 Introduction 1
    1.1   Phonology before *SPE* 1
    1.2   *SPE* phonology 7
    1.3   Phonological theory since *SPE* 11
        1.3.1   Autosegmental phonology 11
        1.3.2   Metrical phonology 15
        1.3.3   Prosodic phonology 17
        1.3.4   Underspecification theory 18
        1.3.5   Lexical phonology 20
    1.4   What is English? 21
    1.5   Overview 22

2 Segmental phonology 25
    2.1   Levels of representation 25
    2.2   English consonants 28
        2.2.1   Glottal stop 28
        2.2.2   Voiceless [w̥] 29
        2.2.3   Affricates 29
        2.2.4   Distinctive features of English consonants 30
        2.2.5   Segments with restricted distribution 32
    2.3   English vowels 34
        2.3.1   Short, lax vowels 34
        2.3.2   Tense vowels and diphthongs 35

		2.3.3 Diphthongs as single units	37
	2.4	Towards systematic phonemics	38
	2.5	Phonology and orthography	42
	2.6	Exercises	44

3 The syllable and the mora 47

	3.1	CV syllables	47
	3.2	More complex syllables	52
	3.3	The syllable in *SPE*	55
	3.4	The internal structure of the syllable	58
		3.4.1 The syllable boundary approach	58
		3.4.2 The autosegmental approach	59
		3.4.3 The constituent structure approach	62
		3.4.4 The moraic approach	62
	3.5	The syllable in English	65
		3.5.1 The onset	65
		3.5.2 The coda	68
		3.5.3 The Coda Condition	70
	3.6	Exercises	76

4 English stress 77

	4.1	Preliminaries	77
	4.2	A parametric approach to stress	78
		4.2.1 Quantity insensitive systems	79
		4.2.2 Quantity sensitive systems	86
	4.3	Stress assignment in English	91
		4.3.1 The English Stress Rule	91
		4.3.2 Stress retraction	96
	4.4	Word Tree Construction	98
	4.5	Destressing rules	102
		4.5.1 Prestress Destressing	102
		4.5.2 Poststress Destressing	104
		4.5.3 Medial Destressing	107
		4.5.4 Sonorant Destressing	108
	4.6	Summary of the stress rules	111
	4.7	The cyclicity of stress rules	111
	4.8	On the treatment of exceptions	115

4.9		Further reading 119
4.10		Exercises 119

5 Prosodic phonology 121

5.1	Prosodic constituents in phonology 121
	5.1.1 Why prosodic constituents? 121
	5.1.2 The prosodic hierarchy 123
5.2	The syllable (σ) and the foot (F) 125
5.3	The phonological word (ω) and the clitic group (C) 132
	5.3.1 The phonological word and Diphthong Shortening 132
	5.3.2 The clitic group (C) 134
5.4	The phonological phrase (φ) 137
5.5	The intonation phrase (I) 142
5.6	The phonological utterance (U) 147
5.7	The ordering of the rules 151
5.8	Conclusion 153
5.9	Exercises 153

6 Lexical phonology: the cyclic rules 155

6.1	Principles of lexical phonology 155
6.2	The interaction of morphology and phonology 158
	6.2.1 An affix sensitive to stress 158
	6.2.2 Zero derivation 160
6.3	The order of affixes 161
6.4	Rule cyclicity 164
6.5	The Strict Cycle Condition 165
6.6	CiV Tensing and s-Voicing 170
6.7	Interaction of stress rules with cyclic segmental rules 172
6.8	Other laxing processes 174
6.9	The morphology and phonology of English strong verbs 181
	6.9.1 Verbs suffixed at stratum 1 181
	6.9.2 Ablaut 183
6.10	Exercises 187

7 Lexical phonology: the postcyclic rules 189

| 7.1 | Vowel Shift .... 189 |

		7.1.1	Basic cases of Vowel Shift	189
		7.1.2	[oy]	196
		7.1.3	Another tensing rule	197
		7.1.4	Summary	199
	7.2	Velar Softening	199
	7.3	Palatalization	200
		7.3.1	Spirantization	204
		7.3.2	*SPE* on *right* and *righteous*	206
	7.4	Types of rule ordering	207
	7.5	Other word-level processes	209
	7.6	Vowel Reduction	211
	7.7	Stem-final Tensing	214
	7.8	Exercises	216

8 Postlexical phonology and conclusion ... 219

	8.1	Postlexical phonology	219
		8.1.1 Stop allophones	220
		8.1.2 *l*-Velarization	221
		8.1.3 Sonorant Devoicing	223
		8.1.4 Diphthong Shortening	223
		8.1.5 Other rules	224
		8.1.6 Summary	227
	8.2	Some other approaches	228
	8.3	General conclusion	235

References ... 239

Index ... 247

Preface

This book is intended as an introduction to the major issues in English phonology. While I have tried to be comprehensive, the treatment is by no means exhaustive. The framework is that of generative phonology, in particular metrical, prosodic, and lexical phonology. Some background in phonology is presupposed, including an understanding of the theory of distinctive features and familiarity with rule writing conventions and other notational conventions.

One of my major goals has been to present an internally consistent synthesis of material derived from many sources. One result is that I see syllabic, metrical and lexical phonology as forming a single integrated system unified by a hierarchy of prosodic categories extending from the mora to the utterance. This necessarily leads to considering the metrical system in terms of trees rather than grids, since grids are on a plane separate from the rest of the metrical structure and cannot be integrated into the prosodic hierarchy. Related to this is my rejection of stress-dependent resyllabification and ambisyllabicity in favour of rules that appeal to higher prosodic structure, such as the foot and the phonological word. All accounts that I am aware of that appeal to ambisyllabicity can be reanalyzed in terms of such units. Since prosodic units are required for independent reasons, I conclude that ambisyllabicity is superfluous. I have also strictly applied the lexical model of morphology in that I assume that inflection as well as derivation is performed in the lexicon. This implies that syntactic rules do not manipulate inflectional morphemes in any way: fully inflected forms, regular and irregular, emerge from the lexicon, where they are manipulated by the syntax as wholes. I have also confirmed the role of rule ordering in phonology. While some investigators would eliminate rules and ordering from phonology in an attempt to predict observed phenomena on the basis of representations and constraints, this does not seem to be a feasible approach when dealing with a substantial body of linguistic data from a single language.

This work has greatly benefited from the advice and assistance of numerous individuals and organizations. I am grateful to the University of Ottawa for having granted me a six-month sabbatical leave in the fall of 1990, when the bulk of the manuscript was prepared. The School of Graduate Studies and Research provided a grant which enabled me to obtain computing equipment which greatly aided the production of the manuscript and the final, camera-ready copy. Margaret Stong-Jensen read through numerous versions of the manuscript and made many valuable suggestions of both style and substance. I thank my students also, who found numerous difficulties in earlier versions of this work and made many suggestions for improvement. I am especially grateful to Kathleen Brannen, Audrey Caldeira, Carolyn Frielink, Sonya McCurdy, Monique McKee, Deanna Smith, Debbie Steele, and Julie Whitnell for their comments on Chapter 4, "English stress." I hope that the incorporation of their comments has resulted in considerable clarification of what is possibly the most difficult area of English phonology. Mohammad Vahedi read through the entire manuscript and made a number of valuable suggestions and corrections. Gwen Foss also read the manuscript and found numerous typographical and stylistic errors. Finally, many thanks to Danielle Heffernan, who read through numerous versions and made many valuable suggestions, helped to check cross-references, helped with the final layout, and helped with the preparation of the index. Of course, none of these individuals or institutions bears any blame for any remaining errors, inconsistencies, or other faults, which are entirely my responsibility.

1 Introduction

Phonology is concerned with the sound patterns of language. We can use the term GENERAL PHONOLOGY to refer to the theory of phonology and the analysis of the sound patterns of the languages of the world. A discussion of the phonology of a particular language, such as English, is the application of this theory to the sound pattern of that particular language. In this book we are primarily concerned with the phonology of English, but we will also refer to certain aspects of general phonological theory.

1.1 Phonology before *SPE*

The publication of Chomsky & Halle's *The Sound Pattern of English* (1968, hereafter *SPE*) was a major landmark of both phonological theory and the phonological description of English. This volume has formed the basis of discussion of phonological issues ever since its appearance, both for those who accept its premises and for those who reject them. The study of phonology has occupied the attention of scholars ever since there has been interest in language from a scientific (as opposed to literary) point of view. The oldest known phonological study is Pāṇini's (third century B.C.) grammar of Sanskrit, which includes a full description of morphology and syntax as well as phonology. The Greek and Roman grammarians compiled elaborate grammars of their languages, including the phonology. Our concerns are primarily with more recent trends in phonology. We will first discuss the development of American structuralist phonology, also known as TAXONOMIC PHONEMICS, and some inadequacies of this theory, and then turn to the manner in which these inadequacies are resolved in the theory of generative phonology. We will then be concerned with certain inadequacies in the *SPE* framework and attempts to resolve these in more recent developments.

Structuralist phonology sets the task of defining the contrasting sound units (PHONEMES) of a language on the basis of a procedure of segmentation and classification of phonetic transcriptions of utterances. Segmentation refers to breaking a sound chain into minimal units that can not be further divided. Classification refers to grouping the phonetic segments so obtained into sets of sounds such that, within each set, there are no sounds that can serve to contrast utterances, but sounds from different sets are potentially available for contrasting utterances. To take the stock example, both English and Thai have both aspirated and unaspirated stops. In Thai, the difference between aspirated and unaspirated segments can distinguish utterances, as in the examples of (1) (from Ladefoged 1971, 12).

(1) phaa   'to split'   tham   'to do'   khàt   'to interrupt'
     pàa   'forest'   tam   'to pound'   kàt   'to bite'
     bàa   'shoulder'   dam   'black'

In English, on the other hand, the presence or absence of aspiration never serves to distinguish utterances. Aspirated stops appear initially in words before a vowel and medially in words before a stressed vowel. Unaspirated stops do not occur in these positions, but do occur in all other positions.[1] The examples in (2) are representative.

(2)   *initially before*   *medially before*   *after word-*   *other positions*
         a vowel   *a stressed vowel*   *initial* s
     a. pin [ph]   appear [ph]   spin [p]   happy [p]
     b. tin [th]   attire [th]   stand [t]   hatter [r]
     c. kin [kh]   acquire [kh]   skin [k]   lacquer [k]

It would not be possible to substitute aspirated [ph] for unaspirated [p] or vice versa in (2a) and have the examples sound like English (although it might sound like English with a foreign accent). We say that aspirated [ph] and unaspirated [p] are in COMPLEMENTARY DISTRIBUTION, i.e., they never occur in the same environment, and so we group them together as one phoneme. The segments themselves are then referred to as ALLOPHONES of the phoneme. Two segments are said to be in FREE VARIATION if they can occur in the same environment but do not serve to contrast utterances. An example is the final stops in words like *tip, pit,* and *pick,*

---

[1] Although this is the stock example of allophonic variation, it is not so easy to describe the environments in which the different allophones of stops occur in English. We will return to this problem in Chapter 5.

which can be released or unreleased (we mark unreleased stops thus: [p̚, t̚, k̚]). Similarly, we can group aspirated [kʰ], unaspirated [k] and unreleased [k̚] as one phoneme; likewise the four segments aspirated [tʰ], unaspirated [t], unreleased [t̚], and the flap [ɾ]. Schematically, we can write the formulas in (3), where virgules (/) enclose phonemes and braces represent sets.

(3) a. /p/ = {[pʰ], [p], [p̚]}
     b. /t/ = {[tʰ], [t], [t̚], [ɾ]}
     c. /k/ = {[kʰ], [k], [k̚]}

Continuing in this manner, structuralist linguists claim that one could ultimately discover all the phonemes of the language and their allophones together with statements concerning the distribution of the allophones. Most structuralist linguists also insisted that this cataloguing of segments into phonemes should be done without reference to any grammatical information, to avoid what they referred to as "mixing levels." Hockett (1942, 20–21), for example, insists that "no grammatical fact of any kind is used in making phonological analysis," and "[t]here must be no circularity: phonological analysis is assumed for grammatical analysis, and so must not assume any part of the latter. The line of demarcation between the two must be sharp."

While this seems entirely straightforward, it is not without difficulties. Phonemic analysis of this type can in fact produce a fairly close approximation to an analysis of a language within the limits that the theory imposes. However, there are numerous difficulties with this theory, which ultimately require us to reject it. An analogy is provided by physics. The Newtonian model of physics, which held sway for several hundred years, is a close approximation to a description of the behaviour of matter and energy in the natural world. However, Newtonian physics has to be rejected in the light of more recent discoveries, such as the structure of subatomic particles and the interconvertability of matter and energy, made famous by Einstein's equation $E = mc^2$. Newtonian mechanics may still prove useful in determining planetary orbits or calculating the trajectory of rockets. Likewise, taxonomic phonemics may be applicable in language teaching, although in a more theoretical discussion it proves to be inadequate.

The difficulties encountered in phonemic analysis did not go unnoticed in the literature of structuralist linguists. Harris (1951), perhaps the most careful attempt to codify the analytical procedures of structural linguistics in both phonology and morphology, discusses a number of them. Chomsky (1964) is a major critique of taxonomic phonemics. We can consider two types of difficulties, which we refer to as NEUTRALIZATION and PSEUDODIFFERENTIATION.

Neutralization occurs when two or more distinct segments of a language are merged in some context. A familiar example of this is word-final obstruent devoicing in German. The words *Bund* 'union' and *bunt* 'colourful' are pronounced identically: [bʊnt]. But if an inflectional suffix *-e* is added, the difference emerges: [bʊndə] versus [bʊntə]. Strictly following the procedure of segmentation and classification would require setting up two phonemic allomorphs of the word for 'union,' /bʊnd/ and /bʊnt/, because /d/ and /t/ contrast in other environments: *Draht* [draːt] 'wire' versus *trat* [traːt] 'stepped.' Worse, this redundancy of representation would be required for literally hundreds of morphemes in the language. If, however, we eliminate the requirement that segments that contrast in some environment are necessarily members of distinct phonemes, you can simply set up one underlying representation for 'union,' namely /bʊnd/, and have one general rule that devoices obstruents in word-final position.

As an example from English, consider the neutralization of *t* and *d* in medial position in words like *writer* and *rider*. In most North American varieties of English, the medial stop in both these words is pronounced as a flap [ɾ]. Because the flap never contrasts with either *t* or *d,* we do not want to analyze the flap as a separate phoneme. Because *t* and *d* do contrast in words like *write* and *ride* or *tie* and *dye,* we set up two phonemes /t/ and /d/. To which of these phonemes does the flap belong? If we say that it belongs to both of them, we have a case of OVERLAPPING ALLOPHONES, which structuralist phonologists tried to avoid because it made it difficult to determine the phonemes purely on the basis of the phonetic record.

This same example also illustrates pseudodifferentiation. In many varieties of English, vowels are noticeably longer before voiced consonants than before voiceless ones. In the case of diphthongs, there is generally a qualitative difference as well; in particular, the diphthong [ɑy] is more like [əy] before voiceless consonants. Thus we have the contrast in (4).

(4) a. write [rəyt]
    b. ride [rɑyd]

But in pairs like *writer* and *rider,* where the medial consonant is neutralized to a flap, the difference in the diphthong becomes the sole phonetic distinction between the two words, as in (5).

(5) a. writer [rəyɾər]
    b. rider [rɑyɾər]

We call this pseudodifferentiation because the two types of diphthongs are contrastive only before flap. In all other environments the two types of diphthongs are in complementary distribution. But because they contrast in the single environment before the flap, the usual criteria of taxonomic phonemics requires that these diphthongs form separate phonemes. To avoid this absurd conclusion, Harris (1951, 70–71) suggests that the phonetic sequence [əyɾ] be phonemicized as /ayt/ as a unit and that the phonetic sequence [ɑyɾ] be phonemicized as /ayd/ as a unit. As Chomsky (1964, 87) points out, "this is a rather vague notion, and it is not at all clear how it would fare once clarified." The implication is that statements of allophone distribution should be replaced by general phonological rules or processes that can interact in producing the observed complexity of phonetic representations. The stop allophones given in (3) would be the result of rules applying to more abstract representations. For example, a general rule providing aspiration for all voiceless stops in a particular position replaces the separate allophonic statements for /p/, /t/, and /k/.

Harris's proposal destroys the generality of two phonological processes in English. One is a process that determines the distribution of the diphthongs [əy] and [ɑy], which we can refer to as Dɪᴘʜᴛʜᴏɴɢ Sʜᴏʀᴛᴇɴɪɴɢ (following Nespor & Vogel 1986). This rule converts /ay/ to [əy] before *any* voiceless consonant, not just *t*. We give a precise formulation of this rule in Chapter 5, section 5.3. Note the diphthong in *wipe, like, rice, fife,* as opposed to *tribe, rise, five.* The second is the rule that determines the distribution of flaps, which we simply call Fʟᴀᴘᴘɪɴɢ. In Chapter 5, section 5.7, we will give a more precise statement of this rule. One environment where it appears is after a stressed vowel before an unstressed vowel. This will suffice for our illustration here. On the uncontroversial assumption that *writer* and *rider* are derived from the verbs *write* and *ride,* respectively, by the addition of an agentive suffix, here represented as /-ər/, and assuming that Diphthong Shortening and Flapping apply to the underlying representations after affixation *in that order,* we obtain the derivations in (6).

(6)   a. /rait + ər/ 'writer'   b. /raid + ər/ 'rider'
           rəitər   —   Diphthong Shortening
           rəɪɾər   raɪɾər   Flapping
           [rəɪɾər]   [raɪɾər] output

It is clear that Diphthong Shortening depends on the underlying representation of the consonant that follows the diphthong, not on the phonetic representation. This ordering of rules is known as a ᴄᴏᴜɴᴛᴇʀʙʟᴇᴇᴅɪɴɢ ᴏʀᴅᴇʀ. If these rules applied in the opposite order Flapping would ʙʟᴇᴇᴅ Diphthong Shortening by destroying the conditions for its application. This is the first of numerous examples where applying rules in a particular order allows us to retain the most general form of the rules. This concept is a major hallmark of phonological theory in *SPE*, and will be especially important in our development of the segmental phonology of English in Chapters 6 and 7.

A second example of pseudodifferentiation was first discussed by Malécot (1960). In many varieties of English, vowels are nasalized if a nasal consonant follows. The nasal consonant may be retained, as in the example of (7b), or it may be absent phonetically, as in the example of (7d).

(7)   a. 'had'   [hæd]
      b. 'hand'   [hænd]
      c. 'cat'   [kæt]
      d. 'can't'   [kæ̃t]

The examples of (7c, d) illustrate a minimal contrast between *can't,* with a nasal vowel [kæ̃t], and *cat,* with an oral vowel [kæt]. This has led to analyses in which nasal vowels are phonemic (i.e., contrastive) in English, for example Pilch (1976, 132). Indeed this is the inescapable conclusion of the assumption that phonological analysis consists of constructing exactly two levels of analysis: the phonetic level, as transcribed by the phonetician, and the phonemic level, constructed on the basis of contrasts and complementarity in the phonetic level. This is again a case of pseudodifferentiation, because nasal vowels contrast with their nonnasal counterparts *only before voiceless consonants.* In other environments the nasalization is completely predictable, as in (7c, d). In discussing this example, Chomsky (1964, 82) observes that a perfectly general and straightforward analysis involves the two rules in (8), applied in this order.

(8)   a. *Vowel Nasalization*

$$V \rightarrow [+\text{nasal}] / \underline{\hspace{1em}} \begin{bmatrix} C \\ +\text{nasal} \end{bmatrix}$$

      b. *Nasal Consonant Deletion*

$$\begin{bmatrix} C \\ +\text{nasal} \end{bmatrix} \rightarrow \emptyset / \begin{bmatrix} V \\ -\text{tense} \end{bmatrix} \underline{\hspace{1em}} \begin{bmatrix} C \\ -\text{voiced} \end{bmatrix}$$

These two rules in this order account for the distribution of nasal vowels in English. The words *cat* and *had* have no nasal consonant, and so will never have a nasal vowel. The vowel of both *hand* and *can't* is nasalized by rule (8a). The nasal consonant is deleted in *can't* by rule (8b), giving rise to the superficial contrast. This order is another example of a counterbleeding order. The nasal consonant is somewhat abstract in that it causes a phonological change (nasalization) without itself being phonetically realized. Nevertheless, because it is transparently related to the modal *can,* this abstractness is motivated. In *hand,* (8b) is not applicable, and so the nasal consonant remains along with the nasalized vowel.

1.2 *SPE* phonology

SPE was the culmination of a number of works on phonological theory, drawing inspiration from several sources. One is the development of distinctive feature theory, which holds that the primitive units of language are not phonemes but smaller units, features, that combine to define phonemes. Another is the development of generative grammar as an explicit system for generating the utterances of a language. Generative grammar recognized the implications of syntactic and morphological representations for phonology. Pike (1947) recognized this also, but most structuralists insisted that the phonemes should be discovered before proceeding to morphological analysis. Finally, generative grammar made extensive use of rule ordering, observing that rules can be made more general if they are stipulated to apply in a particular order. This too has a structuralist precedent in Bloomfield (1939) and ultimately goes back to Pāṇini. Above all, the goal of a generative grammar is to provide the simplest possible grammar for a language, where simplicity (in phonology) is measured in terms of the number of symbols required to represent its underlying representations and the rules that relate these to phonetic representations. *SPE* is now referred to as a LINEAR theory of phonology, in that its representations are a linear sequence of segments and boundaries. Furthermore, *SPE* tied phonology to syntax, claiming that the job of phonology is to interpret the surface syntactic structure phonetically. This surface syntactic structure in turn is derived by inserting lexical items into constituent structure trees, which may have to undergo various sorts of transformations before deriving the surface syntactic structure on which phonological rules can operate.

The surface syntactic structure is ABSTRACT in a number of different senses. Most obviously, its terminal nodes are organized into a hierarchical constituent structure which can influence the phonological derivation.[2] Second, it may contain abstract FORMATIVES (morphemes) with semantic but no phonological content. One such formative specifically discussed in *SPE* is the past tense morpheme, represented as simply *past*. It enters into collocations such as those in (9) with two different verb stems.[3]

(9) a. [[mend] past]
    b. [[sing] past]

In order to derive the phonetic representations, *SPE* invokes (largely inexplicit) READJUSTMENT RULES that replace the formative *past* by the phonological *d* in the case of (9a), but replace the entire form in (9b) by the form [sæng]. Obviously, the readjustment rules are rules of a particularly powerful type. We will suggest that for (9a) the surface syntactic structure actually contains [[mend] d] and that no readjustment rule is needed. For (9b) we will suggest in Chapter 6 that a distinct past morpheme is present in the surface structure, one that has the effect of making the stem vowel [+low].

The third form of abstractness in *SPE*, and the most criticized, concerns the underlying representation of morphemes. An underlying representation can be considered abstract to the extent that it differs from its phonetic forms. It should be emphasized at this point that *SPE*, and generative phonology generally, adheres to the NATURALNESS CONDITION of Postal (1968), which requires that underlying representations be given in terms of the same phonological features as are used for phonetic representations. This is in contrast to some structuralist phonologists who wished to use nonphonetic symbols for underlying forms. Nevertheless, even if they adhere to the Naturalness Condition, underlying representations can be fairly abstract. The underlying representations in the derivations of (6) are not particularly abstract. Although the underlying /t/ appears phonetically as a flap in *writer*, it is phonetically a [t] (but usually glottalized) in *write*. The shortened version of the diphthong is not distinctive, and so its derivation from the longer version is not particularly abstract. Such remarks apply also to the glottalization of the final *t* of *write*. However, *SPE* proposed much more abstract representations than these.

---

[2] In Chapter 5, we will examine evidence that it is not the syntactic surface structure that directly influences the phonological derivation, but rather a prosodic structure derived from the surface structure.

[3] We adopt Halle & Mohanan's (1985) notation of double square brackets [ ] to indicate constituent boundaries in order to distinguish them from regular square brackets [ ], used to indicate distinctive feature complexes or phonetic transcriptions.

One concerns a set of vowel alternations that collectively go by the name Vowel Shift.[4] In order to account for the vowel alternations in such pairs as *sane~sanity, serene~serenity,* and *sublime~sublimity, SPE* set the stem morphemes up with underlying vowels that are underlyingly tense and that have the quality of the lax member of each pair, thus /sæn/, /sɛrēn/, /səblīm/. In the suffixed form, the vowel is laxed by the rule Trisyllabic Laxing, to be discussed in detail in Chapter 7. In the unsuffixed form, the vowels remain tense and are subject to a complex set of rules that change their quality and add a diphthongal element, so that /æ/ becomes [ēy], /ē/ becomes [īy], and /ī/ becomes [āy]. This is abstract because an underlying tense vowel never emerges unchanged in phonetic representations: it is always either laxed or vowel shifted. This treatment of English vowel alternations has encountered some criticism, and a number of psycholinguistic experiments have been performed to test the psychological reality of these underlying representations (see Jaeger 1986, for example). The experimental results are somewhat inconclusive and to a certain extent misleading, in that they impute more phonetic sophistication to human beings than they can reasonably be expected to have (unless of course they have studied linguistics). It is not unreasonable to assume that English speakers relate [æ] and [ēy] on the basis of the alternations that occur in the language. The persistence of conventional spelling, i.e., using the letter <a> for both, as well as the convention of some dictionaries of notating these sounds as [ă] versus [ā] attests to the robustness of the relation between these pairs of sounds. In Chapter 2, we will discuss an additional advantage of deriving English diphthongs from underlying simple vowels, which is that the diphthongs maintain their integrity even before another vowel, so that *Toyota,* for example, is syllabified *toy.o.ta,* and not *to.yo.ta* (as it would be in Japanese).

Other abstract analyses in *SPE* have not fared so well. A particularly notorious case is the analysis of *right* with the underlying form /rɪxt/. The argument for this form is ingenious and intricate, and we will defer full discussion of it until Chapter 7, section 7.3.2, when we will have developed enough analysis to explain it. Although it is completely logical at every step, many linguists found it qualitatively more difficult to accept than vowel shift. For one thing, it involves postulating an underlying segment /x/ which does not appear phonetically in any English word. *SPE* found other uses for this underlying segment, thereby making its postulation appear more plausible. For example, the word *nightingale* was given an underlying representation with a velar fricative in the first syllable: /nɪxtɪngæl/.

---

[4] Strictly speaking, Vowel Shift is one of several rules that together produce the alternations in question. However, the term is also used loosely to refer to the complex of rules and to the alternations produced by them.

This was done in order to account for the appearance of a tense vowel (realized as a diphthong) in the first syllable, in apparent violation of the rule of Trisyllabic Laxing. *SPE* ordered the rules converting the sequence /ix/ to [ɪ̄] after Trisyllabic Laxing. These analyses, though ingenious, are not compelling. We will consider some alternative analyses of such words in Chapter 6.

A major portion of *SPE* is devoted to the analysis of English stress, both in words and in phrases. An important principle of stress assignment is the PHONOLOGICAL CYCLE. This is the idea that the same set of ordered rules can apply several times to the same form, first to the innermost morphological constituent, then to the next larger constituent, and so on, until the maximum domain is processed. Most of the *SPE* stress rules assign primary stress, which they denote by [1 stress]. Lower degrees of stress are denoted by successively larger numbers, e.g., [2 stress] for secondary stress. *SPE* adopts the STRESS SUBORDINATION CONVENTION, according to which, whenever primary stress is assigned within a domain, all previously existing stresses within that domain are reduced by one degree. Within words, this system stresses the word *theatricality* by first assigning primary stress to *thé̀atre*, then assigning primary stress in *theátricàl*, at which point the originally assigned primary stress is reduced to secondary, and finally assigning primary stress in *thèatricálity*, when both previously assigned stresses are reduced by one degree. The same conventions apply within phrases, so that *blàck boárd* 'board that is black' appears with the indicated stresses. A phrase like *sàd plíght* has that stress contour in isolation but the stress contour *sằd plíght* in the sentence *my friend can't help being shocked at anyone who would fail to consider his sad plight*, because "the surface structure might indicate that the word *plight* terminates no less than seven phrases to which the Nuclear Stress Rule applies" (*SPE*, 23), so that primary stress is assigned to *plight* on seven successive cycles. (The Nuclear Stress Rule is the rule that assigns primary stress to the rightmost member of a phrase.) They acknowledge, however, that "the internal relations of stress in *sad plight* are the same" in the sentence as in shorter phrases or in isolation. Recent work on English stress has retained the principle of the cycle for word-internal stress, but uses different means for explaining the stress contour in phrases, a point we will examine in detail in Chapter 4. This system resolves the dilemma posed in SPE of representing the same stress contour of *sad plight* with different numerical values such as 2–1 and 8–1 that we have just seen.

Chomsky & Halle presented *SPE* as "an interim report on work in progress rather than an attempt to present a definitive and exhaustive study of phonological processes in English" (p. vii). Subsequent work has suggested a number of improvements, changes, and complete reanalyses of various aspects of English phonology. In the next section, we will highlight some of the most important recent developments.

1.3 Phonological theory since *SPE*

Five important developments characterize the direction of phonological theory since *SPE*. Three of these challenge the linear character of *SPE*'s representations: AUTOSEGMENTAL PHONOLOGY, METRICAL PHONOLOGY, and PROSODIC PHONOLOGY. Phonology appealing to these models is therefore referred to as NONLINEAR phonology. Another model, UNDERSPECIFICATION THEORY, challenges *SPE*'s assumption that phonological representations are fully specified, and removes as much predictable information from underlying representations as possible. Finally, LEXICAL PHONOLOGY has the effect of enriching the formal apparatus of phonological rules and includes a specific proposal for integrating phonology with morphology. In this section, we will discuss each of these in turn.

1.3.1 *Autosegmental phonology*

One area that *SPE* left quite untouched was tone. In view of the number and variety of tone languages among the languages of the world, and the variety of processes involving tone, this was a lacuna that had to be filled. It turned out that an adequate representation of tone required a radical departure from the linear approach of SPE. This departure came to be called autosegmental phonology (Goldsmith 1976), a term coined as a blend of *autonomous* and *segmental*. The idea is that some features are represented apart from others, on a separate TIER, and are associated to matrices of other features by association lines. An example should help make this clear.

Leben (1973) first noticed that, in Mende, the tonal contours that could appear on morphemes were independent of the segmental content of those morphemes. Leben established five tonal contours that could appear on short vowels in Mende: *high, low, falling, rising,* and *rising–falling*. These could appear on morphemes of one, two, or three syllables as shown in (10).

(10) a. high tone   pélé, kó
     b. low tone   bèlè, kpà
     c. falling tone   kényè, mbû
     d. rising tone   nìká, nàvó, mbǎ
     e. rising–falling tone nìkílì, nyàhâ, mbâ̌

Leben concludes that tone is represented on a TIER separate from the segmental features, and that words get their tones by ASSOCIATION: at the underlying level, tones are not associated with segments. Simple tones (high, low) are represented as a single tone specification. Contour tones are represented as a sequence of simple tones: falling tone is the sequence high–low; rising–falling tone is the sequence low–high–low. Tones are associated to vowels one to one and left to right. If any vowels receive no tone by this procedure, the tone to their left SPREADS to them. If tones are left over after all vowels are associated with tones, then the remaining tones attach to vowels already associated with tones, producing contour tones. This association procedure produces the pattern shown in (10). Separating tonal features from segments, and introducing rules of association, admittedly creates a more complex perspective than the *SPE* linear arrangement, where tones are part of the segmental features defining each segment. Nevertheless, an *SPE*-type analysis would have real difficulty representing contour tones on short vowels at all, except by adopting tone features such as those developed by Wang (1967), which explicitly built in tone contours with such features as [rising], etc. Furthermore, an *SPE*-style analysis could not capture the generalization that there are exactly five tone patterns that can be associated with morphemes of varying length, since there would be nothing common to the forms of (10a), for example, where a high tone is realized on the single syllable of a monosyllabic word but on both syllables of a disyllabic word, or to the forms of (10c), where a falling tone is divided among the two syllables of disyllabic forms but realized on the single vowel of a monosyllabic form.

A second reason for introducing autosegmental formalism is to describe tonal stability. In many tone languages the deletion of a segment does not entail the deletion of its tone. This is difficult to express in the *SPE* framework, where all the features defining a segment are contained within a single feature matrix. However, if tone is represented as a separate tier, we can have a rule that deletes the segmental features, while the tone features remain to be associated with some other segment. An example comes from Yoruba (Pulleyblank 1990), where a verb-final vowel is optionally deleted if the next word begins with a vowel. When this happens, the second vowel acquires the tone of the deleted vowel, as shown in (11).[5]

(11) a. rí igba   rígbá   'see a calabash'
     b. ríaso   ráso   'see cloth'
     c. ríobè   róbê   'see soup'

---

[5] An acute accent indicates high tone, a grave accent indicates low tone, and the circumflex accent indicates falling tone. Mid tone is not marked.

Stability affects not only tone: in Yoruba, nasality is also retained when a vowel is deleted. It is then associated with an adjacent vowel, as seen in (12).

(12)   kpíolú   kpõlú   'divide mushrooms'

In these examples tone features and nasality seem to act independently of other features.

While tone provided the original motivation for the development of autosegmental theory, this theory was later extended to other features whose domain covered more than a single segment. An example is VOWEL HARMONY. In Turkish, a word normally has only back vowels or only front vowels, but not both. Suffixes have different forms for use with back vowel and front vowel words; for example the plural suffix is *-lar* after back vowels and *-ler* after front vowel words.[6] The vowels of stems are fixed. We can say that stems are associated with a morpheme-size feature for [back], which is associated with each vowel of the stem and which spreads to suffix vowels, which initially have no specification for this feature. In this case, we say that suffix vowels are UNDERSPECIFIED for the harmonic feature. Since vowel harmony is relatively easy to express in SPE terms using an iterative rule of vowel assimilation, it provides weaker motivation for autosegmentalism than tone systems do. Nevertheless, an autosegmental analysis of harmony expresses the generalization that each word in Turkish is associated to a single value of [back], rather than associating each vowel separately (and accidentally) with the same value of this feature. Both types of analysis must deal with certain complications, such as those posed by the neutral vowels in Hungarian, Finnish, and Mongolian, where certain vowels are skipped in the harmony process.

This extension of autosegmental theory gives rise to problems of its own. The most obvious of these is the question of what segments can be autosegmental. Some analyses of vowel harmony even allowed the same feature to be specified both segmentally and autosegmentally. Clearly, some constraints were needed. In the most recent versions of autosegmental theory, *all* features are autosegmental, but arranged according to a strict hierarchy. Such a model was proposed in Clements (1985). In (13) we present the version proposed by Sagey (1986), which seems to be the one most commonly accepted today. The feature hierarchy is an area of ongoing research and the exact disposition of features varies from one author to the next.

---

[6] We are ignoring the complication in high-vowel suffixes, which also vary in rounding depending on the roundness of the vowel immediately preceding them.

(13)

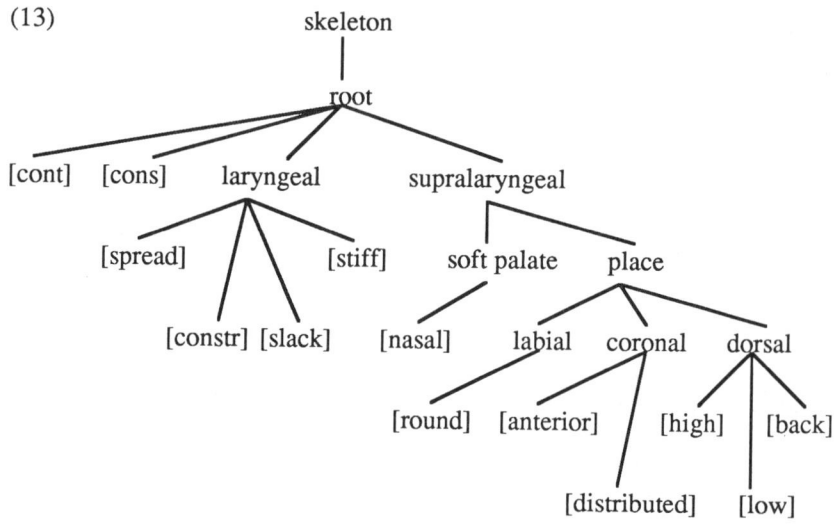

The SKELETON is a linear sequence of TIMING ELEMENTS. These can be represented abstractly either as a series of C (for consonant) and V (for vowel), as argued for in McCarthy (1981), Clements & Keyser (1983), and others, or alternatively as a series of X for consonants and vowels (Levin 1985). The difference in these two approaches is that Levin's Xs get their syllabicity from their position within a syllable rather than by a label on the skeleton. In a more recent analysis the root node is considered to be dominated by a mora constituent within the syllable. We develop this approach in Chapter 3.

In (13), the actual features are given in square brackets, according to the usual convention. The remaining nodes are CLASS NODES, which in turn dominate other class nodes or features. Part of the motivation for this hierarchical arrangement is phonetic, in that features are grouped together on the basis of the articulators involved in their production. Another part of the motivation is phonological: the place node exists because it is very common for place of articulation to be involved in an assimilation rule. For example, when a nasal consonant assimilates in place of articulation to a following obstruent, we can describe the process as the spreading of the place node from the obstruent to the nasal.

The autosegmental formalism provides a way to represent affricates and long segments without using nonarticulatory features. In SPE, affricates were assigned the feature [+delayed release]. This fails to capture the idea that an affricate is a sequence of a stop plus a fricative within the confines of a single segment. An autosegmental representation avoids this problem by associating two values of the feature [continuant] to a single timing slot, as in (14a), where the full details of the hierarchy are omitted for simplicity. Similarly, a long segment can be represented as in (14b), where a single set of features for the vowel [a] are associated to two timing slots. This representation allows us to avoid appealing to a feature [long].[7]

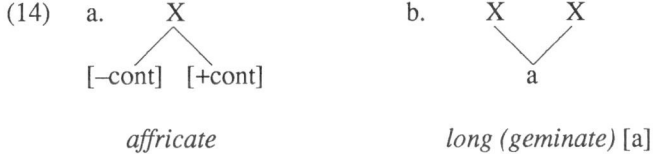

(14) a. affricate   b. long (geminate) [a]

At the present time, representations like (14a) are no longer needed for representing affricates. Recent work (LaCharité 1992) has shown that affricates can be phonologically represented as strident stops, since affrication is never the only difference between stops and affricates. This is certainly true for English, where the affricates [č, ǰ] do not contrast with stops. These affricates are alveopalatal, but the stops are labial, alveolar and velar. This is reflected in our consonant inventory for English discussed in Chapter 2. Representations like (14b) can still be used for the representation of segmental length, but we will do this in terms of moras in Chapter 3, not in terms of timing units.

Autosegmental phonology has not had much influence on English phonology, perhaps because English has neither tone nor vowel harmony, the two domains where Autosegmental formalism has had the most success. Nevertheless, it is important to gain some familiarity with this theory, since it has been very influential in the recent development of phonological theory.

1.3.2 Metrical phonology

The original motivation for the development of metrical phonology was the unease that some workers felt at the *SPE* representation of stress in English. While all other features were binary, i.e., they could assume only the values plus and minus, stress was an n-ary feature, which was allowed to assume numerical values. Primary stress was represented by [1stress], secondary stress by [2stress], and so on. Lack of stress was represented by [0stress]. Not only was stress n-ary, the number of possible values for this feature was unlimited. The reason is that

---

[7] *SPE* avoided the feature [long] in English by using the feature [tense]. But many analyses in the SPE tradition assumed a feature [long]. In Chapter 7 we will see that both length and tenseness are required for an adequate analysis of English vowels, but we will represent length in terms of moras rather than in terms of a feature [long].

stress is assigned to words and phrases, and in principle there is no upper limit on the length of words or phrases. *SPE* also assumed that any stress domain can have only one primary stress. If a stress domain is expanded by the addition of another word or phrase, another cycle of stress rules is required and all stresses save the one assigned primary stress on that cycle are reduced by the stress subordination convention in such a way that they retain their values relative to each other. As a simple example, consider English compounds. In *bláckbòard*, *black* has primary stress and *board* has secondary stress. If we expand this to *bláckbòard eràser*, *black* retains primary stress, *eraser* now has secondary stress, but *board* is reduced to tertiary stress. Since there is no limit on the size of compound nouns produced in this manner, there can be no upper limit on the possible values for the feature [stress]. Clearly, [stress] has a peculiar status within the panoply of *SPE* features. No other feature has values that depend on another value of that feature at an arbitrary distance within some domain.

Liberman & Prince (1977) sought to remedy this problem by setting up relations among constituents to represent relative degrees of prominence. They proposed metrical trees, with binary branches, such that every node of the tree would dominate a strong node (designated *s*) and a weak node *(w)*. Such branching nodes could be embedded within other branching structures, thus capturing the facts of stress subordination without changing stress numbers within complex domains. For example, our *blackboard* example has the metrical structure [sw]. *Blackboard eraser* has the metrical structure [[sw]$_s$ w]. The labelling within *blackboard* does not change just because it is embedded in a larger structure. Thus metrical relations remain binary and local. This also solves the problem that *SPE* noted with the stress contour of the phrase *sad plight*, discussed in section 1.2, which in the long sentence received the stress contour 8–1. In the Liberman & Prince formalism, it would simply be marked [ws] regardless of how deeply embedded it was.

Liberman & Prince retained the feature [stress], reducing it to a binary feature in line with other *SPE* features. This accounts for contrasts such as *gýmnàst* vs *témpest*, where both are labelled [sw]. The difference is that *gymnast* has two syllables labelled [+stress], while in *tempest* only the first syllable is so marked.[8] Later research (e.g., Selkirk 1980b) in metrical structures eliminated the feature [stress] altogether by introducing the concept FOOT. A foot can be defined as a

---

[8] These two words do not have contrastive stress patterns for all speakers. The contrast appears in other pairs, such as *ánnèx* vs *Phóenix*.

domain containing exactly one stressed syllable. Under this conception, *gymnast* has two feet while *tempest* has only one. We will look at metrical structures in English, including the foot, in Chapter 4. We will study these structures in great detail, since the description of stress is one of the key problems in any discussion of English phonology.

It is quite interesting that metrical structures that were developed to provide a more reasonable representation of stress than the *SPE* numerical system turned out to have important consequences for the description of purely segmental phenomena as well, phenomena that *SPE* dealt with inadequately or not at all. The allophones of English stops are predictable only in terms of metrical (and other prosodic) categories. For example, voiceless stops in English are aspirated at the beginning of a foot (see Kiparsky 1979). We will discuss these processes in greater detail in Chapter 5.

1.3.3 Prosodic phonology

The principal motivation for prosodic phonology comes from a consideration of the domains over which phonological rules operate. This in turn requires that explicit provision be made for the way in which phonology fits into a more inclusive model of grammar, specifically its relation to syntax and morphology. *SPE* assumed what is now known as the T-model of grammar,[9] which can be diagrammed as in (15) (modified from Chomsky 1981, 17).

(15)
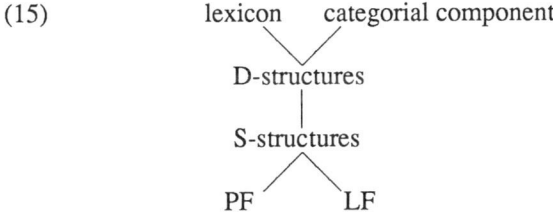

The categorial component generates phrase markers in terms of X-bar theory. For every lexical category X (=N, V, A, P, etc.) a series of phrasal categories X', X" (read "X-bar, X-double-bar") is projected. The highest bar level for N (noun), for example, is N". This is equivalent to NP of older models, which is still used as the

---

[9] So called because it is sometimes diagrammed in such a way as to resemble the letter T, as in (i).

(i)
$$\frac{\text{syntax}}{\text{phonology} \mid \text{semantics}}$$

equivalent of N″. The same pattern holds for the other syntactic categories. The lexicon is a relatively trivial component of this model of grammar, consisting only of a list of morphemes. These combine to form D-structures (formerly called "deep structures") which are operated on by transformational rules to create S-structures (formerly "surface structures"). S-structures are subject to two interpretive components: the phonological component, which produces PF (phonetic form), and the semantic component, which produces LF (logical form). As we mentioned in section 1.2, SPE allows for some readjustment rules to intervene between the output of the syntax and the input to the phonology. In addition to rules spelling out grammatical formatives, they propose readjustment rules that divide complex syntactic expressions into ' "phonological phrases," each of which is a maximal domain for phonological processes' (*SPE*, 9).

The theory of prosodic phonology claims that readjustment is hardly an appropriate term, since phonological rules do not operate on syntactic representations at all, but on phonological representations derived from syntactic structures but bearing little resemblance to the latter. Prosodic phonology includes a category of PHONOLOGICAL PHRASES, thus making this suggestion of *SPE* explicit. But prosodic phonology is not restricted to breaking down phrases of great length or complexity. In prosodic phonology, phonological phrases are part of a hierarchy of prosodic categories, the smallest of which is the syllable[10] and the largest of which is the phonological utterance (which may include more than one sentence). In some ways, prosodic phonology can be considered an extension of metrical phonology, since the prosodic hierarchy includes the syllable and the foot, two important concepts in metrical phonology. Phonological rules can be written to apply within prosodic categories (DOMAIN SPAN rules), at the juncture of two categories of a given type (DOMAIN JUNCTURE rules) or at the end of a category (DOMAIN LIMIT rules). This terminology is derived from Selkirk (1980a), and adopted by Nespor & Vogel (1986), the major discussion of prosodic phonology. We will consider a number of applications of this theory to English in Chapter 5.

1.3.4 Underspecification theory

The theory of underspecification challenges the *SPE* assumption that underlying representations are completely specified, that is, that each segment contains a mark plus or minus (or, in chapter 9, *m* for marked or *u* for unmarked) for every feature. *SPE* required this because of a fear that, by leaving certain features unspecified, the blanks could be interpreted as a third feature value, distinct from both plus and minus. Underspecification theory counters this by requiring that

---

[10] In other treatments of prosodic phonology, the smallest unit in the prosodic hierarchy is the mora, a constituent of the syllable. See the discussion of the mora in Chapter 3, section 3.4.4.

blanks be filled in by appropriate redundancy rules at a point in the derivation before the redundant value is actually referred to. For any feature [F], only one value, say [+F], will be present in underlying representations. The value [–F] is not present underlyingly; it is considered redundant and is filled in by a redundancy rule. But this must occur before any phonological rule can refer to [–F]. In this way, the blank in the underlying form can never be interpreted as distinct from both plus and minus.

This type of representation can allow vast amounts of redundant information to be removed from underlying representations. It also has obvious advantages in describing vowel harmony systems. Since the value for [back] on suffix vowels in Turkish is entirely predictable from the value of this feature in stems, suffix vowels can be left unspecified for [back]. One value of [back] will be present in the lexical entries of stems, say [+back]. If this value is present on a particular stem, it will spread to suffix vowels. If the stem is unspecified for [back], no spreading takes place, and stem and suffix vowels alike are assigned [–back] by default. This means that it is unnecessary to spread both values of the harmonic feature, and that spreading does not have to change the values of underlying forms. In this conception, rules fill in feature values rather than change them.

An analysis in underspecified terms must choose which value of each feature to specify and which features to specify. In her analysis of the Yawelmani vowel system, Archangeli (1984) represents the four vowels of the language in terms of just the two underlying features [high] and [round]. By the end of the derivation, vowels have to be specified for (at least) [low] and [back] as well. However, her underlying features are the ones most important for vowel harmony, which spreads the feature [+round]. In a similar vein, she argues that Japanese, Telegu, and Spanish, each with the same basic five-vowel system {i, e, a, o, u}, have different underlying feature specifications for the vowels, as in (16).

(16)   a. Japanese   b. Telegu   c. Spanish

         i e a o u   i e a o u   i e a o u
[high]   – –   – –   +   +
[low]   +   +   +
[back]   + +   – –   + +

These specifications have implications for various aspects of the phonologies of these languages. To mention just one example, each language has one vowel with no feature specifications underlyingly. An analysis of each language reveals that this vowel functions as the epenthetic vowel in that language: *i* in Japanese, *u* in

Telegu, and *e* in Spanish. According to Harris (1983), Spanish has at least four rules of vowel epenthesis, all of which insert the vowel *e*. In an underspecification framework, epenthesis need only insert a vowel slot, since the complete set of features can be provided by redundancy rules.

Underspecification theory has had some influence on English phonology. In an unpublished paper, Kiparsky (1984) has suggested an underspecification account of English vowel shift (see the discussion in Chapter 7). Borowsky (1986) suggested an underspecification account of *right* and *righteous* which avoids the abstract underlying velar fricative (see the discussion in section 1.2 and in Chapter 7).

1.3.5 Lexical phonology

The last post-*SPE* development in phonology that we will be concerned with is lexical phonology. This model challenges two aspects of the T-model given in (15) that are not addressed in the other developments we have been discussing. First, it challenges the implicit assumption that the phonological component is strictly interpretive, that is, that it applies exclusively to the output of syntactic structures. Instead, it proposes that phonology is divided into two major components: the LEXICAL PHONOLOGY, which operates *within* the lexicon, and the POSTLEXICAL PHONOLOGY, identified with the phonological component in (13), which applies after lexical items have been concatenated into sentences. The lexical phonology in turn may be divided into a series of STRATA, each of which is correlated with a corresponding STRATUM of morphology.

This model therefore provides an explicit place for morphology, which is lacking in the simple T-model given in (15). This makes it unnecessary to invoke readjustment rules to perform the morphological conversions that we saw in section 1.2 that generate *sang* and *mended*. We can simply say that there is a morpheme /-d/ in the lexicon with the meaning 'past,' which can be attached to every regular verb. The past tense *sang* can be derived by a MORPHOLOGICAL RULE in the lexicon that applies to the majority of verbs of this phonological shape, and which has the effect of changing the vowel to [+low], one form of ABLAUT in English. In Chapter 6, we will develop a means of representing ablaut as morphemes rather than as processes.

The rules of the lexical phonology are subject to certain constraints that do not apply to postlexical rules. For one thing, lexical rules are STRUCTURE PRESERVING, meaning that they do not derive segments (or segment types) that do not appear in underlying representations. The various lexical strata operate in a strict order, so that it is impossible to return to an earlier stratum once a later stratum has begun its part in a derivation. The earlier lexical strata are further subject to the STRICT

CYCLE CONDITION, which prevents rules on these strata from changing structure in underived environments. We will clarify all these aspects of lexical phonology in Chapter 6, when we look at the first lexical stratum in English. For English, we will claim that we need two lexical strata, of which only the first is cyclic.

1.4 What is English?

In a work devoted to English phonology, we should try to be specific about what we mean by English. A language cannot be equated with the contents of a dictionary or a grammar book, or even the two together. A language is a mental object, the knowledge acquired by a person which allows him or her to produce and understand an infinite number (in principle) of utterances never before uttered. The qualification "in principle" is needed because no human being can ever experience an infinite number of utterances in the space of a finite lifetime. Human language is *creative* in that each utterance, outside of a few formulaic expressions like "good morning," is created anew in accordance with the grammar, without reference to previous utterances. Creativity is generally said to be characteristic of syntax, where a simple listing of possible utterances seems genuinely impossible. It is sometimes said that the same claim is difficult to make in phonology, because phonology deals with a smaller set of items, often claimed to be the set of words in the language, which, it is said, is a finite if rather large set. However, even if we confine ourselves to words, we find the creative spirit here too. Speakers can generally produce a correct pronunciation of unfamiliar words (often, in fact, several acceptable pronunciations!) and furthermore create new words in accordance with the morphological patterns of the language, to which an acceptable pronunciation can be given. The creation of new words to correspond to new ideas and technological advances is the norm in most societies. Thus, the set of words is no more finite than the number of utterances. Even if creativity in the lexical arena is rarer than in sentence construction, it is still clear that we need phonological rules to predict the pronunciation of new words. We can assume that these same rules play a role, even if only a passive one, in the pronunciation of familiar old words as well.

Phonology is concerned with more than the pronunciation of individual words. The lexical phonology is confined to specifying the pronunciation of individual words, but the postlexical phonology includes aspects of the pronunciation of phrases and sentences (and longer utterances). Here, we must admit a degree of productivity to the phonology. We have already established that syntax is productive in a nontrivial way, and hence the phonology of utterances must be equally productive.

The next question to deal with is what variety or varieties of English we should be concerned with. Inasmuch as this is not intended to be a treatise on English dialectology, we will for the most part avoid nonstandard dialects. As for the standard varieties, we will refer primarily to standard Southern British English (from the point of view of pronunciation referred to as RP, or "received pronunciation," i.e., received at court), and standard North American English. Standard RP is fairly well codified, and is taught prescriptively in British public schools. Standard North American English is less well codified, and therefore less easy to define. It is generally regarded as that North American variety lacking the strong regional characteristics found in Eastern New England and the southern United States. Even so, standard North American English admits of considerable variation. Despite this variety, North American speakers can generally understand each other, and in fact RP is mutually comprehensible with standard North American varieties. Speakers are capable of producing a range of linguistic varieties depending on the social circumstances of the colloquy. This implies that a speaker's knowledge of his or her language is not restricted to a particular dialect or idiolect, but actually encompasses a range of varieties or styles of the language. If we use Bailey's (1973) term LECT to refer to a single variety of a single speaker in a single style, we might say that each speaker's grammar is POLYLECTAL, that is, comprising a variety of styles and dialects. Pushing this idea to its logical conclusion, Bailey has proposed that each speaker commands a PANLECTAL grammar, one which contains the rules required for all (or at least a wide range of) idiolects, rules which are brought into play in understanding speakers of other dialects. Often two varieties will contain the same rules, but the order will differ. If the speaker knows the rules, he will use them in one order when speaking and he can understand a speaker who uses the same rules in the opposite order. This idea may be vague, and at times simply unworkable. However, it certainly seems true that a speaker must have a more extensive grammar than is needed to produce utterances in a single idiolect. The production grammar of a speaker is more restricted than his comprehension grammar, and is probably in a subset relation with the latter. Our transcriptions will be at least partially panlectal, presenting distinctions that may not all be present in a single lect, but from which the pronunciation in actually occurring lects may be deduced.

1.5 Overview

In this chapter, we have introduced some of the issues that we will deal with in greater detail in coming chapters. In Chapter 2, we will examine the segments that constitute English utterances and their distribution, paying special attention to the representation of diphthongs and affricates. In Chapter 3, we will broaden our investigation by examining syllable structure in English. We will consider how certain questions about sound distribution can be stated better in terms of the prosodic units syllable and mora than in terms of the sequence of sounds. In Chapter 4, we will discuss how English stress provides evidence for a higher level of prosodic structure, the foot. Chapter 5 introduces further elements of the prosodic hierarchy, the phonological word (ω), the clitic group (C), the phonological phrase (φ), the intonation phrase (I), and the phonological utterance (U). This hierarchy is based on Nespor & Vogel (1986). We will be concerned primarily with its application to English and offer a revision of some of their formulations. Chapter 6 introduces lexical phonology and the interaction of morphological and phonological operations in the lexicon. In this chapter, we will be primarily concerned with the first stratum of the lexicon where phonological rules operate cyclically, reserving the postcyclic rules of the second lexical stratum for Chapter 7. Chapter 8 discusses postlexical phonology, and introduces some criteria for assigning rules to the postlexical component. It goes on to discuss some alternative approaches to the questions considered in the earlier parts of the book. The chapter ends with a brief summary and conclusion.

2 Segmental phonology

2.1 Levels of representation

This chapter probes the segmental system of English. It is a traditional concern of phonology to compile a catalogue of what sounds are found in a given language. This is not as straightforward a task as one might think. It is not always easy to tell if a given sound forms part of the sound system of a language or not. For example, nasalized vowels occur in English, sometimes even in minimal phonetic contrast with their nonnasalized counterparts, as we saw in the examples given as (7) in Chapter 1. We repeat some of these examples here as (1).

(1) a. 'cat' [kæt]
    b. 'can't' [kæ̃t]
    c. 'canned' [kæ̃nd]

Such examples are not accepted as evidence that vowel nasalization is distinctive in English, any more than the examples of *writer* and *rider,* discussed in section 1.1 of Chapter 1 are accepted as demonstrating the distinctiveness of the shortened diphthong [əy] as opposed to its unshortened counterpart [ɑy]. For the latter distinction we proposed two ordered rules of Diphthong Shortening and Flapping, which produce the correct phonetic representations, assuming uncontroversially a distinction between voiced and voiceless stops, as in the final segments of *ride* and *write*. In the case of nasalization we proposed the two ordered rules given in (8) of Chapter 1. The derivations in (2) (overleaf) show how such forms are derived.

Since our model of grammar includes phonological rules, we must assume that there are distinct LEVELS OF REPRESENTATION for phonological forms. As we have seen, phonological rules can result in neutralization (as when underlying /t/ and /d/ both become flap [ɾ] by the Flapping rule) or introduce new segment types,

(2) underlying[1]   /kænt/   /kæt/   /kænd/
     Vowel Nasalization   æ̃   ———   æ̃
     Nasal Consonant Deletion Ø   ———   ———
     phonetic representation [kæ̃t]   [kæt]   [kæ̃nd]

as with Aspiration. So far, we have been assuming two levels of representation. The first is the UNDERLYING REPRESENTATION, or the SYSTEMATIC PHONEMIC level of Chomsky (1964), which encodes all the systematic distinctions present in the language. The second is the SYSTEMATIC PHONETIC level of Chomsky (1964), defined by McCawley (1968, 14) as

> a representation in which all phonetic characteristics are represented which are governed by linguistic regularity in the language. Those characteristics of pronunciation which are caused not by language but by extra-linguistic factors (such as the size and shape of the speaker's vocal organs, his state of mental alertness, the possible presence of chewing gum in his mouth, etc.) are excluded from a phonetic representation. The characteristics recorded in a phonetic representation are thus, roughly speaking, those which, if deviated from, would yield a "foreign accent."

We may now ask whether there are any other levels of representation that are significant for phonology. Chomsky (1964) observes that most linguists assume a physical phonetic level, which Bloomfield (1933, 85) characterized as a "mechanical record of the gross acoustic features, such as is produced in the phonetics laboratory." This level can be thought of as resulting from the PHONETIC IMPLEMENTATION (Mohanan 1986, 153) of phonetic representations in conjunction with mental states, aesthetic factors, chewing gum, etc. American structuralist phonologists posited a fourth level, intermediate between the systematic phonemic and the systematic phonetic levels, which they called the phonemic level (referred to by Chomsky as the TAXONOMIC PHONEMIC level).[2] Chomsky denied the relevance of any level between the systematic phonemic and the systematic phonetic levels. However, there does seem to be some truth to the claim that there is a difference between purely allophonic rules, such as those which produce aspirated voiceless stops and flaps in English, and morphophonemic rules, which involve alternations in distinctive segments. Morphophonemic rules include the rules involved in Vowel Shift, discussed in section 1.2 of Chapter 1, responsible for alternations such as the one in *sane~sanity*. The trouble with structuralist

---

[1] These forms are actually the lexical representations, in the terminology developed in this section. Since no lexical rules apply to these forms, this distinction does not affect the matter at hand.

[2] See discussion in section 1.1 of Chapter 1.

methodology is that it is incapable of making the correct assignment of phonemes. Since minimal contrasts imply phonemic distinctions, we run into the inevitable paradox of concluding, contrary to our intuition, that shortened diphthongs and nasalized vowels are phonemic in English.

The theory of lexical phonology (discussed in detail in Chapter 6) resolves this paradox in the following way. It proposes a systematic distinction between the rules of the lexical phonology, which apply within the lexicon, and the rules of the postlexical phonology, which apply outside the lexicon to representations that have been concatenated syntactically. We can make the following reasonable assumptions. The allophonic rules, such as those responsible for flapping and aspiration, are postlexical. Morphophonemic rules are lexical. Following Mohanan (1986), we can define LEXICAL REPRESENTATIONS as those which result from the application of lexical rules. The system can be schematized as in (3), with some refinements to follow in Chapter 6.

(3)

	level	*source*	*characteristics (in English)*
a.	underlying (systematic phonemic)	listed underlying representations	no flapping, no glottalization, no diphthongs, no velar nasal
b.	lexical	derived from (a) by lexical rules	diphthongs, velar nasal introduced
c.	systematic phonetic	derived from (b) syntactic concatenation and postlexical rules	glottalization, aspiration and flapping introduced
d.	physical phonetic	derived from (c) and nonlinguistic factors by phonetic implementation	segments no longer discrete, optional deletion of unstressed vowels, etc.

It would be difficult if not impossible to catalogue the segments that appear on the physical phonetic level. Actual speech is infinitely varied, and no two utterances are ever exactly alike. It is not difficult to catalogue the segments of the systematic phonetic level. However, there is a certain amount of redundancy in such a catalogue, since, for example, this catalogue would list the aspirated allophone for each of the voiceless stops in English (as in (3) of Chapter 1), and would thus fail to capture the generalization that the aspiration in each case is produced by a general rule. We will introduce this rule in Chapter 5. A catalogue of systematic phonemic segments is also useful, but its content depends on fairly complex arguments, which we have deferred until Chapters 6 and 7. With these points in mind, it seems best to start with the lexical level.

2.2 English consonants

First, we present a table of the consonants that appear at the lexical level in English.

	bl		ld		dn		al		pa		pl	ve		gl
	vl	vd	vl	vd	vl	vd	vl	vd	vl	vd	vd	vl	vd	vl
stops	p	b					t	d				k	g	
affricates									č	ǰ				
fricatives			f	v	θ	ð	s	z	š	ž				h
nasals		m						n					ŋ	
laterals								l						
approximates		w						r			y			

Key to abbreviations: bl=bilabial, ld=labiodental, dn=dental, al=alveolar, pa=palatoalveolar, pl=palatal, ve=velar, gl=glottal, vl=voiceless, vd=voiced

Table 1

From the structuralist point of view, Table 1 represents the phonemic consonants of English. The velar nasal is not an underlying segment of English, but, since it is derived by lexical rules, it is included in our table of lexical segments. The rules required for deriving the velar nasal are discussed in section 2.2.5. All the other segments in Table 1 are underlying segments that are preserved at the lexical level. An additional segment that occurs phonetically in English, the glottal stop, is neither underlying nor lexical, and so it doesn't appear in Table 1. We will comment on this in the next subsection before moving on to some additional problematic cases.

2.2.1 *Glottal stop*
The glottal stop has three sources in English. The first occurs in emphatic pronunciation of vowel-initial words, for example, *I want an apple* [ʔæpl̩], *not a pear*. The second is as an intrusive element between two vowels when the second vowel is stressed, as in *myopic*. In this usage it alternates with a glide [w] or [y]. The third is an allophonic realization of *t* (and other voiceless stops in certain varieties), as in *kitten* [kɪʔn̩]. We will discuss the allophones of the voiceless stops further in Chapter 5, where we will show that the distribution of allophones is actually quite complex, and can be reasonably described only in terms of prosodic categories.

Structuralist phonemics did not consider the glottal stop phonemic either, but structuralist methodology can be seen as leading in that direction. Instead of observing that [ɛg] and [ʔɛg] are noncontrastive (both meaning 'egg'), one might observe that [ʔɛg] contrasts with [bɛg] and conclude that glottal stop is a phoneme (Mohanan 1986, 178–9). In lexical phonology, there is no reason to posit glottal stop as either underlying or derived by lexical rules. We conclude that, in all its uses described here, it is derived by postlexical rules.

2.2.2 Voiceless [ʍ]

Some dialects of English systematically distinguish pairs of words like *witch* and *which* by pronouncing the latter with what might be described phonetically as a voiceless [ʍ]. We have not included this in Table 1 because it seems best to analyze it as a sequence [hw], parallel to the sequence [hy] in words like *hue*. In Old English, there were a number of initial consonant clusters consisting of [h] plus a sonorant, such as *hring* 'ring,' *hlāford* 'lord,' *hnutu* 'nut,' as well as *hwīt* 'white.' The [h] has been progressively lost from such clusters, and none of them survive in RP. In some forms of North American English and in Scottish English, the cluster [hw] remains but no other clusters beginning with [h]. Analyzing this sound as a cluster allows us to maintain the generalization that all sonorants in English are voiced. It also maintains a parallelism to sequences like [hy] in *hue* (where the [h] also drops in some dialects).

2.2.3 Affricates

The English consonant inventory contains two affricates, [č] and [ǰ]. The question that arises is whether to consider each of these as one segment or as a sequence of a stop plus a fricative. The notation is potentially significant here. The symbols we use for affricates imply that they are single segments. The notation of the International Phonetic Association (IPA), on the other hand, implies an analysis as two segments: [tʃ] and [dʒ] respectively. The IPA does provide the option of writing these as ligatures, [ʧ] and [ʤ], but the implied analysis of a stop plus fricative sequence is still evident. We can bring several types of considerations to bear on this question. Native speakers have the intuition that each affricate is a single segment, despite the two or three letters <ch>, <tch> required to spell [č] (Wells 1982, 48–49). PHONOTACTICS, the study of the distribution of segments, provides another source of evidence. English words do not begin with a sequence of stop plus fricative, with a few marginal exceptions like *tsetse (fly)*. This suggests that English has a constraint against syllable-initial stop–fricative sequences. If affricates are analyzed as single segments, they will not be subject to this constraint. A further source of evidence comes from other languages which do not have a prohibition against syllable-initial stop-fricative sequences. Polish, for example, contrasts syllable-initial [č] with syllable-initial [tš], as in *czy* [či] 'whether' vs *trzy* [tšɨ] 'three.' Careful acoustic measurements of these words show a considerably longer fricative portion in the stop-fricative sequence than in the affricate (Brooks 1965). This shows that affricates have to be considered a separate category of segments on a language universal basis. In fact, such contrasts exist in English, though only across a morpheme boundary, as shown by pairs like *scorching* and *courtship*. A third type of evidence comes from backward speech (Cowan et al. 1985). Some speakers can fluently reverse the order of phonemes in words. When producing a word like *choice* backwards, subjects produced [soyč], showing that they perceive the affricate as a unit.

2.2.4 Distinctive features of English consonants

Ever since Jakobson & Halle (1956), phonology has viewed the fundamental unit not as the segment but as the phonological DISTINCTIVE FEATURE. The features detailed in Jakobson, Fant, & Halle (1963) were primarily ACOUSTIC in nature, but *SPE* detailed a system of features based on articulation, which has remained standard in generative phonology. To be sure, recent work has made further refinements in the system, one of the most important of which is to group features into NODES representing articulators (e.g., 13 in Chapter 1). Researchers have also tried to eliminate the one *SPE* feature which remained acoustic in nature, [strident]. This work has not yet found much application in English phonology. For the most part we will confine our attention to the traditional *SPE* features. The consonants listed in Table 1 can be classified in terms of *SPE* features as in Table 2.

	p	b	t	d	k	g	č	ǰ	f	v	θ	ð	s	z	š	ž	h	m	n	ŋ	l	r	w	y
consonantal	+	+	+	+	+	+	+	+	+	+	+	+	+	+	+	+	−	+	+	+	+	−	−	−
sonorant	−	−	−	−	−	−	−	−	−	−	−	−	−	−	−	−	−	+	+	+	+	+	+	+
continuant	−	−	−	−	−	−	−	−	+	+	+	+	+	+	+	+	+	−	−	−	+	+	+	+
coronal	−	−	+	+	−	−	+	+	−	−	+	+	+	+	+	+	−	−	+	−	+	+	−	−
anterior	+	+	+	+	−	−	−	−	+	+	+	+	+	+	−	−	−	+	+	−	+	−	−	−
strident	−	−	−	−	−	−	+	+	+	+	−	−	+	+	+	+	−	−	−	−	−	−	−	−
back	−	−	−	−	+	+	−	−	−	−	−	−	−	−	−	−	−	−	−	+	−	−	+	−
voiced	−	+	−	+	−	+	−	+	−	+	−	+	−	+	−	+	−	+	+	+	+	+	+	+

Table 2

Table 2 represents a fully specified matrix for English consonants. In accordance with underspecification theory (section 1.3.4) we can remove many of the specifications in the table and allow default rules to supply them. For example, since all the sonorants in table 2 are voiced, this feature can be removed from the specification of the sonorants. Similarly, while [l] is typically [–back], it becomes [+back] in various contexts depending on dialect (see the discussion of *l*-Velarization in section 5.2). Therefore, no underlying specification for [back] is needed for [l]. Similarly, many phonologists consider [+coronal] to be the universally unmarked point of articulation, and would advocate removing specifications for [+coronal] from table 2. We will, however, leave the table fully specified to make it easier to construct natural classes.

Some other NONDISTINCTIVE FEATURES play a significant role in English phonology. Since we will be concerned with the allophones of stops in English, especially in Chapter 5, we should consider the features that characterize them. Halle & Stevens (1971) investigate the speech mechanisms that underlie phonetic features such as voicing, aspiration, glottalization, and tone. They propose four features: [spread glottis], [constricted glottis], [stiff vocal cords], and [slack vocal cords]. Because the glottis cannot be simultaneously spread and constricted (although it can be neither), and because the vocal cords cannot be both stiff and slack (but can be neither), these features together define nine laryngeal configurations. Table 3 shows the results of applying these features to obstruents, glides, and vowels.

	1	2	3	4	5	6	7	8	9
obstruents	b_l	b	p	p_k	b^h	p^h	ɓ	ʔb	p'
glides	w, y			fi	ɦ	h, w̥, y̥	ʔ̬		ʔ, ʔw, ʔy
vowels	V	V̇	V̇	voiceless vowels	breathy vowels			creaky voice vowels	glottalized vowels
spread glottis				+	+	+	–	–	–
constricted glottis	–	–	–	–	–	–	+	+	+
stiff vocal cords	–	–	+	–	–	+	–	–	+
slack vocal cords	–	+	–	–	+	–	–	+	–

Table 3

This proposal allows us to account for an impressive array of contrasts that appear in a variety of languages. Let us explain some of the unfamiliar symbols that appear in this chart. The symbol p_k represents a moderately aspirated stop, found in Korean, as opposed to the fully aspirated stop [pʰ]. The symbol ʔ represents a voiced glottal stop "that appears to be attested in Jingpho" (Halle & Stevens 1971, 208). The symbol [b₁] represents a lax voiceless stop, as in Danish. The symbol [ʔb] represents a preglottalized [b], for which Halle & Stevens give no examples. The grave and acute accents on the symbol V in columns 2 and 3 represent low and high tones respectively; comparison with the obstruent row shows the correlation of low pitch with voiced obstruents and of high pitch with voiceless obstruents, which is characteristic of many languages. We will not discuss the remaining contrasts in this table, which are interesting in their ability to characterize many language contrasts. In this book, we use the feature [+spread (glottis)] to represent aspiration in English and [+constricted (glottis)] to represent glottalization.

2.2.5 Segments with restricted distribution

Not all segments can appear in all environments. Some segments are quite restricted in their distribution. Let us consider the velar nasal first. This segment cannot appear at the beginning of a word in English, nor can it appear in the onset of a stressed syllable.[3] *SPE* proposed to explain this by analyzing the velar nasal as derived in all cases by assimilation to a following velar consonant. In their treatment the velar nasal is nowhere an underlying segment. The velar nasal appears in a transparent assimilation environment in words like *sink*. For words like *sing, SPE* proposed that the [g] is deleted by a rule that follows the assimilation. The rules required are those in (4).

(4) a. n → ŋ / __ $\begin{bmatrix} -\text{son} \\ -\text{ant} \\ -\text{cor} \\ -\text{strid} \end{bmatrix}$ (an alveolar nasal becomes a velar before a velar consonant or [h])

b. g → ∅ / [+nasal] __] (g drops after a nasal at the end of a morpheme)

---

[3] More concisely, the velar nasal can appear anywhere except at the beginning of a FOOT. We define the foot as a unit containing one and only one stressed syllable. Feet in English generally begin with a stressed syllable, but at the beginning of a word it is possible to have one unstressed syllable before the stressed syllable of a foot. This will be formalized in Chapter 4.

The rules must apply in this order. The velar stop must be present in order for the preceding nasal to assimilate to it. Prior deletion of the stop would bleed the assimilation rule (4a), so that this analysis is another example of a counterbleeding order (cf. the discussion of Diphthong Shortening and Flapping in section 1.1 of Chapter 1). Since the environment for *g*-Deletion is at the end of a morpheme (that is, before a morphemic bracket), (4b) will delete both *g*s of *singing,* with the morphological analysis [[sing] ing]. However, there are a few monomorphemic words, such as *hangar* and *dinghy,* with [ŋ] in intervocalic position, where (4b) would not delete [g]. In these cases, *SPE* suggested underlying representations like /xænxr/, where /x/, as a velar fricative, would cause assimilation and then delete. As we discussed in section 1.2 of Chapter 1, *SPE* uses the velar fricative to analyze words such as *right* and *righteous.* But, in their analysis, this segment was always either deleted or converted to [h]. Borowsky (1986, 69) suggested a more concrete analysis for *hangar,* with the underlying form /hænhər/. In fact, rule (4a) implicitly includes /h/ as a segment that can cause assimilation of a preceding nasal. Furthermore /h/ is itself a segment with a restricted distribution.[4] It can appear only at the beginning of a foot (see footnote 3). In the usual pronunciation of *vehicle,* there is no [h] phonetically.[5] In *vehicular,* where /h/ is the onset of the stressed syllable, it is pronounced. The place name *Birmingham* has two pronunciations, ['bərmɪŋəm] or ['bərmɪŋ‚hæm]. In the first, there is only one foot, and /h/ is not realized. In the second, the secondary stress on the final syllable indicates a foot on that syllable, and the /h/ is realized at the beginning of this foot.

The voiced alveopalatal fricative /ž/ is restricted in its distribution in almost exactly the same way as the velar nasal /ŋ/. This suggests that we seek some explanation for its distribution also. In Chapter 7, we suggest that some instances of /ž/ are derived from /z/ plus /y/, as in *confusion* from *confuse.* This is unlikely to be the source of all occurrences of /ž/ in English, since we have it also in *vision, azure, cortège,* where the relevant environment would be difficult to motivate. This segment is relatively rare in English, but it does seem to be underlying. Its distributional similarity to the velar nasal is taken to be accidental, not the result of phonological rules, as is the case with the latter. The occurrence of [ž] in

---

[4] The velar fricative is a segment whose distribution is restricted to nowhere. Using /h/ to condition velar assimilation is therefore less abstract, because the limited distribution of /h/ is visible in phonetic forms.

[5] The pronunciation ['vi‚hɪkəl] reflects two feet, with the /h/ at the beginning of the second, so it can be realized. The usual pronunciation [vɪtkəl] presents a conflict between this rule for the distribution of /h/ and the principle that syllables prefer to have onsets, discussed in section 2.2.3 and section 3.1 of Chapter 3.

English is largely the result of borrowings from French, whereas the velar nasal was always present phonetically in English, as a result of assimilation to a following velar obstruent, and only became a lexical segment when certain velar obstruents were lost as a result of historical change.

We can make a case for treating the velar nasal differently from the voiced alveopalatal fricative by noting the relative degree of difficulty each of these sounds represents for English speakers learning other languages that feature these sounds under less restrictive conditions. English speakers have little difficulty learning to pronounce French words like *jour, Georges, général,* where [ž] occurs initially. English speakers have a much harder time with the Vietnamese name Nguyen [ŋuyɛn]. They tend to pronounce it something like [əŋguyɛn] in order to conform to English phonotactic patterns. This suggests treating these two segments differently. The velar nasal is restricted to non-foot-initial position because it is derived from an underlying sequence that cannot occur foot initially, while [ž] is restricted to the same environments for accidental historical reasons.

2.3 English vowels

2.3.1 Short, lax vowels

The short vowel system is relatively straightforward. We give the phonetic short, lax vowels in Table 4, classified in terms of distinctive features, along with an example of each.

	−back	+back	
		−round	+round
+high −low	bit [ɪ]	[ɨ]	book [ʊ]
−high −low	bet [ɛ]	but [ə]	[ɔ]
−high +low	bat [æ]	balm [ɑ]	bomb [ɒ]

Table 4

There is no controversy with the vowels in the first column. The back vowels are more of a problem. The high back unrounded vowel [ɨ] occurs in some American pronunciations of the adverb *just,* as in *just a minute.* The mid back round vowel [ɔ] apparently does not occur in North American pronunciation at all in its short lax form, although Halle & Mohanan (1985) consider this to be the vowel of *baud* in RP. A tense version of this vowel, [o], occurs finally in words like *echo*. Notice that I do not use the symbol [ɔ] for the low tense round vowel of *law, all:* for this vowel I use the symbol [ō], where the macron indicates tenseness. The lax version of this latter vowel occurs in *bomb*, for those dialects that distinguish this from *balm,* with an unrounded vowel. Finally a note on the symbol [ə] for the vowel of *but,* which is often written [ʌ]. It is a matter of convention to reserve the symbol [ə] for the unstressed reduced vowel that appears at the end of *sofa* or the beginning of *about*. However, this convention contradicts a fundamental principle of phonology, which states that we should not represent differences that are completely predictable as though they were distinctive. The vowels [ʌ] and [ə] are phonetically very similar, and they differ only in that [ʌ] occurs only stressed while [ə] occurs only unstressed. It therefore behooves us to use the same symbol for both, and we have chosen [ə] for this purpose. We consider [ʌ] to be the tense counterpart of [ə].

The vowels of Table 4 share another characteristic: they cannot stand at the end of a stressed monosyllabic word. This is shown in (5).

(5)

final lax vowel	*lax vowel plus consonant*		*final tense vowel*	
*[bɪ]	bit	[bɪt]	bee	[biy]
*[bɛ]	bet	[bɛt]	bay	[bey]
*[bæ]	bat	[bæt]	spa	[spā]
*[bʊ]	put	[pʊt]	gnu	[nu]
*[bɒ]	cot	[kɒt]	law	[lō]

In a somewhat different terminology, the lax vowels are referred to as CHECKED vowels, because in a stressed monosyllable they must be followed ('checked') by a consonant in the coda. The tense vowels, on the other hand, are considered FREE vowels, because they are not constrained in this manner (although they may be followed by coda consonants, as in *beet, bait,* etc.).

2.3.2 Tense vowels and diphthongs

The long vowels of English are uniformly tense, and, in most dialects, diphthongized. There is some controversy over whether to analyze these vowels as underlyingly long, underlyingly tense, or underlyingly diphthongs. Table 5 gives the phonetic values of these segments, again on the basis of the distinctive features that comprise their most prominent element.

	−back	+back	
		−round	+round
+high, −low	bee [iy]	music [yɨw]	gnu [uw]
−high, −low	bay [ey]	doe [ʌw]	boy [oy]
−high, +low	cow [æw]	buy [āy]	law [ō]

Table 5

One immediate problem is whether the high nuclei[6] in this table are really diphthongs. These could be considered simply as long tense vowels, without a diphthongal element. A related problem is whether the nuclei in *bay* and *doe* should be considered true diphthongs or simply diphthongized vowels, since the tense vowels [e] and [ʌ] do not contrast with these diphthongs. Finally, certain questions may arise concerning some of our transcriptions. Halle & Mohanan, for example, transcribe *doe* (they use *boat*) with the nucleus [ow], and *boy* with the nucleus [ōy].[7] Hoard (1972), however, claims that the nucleus of *boy* begins with a mid vowel. We will follow Hoard's transcription here. The nucleus of *doe* and *boat* begins with an unrounded vowel in RP and some varieties of North American English, notably in New England. If we note that both are possible, we can develop rules that can generate both when we consider the underlying representations of English vowels in Chapter 7.

The nucleus of the first syllable of *music* is transcribed as [yuw] by Halle & Mohanan (1985). The vowel portion of this nucleus is unround in many dialects, as indicated in Table 5. The round version, however, can easily be produced by an extension of rules that we will need elsewhere. This nucleus is actually a triphthong phonetically. The initial [y] of this nucleus is due to an insertion rule. We argue for this position on the grounds that syllable-initial clusters of the form Cy are invariably followed by the nucleus portion [ɨw]. Without a rule inserting y in these positions, we would be unable to explain the observed restriction on these clusters.

---

[6] I use the term nucleus to refer to the vocalic portion of a syllable, the part between the onset and the coda, whether this portion is a single vowel or a diphthong. This terminology will be developed further in Chapter 3.

[7] In their notation [ɔ_t y], where the subscript *t* indicates tenseness. As explained in section 2.3.1, I reserve the symbol [ɔ] for a lax mid back round vowel.

The nucleus of *loss* (where distinct from both *balm* and *bomb*) is the only tense vowel whose final offglide is neither *y* nor *w*. In fact, this nucleus is simply tense [ō] in Halle & Mohanan's treatment. We will consider the rules responsible for these phonetic variations in Chapter 7.

2.3.3 Diphthongs as single units

The high nuclei are frequently phonetic diphthongs, as in RP [ɩy] for [iy]. The nuclei of *buy* and *doe* are diphthongs in RP and in General North American, but monophthongs in Scots. There seems to be a major dichotomy between the lax vowels (checked, as we called them in section 2.3.1) and tense (free) vowels. This suggests that we treat all tense vowels in a parallel fashion, which in turn suggests that we treat them all as diphthongs phonologically, since three items from Table 5 are clearly diphthongs: [æw], [āy] and [oy]. However, even though they are phonetically a sequence of two articulations, we will treat them as single units underlyingly. This single-unit treatment is sometimes coded in phonetic representations by the use of a ligature, e.g., [a͡i], the notation used by MacKay (1987) for our [āy]. There is evidence for treating diphthongs in English more transparently as single units, that is as pure vowels underlyingly. Thus underlying the diphthong [āy] is the pure vowel [īː].

There are three sources of evidence for the claim that English diphthongs are single units phonologically. One is from backward speech, mentioned already in connection with the single-phoneme analysis of affricates in section 2.2.3. There we observed that backward speakers produce [soyč] as the backward form of *choice*. This indicates not only the single-phoneme interpretation of the affricate [č], but also of the diphthong [oy]. Interpreting the diphthong as a sequence of two segments would predict a backwards rendering as [syoč].

A second source of evidence for the single-phoneme interpretation of diphthongs comes from syllabification, which we treat in detail in the next chapter. There we discuss the Onset Principle, which requires that syllables have onsets if possible. That is, a sequence ... VCV... will universally be syllabified ... V.CV... rather than ... VC.V..., where a single period indicates the syllable boundary. Now consider the syllabification of such a sequence where C is a glide *w* or *y*, as in *Toyota*. In Japanese, this word is syllabified *to.yo.ta*, following the Onset Principle. But, in English, the syllabification is clearly *toy.o.ta*. We will have to claim either that English violates the Onset Principle in certain cases of intervocalic glides, or that English diphthongs are simple vowels at the time syllabification takes place. In this study we make the latter choice. Syllabification takes place quite early in the lexical phonology of English, on stratum 1, before stress assignment takes place. We will assume that the nuclei of Table 5 are simple tense vowels at that point, so that syllabification takes place with no violation of the Onset Principle. We then assume that Vowel Shift[8] and related rules are assigned to stratum 2 of the lexicon, and that no resyllabification takes place at that point. This analysis predicts the observed syllabifications in English. In Japanese, since the glides are underlying, they are syllabified with the following vowel, in accordance with the Onset Principle.

A third source of evidence for treating diphthongs as single units comes from the vowel shift alternations discussed briefly in section 1.2 of Chapter 1. Some examples of the alternations are given in (6).

(6)   *Tense vowel (diphthong)*   *Lax vowel*   *Underlying*

         a.   div*i*ne   [ɑy]   div*i*nity   [ɪ]   /ī/
         b.   ser*e*ne   [iy]   ser*e*nity   [ɛ]   /ē/
         c.   s*a*ne   [ey]   s*a*nity   [æ]   /ǣ/

Each line of (6) is representative of a wide range of examples. *SPE* sought a common underlying representation for each stem. It turns out that the most economical underlying representation contains a *tense* version of the vowel that appears in the *lax vowel* column, as shown in the *underlying* column. We present the details of this analysis in Chapter 7, adopting the *SPE* analysis of these nuclei as underlying tense vowels. For purposes of stress assignment, it will be necessary to assume that they are also long. We do this in consideration of Halle's (1977) suggestion that some vowels are long, and so affect stress assignment, but are nontense, and so do not undergo Vowel Shift.

2.4 Towards systematic phonemics

Let us return briefly to the levels of representation listed in (3), and clarify some of the characteristics of each level, starting from the physical phonetic level. Mohanan (1986) claims that this level results from the phonetic implementation of the systematic phonetic level, taking nonlinguistic factors into account, such as mental states and aesthetic factors. At this level, features assume scalar (nonbinary) values and phonetic segments are no longer discrete. Scalar valued features are needed to specify that the *b*s at the beginning and end of *bib,* said in isolation, are voiced to a lesser degree than the *b* of *abbey,* although at the systematic phonetic level both are specified as [+voiced] (Mohanan 1986, 157).

---

[8] See the discussion in section 1.2 of Chapter 1.

Phonetic segments are no longer discrete in physical phonetics, since articulatory gestures do not necessarily coincide. The word *inn,* with the partial systematic phonetic representation in (7a), is converted into (7b) by phonetic implementation (Mohanan 1986, 159).

(7) a.

	ɪ	n
nasal	−	+
continuant	+	−

b.

	ɪ	n
nasal	−	+
continuant	+	−

In (7b), nasality begins before the tongue contacts the hard palate. This means that the vowel is nasalized toward the end of its articulation, before the nasal consonant is fully articulated. In actual speech there will be many instances of such overlapping articulatory gestures. Another example is the distinction between words like *prince* and *prints.* Most English speakers distinguish these two words, which would have the systematic phonetic representations [prins] and [prints] respectively. Yet most English speakers insert a short *t* in words like *prince,* which can be transcribed [prɪnᵗs]. This is again the result of overlap in the articulatory gestures: the soft palate is raised (ending the nasal articulation) prior to the release of the tongue tip (resulting in the transition from the stop to the fricative articulation). The result is that a portion of the utterance of *prince* has an articulation that is like *t,* but much shorter than the same articulation in *prints* (Mohanan 1986, 162).

Another characteristic of the physical phonetic level in English is the reduction or deletion of unstressed vowels between consonants. Words like *potato* and *divinity,* with the systematic phonetic representations [pʰə'tʰeyɾo] and [dɪ'vɪnɪṭi], respectively, can shorten the vowel of the first syllable by varying degrees up to and including total disappearance. This is a gradient operation, in contrast to the total disappearance of the last vowel of *idea* when it combines with the suffix *-ology* to form *ideology* (Mohanan 1986, 167–168).

The systematic phonetic level contains all the information required to produce natural speech. So, for English, the glottalization of stops in syllable-final position, the aspiration of stops in foot-initial position, and the flapping of certain intervocalic alveolar stops will be specified at this level. These phenomena are produced by postlexical rules. The systematic phonetic level does not contain information regarding partial nasalization of the vowel of *inn,* the intrusive short *t* in *prince,* or the reduction or deletion of the vowel of *potato,* since these are a matter of phonetic implementation. This does not mean that these phenomena are not grammatically conditioned. Mohanan (1986, 168–9) argues that vowel reduction similar to that in *potato* occurs in Malayalam and Warlpiri. In Malayalam the vowels may shorten considerably but may not delete completely when between identical stops, but in Warlpiri they can disappear completely under the same conditions. This shows that even phonetic implementation must be built into the grammars of individual languages.

The lexical level is derived from underlying representations by the operation of lexical rules. In Chapter 7 we argue that the rules in (4) that produce the velar nasal are lexical rules of stratum 2. It follows that velar nasals are present at the lexical level but not at the underlying level. Likewise, since Vowel Shift and Diphthongization are rules of stratum 2 of the lexicon, diphthongs are present at the lexical level but not at the underlying level. Mohanan (1986, 152) refers to the inventory of segments appearing at the lexical level as the LEXICAL ALPHABET.

Finally, we consider the underlying level. Mohanan uses the term UNDERLYING ALPHABET to refer to the inventory of segments that appear at this level. Chomsky (1964) called this the systematic phonemic level and emphasized the importance of giving each morpheme of the language a unique underlying representation wherever possible. If we are forced to, we may propose two or more underlying representations, called ALLOMORPHS, to represent a single form, but we try to derive the various phonetic representations of a morpheme from a single underlying representation, wherever possible, by invoking phonological rules. This follows from the premise that the overall grammar should be as SIMPLE as possible, where simplicity refers to the number of features required to state all the underlying forms and the rules needed to produce phonetic forms. If many lexical items vary in a similar way that is predictable by a rule, then it is simpler to state the rule than to design distinct allomorphs for each lexical item.

Let us consider a simple example, discussed in *SPE* 11–13. In (8) we have the systematic phonetic representation of three related words.

(8) a. telegraph [ˈtʰɛlɪˌgræf]
 b. telegraphy [tʰɪˈlɛgrəfi]
 c. telegraphic [ˌtʰɛlɪˈgræfɪk]

The stem *telegraph* appears in three different phonetic shapes. Although there are some differences, the three forms show many similarities. They differ primarily in the vowels and in the location of stress. If we assume that the stress of these forms is predictable by rules (which we discuss in detail in Chapter 4), then we can say that the vowel quality depends on stress. Roughly speaking, vowels retain their full range of qualities only when stressed. In unstressed position vowels are REDUCED to one of two qualities: [ɪ, ə]. If we were to enter the unstressed, reduced form of vowels in lexical representations, we would be unable to determine what quality the vowel will have when it appears in stressed position. On the other hand, if underlying representations contain the unreduced vowels, we can say that an underlying vowel retains its quality if it is stressed; otherwise, a reduced quality appears. This means that we propose (9) as the underlying form for *telegraph*.

(9)   /tɛlɛgræf/

The form in (9) does not appear in that shape unaltered in any of the phonetic forms. This form is somewhat more ABSTRACT than the phonetic forms in (8). In *SPE* a number of other abstract analyses were proposed, some quite a bit more abstract than (9). All the segments of (9) appear in at least one of the phonetic forms of the morpheme, but they do not all occur in the same form. This is not true of the underlying /x/ which *SPE* proposed for *right*. The ABSTRACTNESS CONTROVERSY arose in response to what some saw as an excessive abstractness in *SPE*-type analyses. Kiparsky (1968b) proposed the ALTERNATION CONDITION, cited in (10) to prevent ABSOLUTE NEUTRALIZATION, the merger of two or more segments regardless of context.

(10)   *Alternation Condition*
        Obligatory neutralization rules cannot apply to all occurrences of a morpheme.

Contextual neutralizations, such as the merger of /t/ and /d/ to flap [ɾ], are permitted by this condition, but neutralizations without context, such as the merger of *SPE*'s /x/ with zero, are disallowed. Vowel Shift, although it occurs regardless of context, is allowed by the alternation condition because it is not a neutralization. The alternation condition generated a considerable amount of controversy, primarily because it disallowed a number of well-motivated analyses along with *SPE*'s abstract /x/. Kiparsky (1982b, 150ff) argues against it, in fact. He gives the example of the glide /y/ which SPE proposed as the final segment in words with the suffixes *-ory* and *-ary*, as well as words like *galaxy* and *industry*. In terms of the stress rule of Chapter 4, *galaxy* would have penultimate stress if its final segment were a vowel rather than a glide. Similarly, words like *secrecy* would be expected to undergo Trisyllabic Laxing if its final segment were a vowel underlyingly, producing *[sɛkrɪsi]. But the rule that turns such final glides to vowels, given in (11), is an obligatory neutralization rule under Kiparsky's definition, and so would not be permitted in *galaxy, secrecy* under the Alternation Condition (10).

(11) y → i / ___]

Vennemann (1974) and Hooper (1976) proposed a much more restrictive constraint on abstractness, which they called the Strong Naturalness Condition, although it bears no relation to Postal's Naturalness Condition, referred to in section 1.2 of Chapter 1. This condition disallows even such benign abstractness as (9).

While there was a general feeling that some restrictions should be placed on abstractness, none of the solutions proposed could escape from the charge of arbitrariness. They often forced analyses to be even more concrete than those of structuralist phonology, and for this reason were generally unsatisfying. This problem could not be solved purely in terms of *SPE* theory, but had to await the development of more sophisticated techniques of analysis. The culmination of this development has been the theory of lexical phonology. Lexical phonology is able to satisfy both sides of the abstractness controversy. It satisfies the antiabstractness position by placing abstract underlying forms in the lexicon, along with the rules that produce the most abstract kinds of alternations, such as those illustrated in (6). This procedure corresponds to what some antiabstract phonologists called LEXICALIZATION of such processes, but avoids their claim that all such forms are simply listed outright, which they justified by the lack of clear phonetic motivation for the rules required. It also satisfies the abstract camp in permitting rather abstract forms, within certain constraints.

2.5 Phonology and orthography

It has long been recognized that English orthography corresponds only indirectly to English pronunciation. Some have even gone so far as to claim that English spelling is not ALPHABETIC. This claim depends on a rather idiosyncratic definition of an alphabetic system as one with "a one-to-one correspondence between distinctive speech sounds and letters of an alphabet" (MacKay 1987, 46). Even if we take the expression "distinctive speech sound" to refer to the units of the lexical alphabet, this "one-to-one" constraint is too restrictive, because it does not allow any writing system to be called alphabetic. Even such languages as Spanish and Finnish, which are often cited as having such a one-to-one correspondence between letters and distinctive sounds, have certain idiosyncrasies of spelling; for example, Spanish uses both <c> and <qu> to represent the sound [k], and Finnish does not record the so-called "glottal stop," actually a doubling of a consonant at the beginning of a word following certain vowel-final forms.

A better definition of an alphabetic system is one which uses an alphabet, a relatively small set of graphemes (letters) that correspond to phoneme-size units of sound in the language. This distinguishes an alphabet from a SYLLABARY, in which the individual symbols correspond to larger units, either syllable-sized or mora-sized units. See Figures 1, 2, and 3 of Chapter 3 for some examples of syllabaries.

At the other extreme is *SPE*'s claim (1968, 49) that "conventional orthography is...a near optimal system for the lexical representation of English words." They base this opinion on "the fundamental principle of orthography...that phonetic variation is not indicated where it is predictable by general rule" (1968, 49). In section 2.4 we examined the distinct pronunciations of the morpheme *telegraph* when it appears alone and with different suffixes. This variation is predictable by rules of stress placement and vowel reduction, which we will examine in greater detail in Chapters 6 and 7. Because this variation is predictable, it is not indicated by distinct spellings. Furthermore, the use of a common spelling for the different phonetic manifestations of *telegraph* makes it easier to recognize the common morpheme in the forms of (8).

The alternations in (6) that result from the rule of Trisyllabic Laxing discussed at the end of section 2.4 are another case like *telegraph*. Even though the stressed vowels of *divine* and *divinity* are phonetically quite different, they are represented orthographically by the same letter, *i*, justified because the alternation is governed by a rule. The orthography preserves the identity of the morpheme that appears in two phonetically distinct manifestations.

This is not to deny that there is a certain degree of idiosyncrasy in English spelling. For example, there is the <b> in *debt* was inserted because someone thought it ought to be related to Latin *debitum,* from which it is ultimately derived, although it is directly derived from French *dette*. The <s> in *island* comes from falsely relating it to French *isle,* from Latin *insula. Island,* however, is derived from Old English *īeg-land* 'island land' or *ēa-land* 'river land.' But, on the whole, English spelling is quite systematic, and relates to sound, though indirectly. Even George Bernard Shaw's (apocryphal) suggestion that *fish* could be spelled <ghoti> supports this claim rather than denying it. Shaw took the <gh> from *enough,* the <o> from *women,* and the <ti> from *nation*. But this is nonsense, because it does not correspond to the regularities of English orthography. The sequence <gh> is used for [f] only at the end of words (and before certain suffixes, as in *laughter*), never at the beginning, where it always spells [g], as in *ghost*. <o> corresponds to [ɪ] only in the single case of *women,* and <ti> corresponds to [š] only when it is followed by another vowel (and not preceded by [s]), as in *nation, partial.*

Shaw's will provided for a prize for the best design of a totally new alphabet for English. The winning entry is given in Table 6, along with a reading passage (from Algeo 1982, 5). This alphabet forms the basis for an exercise in this chapter.

2.6 Exercises

1. Transcribe the following words, as narrowly as you can, following your own pronunciation and/or that of a friend. Include indications for stress (primary and secondary). If you are unsure of a word, transcribe your best guess of its pronunciation before consulting a dictionary. Save the results for further exercises in Chapters 3 and 4.

migratory	opodeldoc	retrogradation	legendary
syntactician	Menomini	synonymy	Aztec
quinquenniad	triptych	helicopter	pterodactyl
abnegate	micrometer (unit of measure)		uncinal
micrometer (measuring instrument)	paludism		

2. Read the passage in the Shaw alphabet given in Table 6 with the aid of the Shaw Alphabet Reading Key. Discuss the ways in which related sounds, e.g., voiced and voiceless pairs of consonants, are represented. Does the same orthographic relation hold between unrelated sounds (or sounds related in a different way)? Is this alphabet suitable for all dialects?

SEGMENTAL PHONOLOGY   45

The following is a short text in the Shaw Alphabet composed by John Algeo, reproduced from Algeo (1993) by permission of the author.

[handwritten Shaw Alphabet text]

THE SHAW ALPHABET READING KEY
The letters are classified as Tall, Deep, Short, and Compound.
Beneath each letter is its full name: its *sound* is shown in **bold** type.

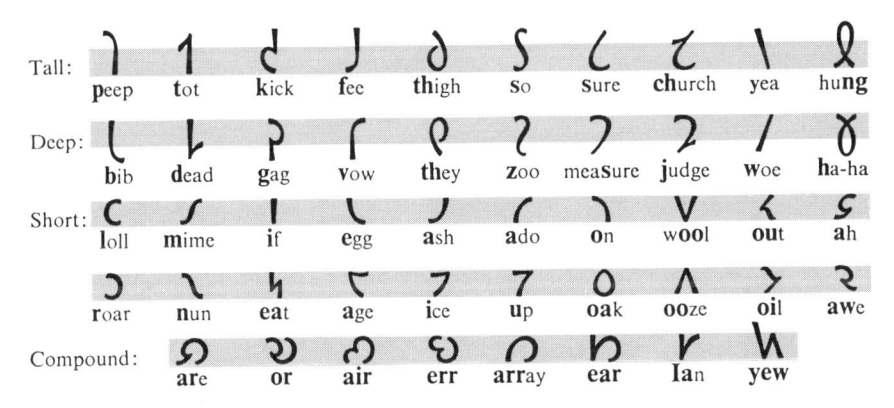

Tall:	**p**eep	**t**ot	**k**ick	**f**ee	**th**igh	**s**o	**Sh**ure	**ch**urch	**y**ea	hu**ng**
Deep:	**b**ib	**d**ead	**g**ag	**v**ow	**th**ey	**z**oo	mea**S**ure	**j**udge	**w**oe	**h**a-ha
Short:	**l**oll	**m**ime	**i**f	**e**gg	**a**sh	**a**do	**o**n	w**oo**l	**ou**t	**a**h
	roar	**n**un	**ea**t	**a**ge	**i**ce	**u**p	**oa**k	**oo**ze	**oi**l	**a**we
Compound:	**are**	**or**	**air**	**err**	**arr**ay	**ear**	**Ia**n	**yew**		

The four most frequent words are represented by single letters: the ҫ, of ſ, and ι, to ʇ.
Proper names may be distinguished by a preceding 'Namer' dot: e.g. ·ɔoſ, Rome.
Punctuation and numerals are unchanged.

Table 6. The Shaw alphabet

3 The syllable and the mora

3.1 CV syllables

The syllable is the basic unit of pronunciation. Every utterance must consist of one or more syllables, and speakers are generally aware of how many syllables there are in words of their language. In the simplest case, each syllable consists of a consonant plus a vowel, often referred to as a CV syllable. We can think of a sequence of such syllables, CVCV..., as a rhythmic rise and fall in sonority, with the vowels as sonority peaks and the consonants as sonority valleys.

The CV syllable is often regarded as the most basic, or CORE syllable. This is suggested by languages like Samoan, which do not allow syllables more complex than CV, and where the majority of syllables are of this type. In Samoan (Marsack 1962), all syllables end in a vowel and two consonants never occur together in a word. A great many Samoan words consist entirely of CV syllables, such as *vave* 'quick,' *manu* 'animal,' *pata* 'butter,' *tusitala* 'author.' Two vowels together generally form a diphthong, as in *moe* 'sleep' and *loi* 'ant.' Although the predominant syllable type in Samoan is CV, some vowel-only (V) syllables also occur. This is exemplified in two cases. One is sequences of vowels which do not form a diphthong (HIATUS), as in *solofanua* 'horse.' The other is words that begin with a vowel, as in *ola* 'live.'

Bell & Hooper (1978, 8–9) summarize a number of other cross-linguistic generalizations which seem to conspire to afford a special status to the CV syllable. Although hiatus occurs in Samoan, it is not permitted within the (phonological) word in about half the world's languages, e.g., Berber. The exclusion of word-internal CC sequences, which we saw in Samoan, characterizes between ten and fifteen percent of the world's languages. Of the languages that permit such word-internal CC sequences, about ten to fifteen percent permit none initially or finally. In about twenty to forty percent of languages a word must begin with a consonant, e.g., Hottentot; conversely in ten to twenty-five percent of languages words must end in a vowel, e.g., Luganda. There are probably no languages in which words must begin with a vowel or end in a consonant.

A second indication that CV is the core syllable comes from so-called syllabic orthographies. The Japanese Hiragana syllabary, used for words for which no conventional kanji is in use, and for inflectional suffixes, has separate symbols for each V, CV, and CyV syllable of the language (see Figure 1, opposite). Syllable-final consonants are limited to a gemination of a following obstruent onset or a nasal that is homorganic with a following stop. This latter has a special symbol (shown in the figure in row 11 as the lone hiragana symbol transliterated *n*). A geminated obstruent is indicated by a small version of the symbol for *tsu*. Thus a word like *kitte* 'stamp' could be written きって in hiragana, while *hakkiri* 'clear' would be はっきり. A syllable with a long vowel is represented by adding the appropriate vowel symbol after the (C)V syllabic; thus *kiito* 'raw silk' could be written きいと.[1] This makes the system MORAIC rather than syllabic. There is a single symbol for (C(y))V syllables, but not for more complex syllables CVC, CVn, or CVː, which require two symbols each. The length of the vowel in a syllable with a long vowel, or the final consonant in a syllable ending in a consonant, constitutes an additional mora, juxtaposed to the mora which the basic (C)V syllable constitutes. In section 3.4.4 we will consider the role of the mora in syllable structure in more detail.

The modern Eskimo syllabary illustrates a similar moraic system (Figure 2, page 50). The (C)V symbols refer either to a single vowel or to a sequence of consonant plus vowel. A dot over any syllabic indicates that the vowel of that syllabic is long. Other symbols, reduced versions of the *Ca* syllabic, represent syllable codas (the so-called finals). In (1) we give some examples of the use of the Eskimo syllabary.

(1)   a.   ᐃᓄᒃᑎᑐᑦ   Inuktitut
               ᐲᑕ   Peter

Figure 3 (page 51) shows the Cherokee syllabary, invented by Sequoya, a native scholar. Sequoya knew the Latin alphabet but was not literate in English. His syllabary consists primarily of Latin letters and variants of these, with a number of apparently newly invented symbols. This syllabary is also moraic.

---

[1] For historical reasons, a consonant followed by long [eː] is written C*e*+*i* and a consonant followed by long [oː] is written C*o*+*u*. These words would ordinarily be written in kanji. The hiragana versions are possible, however, and illustrate the principles of kana orthography quite nicely. I am indebted to Phil Hauptman for discussion of these Japanese data.

V	あ	a	い	i	う	u	え	e	お	o
kV	か	ka	き	ki	く	ku	け	ke	こ	ko
sV	さ	sa	し	ši	す	su	せ	se	そ	so
tV	た	ta	ち	či	つ	tsu	て	te	と	to
nV	な	na	に	ni	ぬ	nu	ね	ne	の	no
hV	は	ha	ひ	hi	ふ	fu	へ	he	ほ	ho
mV	ま	ma	み	mi	む	mu	め	me	も	mo
yV	や	ya			ゆ	yu			よ	yo
rV	ら	ra	り	ri	る	ru	れ	re	ろ	ro
	わ	wa							を	o
	ん	n								
gV	が	ga	ぎ	gi	ぐ	gu	げ	ge	ご	go
zV	ざ	za	じ	ji	ず	zu	ぜ	ze	ぞ	zo
dV	だ	da	ぢ	ji	づ	zu	で	de	ど	do
bV	ば	ba	び	bi	ぶ	bu	べ	be	ぼ	bo
pV	ぱ	pa	ぴ	pi	ぷ	pu	ぺ	pe	ぽ	po
kyV	きゃ	kya			きゅ	kyu			きょ	kyo
šV	しゃ	ša			しゅ	šu			しょ	šo
čV	ちゃ	ča			ちゅ	ču			ちょ	čo
nyV	にゃ	nya			にゅ	nyu			にょ	nyo
hyV	ひゃ	hya			ひゅ	hyu			ひょ	hyo
myV	みゃ	mya			みゅ	myu			みょ	myo
ryV	りゃ	rya			りゅ	ryu			りょ	ryo
gyV	ぎゃ	gya			ぎゅ	gyu			ぎょ	gyo
jV	じゃ	ja			じゅ	ju			じょ	jo
byV	びゃ	bya			びゅ	byu			びょ	byo
pyV	ぴゃ	pya			ぴゅ	pyu			ぴょ	pyo

Figure 1. Japanese Hiragana syllabary.

	Ci		*Cu*		*Ca*		*finals*
ᐃ	i	ᐁ	u	ᐊ	a		
ᐱ	pi	ᐳ	pu	ᐸ	pa	ᐟ	p
ᑎ	ti	ᑐ	tu	ᑕ	ta	ᐟ	t
ᑭ	ki	ᑯ	ku	ᑲ	ka	ᐠ	k
ᑭ	gi	ᒍ	gu	ᒐ	ga	ᐞ	g
ᒥ	mi	ᒧ	mu	ᒪ	ma	ᐦ	m
ᓂ	ni	ᓄ	nu	ᓇ	na	ᐣ	n
ᓯ	si	ᓱ	su	ᓴ	sa	ᐢ	s
ᓕ	li	ᓗ	lu	ᓚ	la	ᐪ	l
ᔨ	ji	ᔪ	ju	ᔭ	ja	ᐨ	j
ᕕ	vi	ᕗ	vu	ᕙ	va	ᐯ	v
ᕆ	ri	ᕈ	ru	ᕋ	ra	ᐨ	r
ᙯ	qi	ᙰ	qu	ᖃ	qa	ᖅ	q
ᖏ	ŋi	ᖑ	ŋu	ᖓ	ŋa	ᖕ	ŋ
ᑦ	łi	ᒀ	łu	ᒡ	ła	ᑊ	ł

Figure 2. Eskimo syllabary.

While onset clusters plus vowel, such as *dla, tsa,* have their own symbols, the coda consonant *s* is represented by its own symbol (without a vowel). This appears to be the only coda consonant used. The only exception to this statement is the symbol for *nah*. However, this is often transcribed *noh* and furthermore "seems never to have been used in actual Cherokee texts" (Trager 1972, 231).

The CV syllable figures prominently in some reduplication systems (McCarthy & Prince 1986). The idea that the simplest syllable is CV, rather than just V, has been used to motivate the ONSET PRINCIPLE in Itô (1989, 223), which is stated in (2).

(2)   Onset Principle

      Avoid $[_\sigma$ V   (i.e., avoid a syllable that begins with a vowel)

This principle claims that a syllable will have an onset whenever possible. Thus, a sequence CVCV will always be syllabified CV.CV, never CVC.V (where the period represents the syllable boundary). In fact, we will go beyond this in proposing that syllable onsets are MAXIMAL. That is, between vowels, a sequence of consonants will be divided such that the largest number consistent with the onset conditions of the language is associated as an onset to a following vowel.

	a	e	i	o	u	ʌ
	D	R	T	Ꮼ	Ꭳ	i
ka	ga	ge	gi	go	gu	gʌ
Ꭹ	Ꮧ	Ի	y	A	J	E
	ha	he	hi	ho	hu	hʌ
	Ꮣ	Ꭾ	Ꭿ	Ꮀ	Γ	Ꮁ
	la	le	li	lo	lu	lʌ
	W	♂	Ꮅ	Ꮆ	M	Ꮊ
	ma	me	mi	mo	mu	
	Ꮉ	Ꮋ	H	Ꮍ	Ꮎ	
hna	nah	na	ne	ni	no	nu	nʌ
Ꮏ	G	Θ	Ꮑ	h	Z	Ꮓ	Ꮕ
	kwa	kwe	kwi	kwo	kwu	kwʌ
	Ꮖ	ω	Ꮘ	Ꮚ	ω	Ꮛ
s	sa	se	si	so	su	sʌ
Ꮝ	Ꮜ	4	Ꮟ	Ꮰ	Ꮡ	R
	da	de	di	do	du	dʌ
	Ꮣ	Ꮥ	Ꮧ	V	S	Ꮩ
	ta	te	ti			
	W	Ꮦ	Ꮨ			
dla	tla	tle	tli	tlo	tlu	tlʌ
Ꮬ	Ꮭ	L	C	Ꮯ	Ꮱ	P
	tsa	tse	tsi	tso	tsu	tsʌ
	Ꮳ	V	Ꮵ	K	Ꮷ	Ꮸ
	wa	we	wi	wo	wu	wʌ
	Ꮹ	Ꮻ	Θ	Ꮼ	Ꮽ	6
	ya	ye	yi	yo	yu	yʌ
	Ꮾ	β	Ꮿ	Ᏽ	Ᏻ	B

Figure 3. Cherokee Syllabary.

The remaining consonants can become a coda of the syllable of the preceding vowel.

Although we have so far assumed that vowels are always syllable peaks, it is also possible to have other sonorants in this function. For example, in *paludism, bottle, bottom,* the word-final sonorant is syllabic. There may be some constraints on this type of syllable; for example, they are never stressed, and the syllabic sonorant cannot be followed by a coda consonant except for inflectional suffixes, as in *bottled*.

3.2 More complex syllables

Languages like English have more complex syllables than languages like Japanese and Eskimo. Two factors have to be taken into consideration in accounting for these languages. First, what types of consonant clusters can appear before and after the vowel of a syllable? Second, where do we divide complex sequences of consonants at syllable boundaries?

Taking the second question first, we will presume that a complex sequence of consonants between vowels is syllabified so as to maximize the onset of the second syllable, in accordance with constraints on possible onsets in the language. The syllabification of *extra* in English is /ɛk.strə/, rather than /ɛks.trə/, or /ɛkst.rə/, since *str-* is a possible syllable-initial sequence. We will return to the question of syllable sequences in section 3.5.3.

Turning to the first question, we will appeal to a hierarchy of sonority. Intuitively, the idea is that the vowel represents the sonority peak of the syllable. Any consonants preceding the vowel should show increasing sonority, going from the beginning of the syllable toward the vowel, while those consonants that follow the vowel should show decreasing sonority, going from the vowel to the end of the syllable. While there are different versions of the sonority hierarchy, we will use the one proposed by Kiparsky (1979). We give this in (3), where the arrows show increasing sonority from the stops to the low vowels.

(3) *Sonority hierarchy*
stops, fricatives, nasals, l, r, w, y, u, i, o, e, a
w ←——————————————————→ s
less sonority   greater sonority

Selkirk (1984b, 116) proposes the Sonority Sequencing Generalization (SSG), which we quote in (4).

(4)   *Sonority Sequencing Generalization (SSG)*
        In any syllable, there is a segment constituting a sonority peak that is preceded and/or followed by a sequence of segments with progressively decreasing sonority values.

Some examples of well-formed syllables (which happen also to be English words) are given in (5).

(5)   brand, print, grind, snark, snarl, swarm

However, not all sequences allowed by the SSG are well-formed syllable onsets in English. For example, English does not allow words beginning with a stop plus nasal. This means that **bnik* is not a possible English word, while *blik* is only accidentally missing from the English lexicon, since *bl* is a possible syllable onset in English *(black, blue)*. English also disallows syllable-initial stop sequences *(*ptik)*, so that it is possible to give a general statement to cover both cases. Kiparsky (1979, 434) formulates a constraint against syllable-initial sequences of two noncontinuants, which we can give as (6).[2]

(6)   *[$_\sigma$ [–cont] [–cont] ...

This constraint is specific to English, as shown by the existence of French words such as *pneu* 'tire' that violate (6) but are well formed by (3) and (4). French also has words like *ptomaïne* 'ptomaine,' which violate (6) and are excluded by (4). One stop cannot be weaker than another stop by (3). However, it might be possible to refine the hierarchy to allow certain points of articulation to stand in a strongweak relation: thus, the onset *pt-*, which appears to be commoner than the onset *tp-* could be represented by making *t* stronger than *p*.

Other onsets that would be allowed by the sonority hierarchy but which do not occur in English are *tl-, dl-,* and *θl-*. Kiparsky rules these out by a constraint that we can state as (7).

(7)   *[$_\sigma$ $\begin{bmatrix} +\text{cor} \\ -\text{strid} \end{bmatrix}$ [l]

Similarly, a sequence of two sonorants is excluded from the onset. This is expressed as (8).

---

[2] We have not given this constraint in terms of Kiparsky's metrical syllable structure. We will return to the internal structure of the syllable in section 3.4.

(8) $*[_\sigma \text{[+son] [+son]}]$

A sequence of stop (oral or nasal) followed by a fricative is excluded, with the possible exception of *tsetse (fly)* and certain other borrowed words.

(9) $*[_\sigma \text{[-cont]} \begin{bmatrix} -\text{son} \\ +\text{cont} \end{bmatrix}]$

On the other hand, Kiparsky notes that some sequences *not* permitted by the SSG (4) are allowed in English. Examples are syllable-initial sequences of *s* plus voiceless stop. Because stops are less sonorous (weaker) than fricatives by (3), such sequences should not occur. For these he proposes "a special dispensation which allows a cluster of descending sonority in the onset provided its first member is [s]; that is, *sp, st, sk* may begin syllables even though s is [stronger on (3)] than p, t, k..." (Kiparsky 1979, 434). We can express this as in (10).

(10) $[_\sigma \text{s} \begin{bmatrix} -\text{son} \\ -\text{cont} \\ -\text{voiced} \end{bmatrix}]$ ... is OK

The commonness of *s* plus stop clusters in English may make it seem strange that a special dispensation is required to permit them. Two types of evidence can be brought to bear on this question. First, some languages, such as Spanish, lack such clusters entirely. The Spanish name of the language, *español,* shows that the language avoids these clusters by inserting a vowel before them. Since the syllable boundary is then between the two consonants, there is no cluster in the onset. Many Spanish speakers who learn English as a second language have difficulty producing these clusters when speaking English.

Kiparsky argues more indirectly for the special status of *s* plus stop clusters in various languages. For example, he notes that these clusters alliterate as units in the verse patterns of languages like Old English. In general, a line of Old English poetry requires two words, one in each half line, to have a stressed syllable beginning with the same consonant. The first half line may have two such words, but the second half line will always have one. Vowel-initial words alliterate regardless of the quality of the vowels. With consonant clusters, *pl-,* for example, can alliterate with any other *p-* in a stressed syllable. But the cluster *st-* can alliterate only with another *st-;* likewise *sp-* and *sk-.* Some examples of alliteration in verse are given in (11) (from Diamond 1970). Alliterating consonants and clusters are italicized.

(11) Þā stōd on stæðe　　sūþ-līče clipode
　　　wičinga ār　　wordum mælde
　　　'Then a messenger of the vikings stood on the shore called out sternly,
　　　spoke with words...' (The Battle of Maldon, lines 25–26)

　　　crēad cnearr on flot,　　cyning ūt ʒewāt
　　　on fealone flōd,　　feorh ʒenerude
　　　'...the ship hastened to sea, the king went out on the dark flood, saved his
　　　life.' (The Battle of Brunanburg, lines 35–36)

　　　Hē ǣrest scōp　　ielda barnum
　　　heofon to hrōfe　　hāliʒ scieppend
　　　'He, the holy creator, first created heaven as a roof for the sons of men...'
　　　(Caedmon's hymn, lines 5–6)

In Gothic, the preterite (a past verb form) is formed by reduplicating the stem-initial consonant and inserting the vowel [ɛ]. For data see also Kim (1990).[3]

(12)　　　*infinitive*　　*preterite*　　*gloss*
　　a.　　háita　　　　　haí-háit　　　'be called'
　　b.　　grēt-an　　　　gaí-grōt　　　'weep'
　　c.　　skáid-an　　　 skaí-skáiþ　　'divide'

In most cases, only the first consonant is copied, as in (12a, b). But if the verb stem begins with s plus stop, as in (12c), the entire cluster is copied. Here, as in the Old English example, clusters of s plus stop have special status.

3.3　The syllable in *SPE*

SPE did not use the syllable as an element of phonological structure or phonological rules. This may seem surprising, inasmuch as the syllable has a long and distinguished tradition, going back at least to the ancient grammarians of Latin and Greek (for some discussion, see W. S. Allen 1973, 27). A consistent definition of the syllable has been difficult to achieve, however. As Pulgram (1970, 11) puts it "...the syllable has been employed in synchronic and diachronic investigations without being defined—on the assumption, it seems, that everyone knows what it is. Everyone does not know."

Perhaps for these reasons, both American structuralist phonology and early

---

[3] The digraph *aí* in these examples represents [ɛ].

generative phonology shunned the syllable as a formal unit, while using it for informal descriptions. In such classic works of American structuralism as Bloomfield (1933) and Hockett (1958), the syllable is either not mentioned or receives only scant attention. The term "syllable" does not appear in the index of *SPE,* which builds on the older structuralist tradition. *SPE*'s disregard for the syllable is in line with the SIMPLICITY METRIC, which evaluates grammars on the basis of the total number of symbols required to express them. If a grammar can express the appropriate generalizations without appealing to the syllable, then the syllable must be seen as so much excess baggage that the grammar can do without. In fact, *SPE* achieved a remarkably comprehensive description of English stress and (morpho-)phonological segmental alternations without any appeal to the syllable.

However, a number of later studies formulated in the *SPE* framework proposed rules that did not express the appropriate generalizations without using the syllable. For example, Kahn (1976, 11) cites (13) as the environment where phonetic [r] is lost in so-called "r-less" dialects of English.

(13) $\underline{\quad} \left\{ \begin{matrix} \# \\ C \end{matrix} \right\}$

This is not a natural environment. Consonant and word boundary do not form a natural class, since they have no common features. Lightner (1972, 33) points out that this is not an isolated case. There are many examples of rules of this type in the world's languages. One is the rule that Kenstowicz & Kisseberth (1979, 96) give for Epenthesis in Yawelmani, in (14).

(14) $\emptyset \rightarrow i / C \underline{\quad} C \left\{ \begin{matrix} \# \\ C \end{matrix} \right\}$

Schane (1968c, 48) proposes (15) for French vowel nasalization.

(15) $V \rightarrow [+\text{nasal}] / \underline{\quad} \left[\begin{matrix} C \\ +\text{nasal} \end{matrix} \right] \left\{ \begin{matrix} \# \\ C \end{matrix} \right\}$

It is the common disjunctive environment {#, C} that is the culprit in these rules. In fact, all three rules refer to the syllable as the conditioning environment. In (13), the loss of [r] in English occurs in syllable codas. In Yawelmani, Epenthesis provides a nucleus in order for a consonant to its right to be syllabifiable. French nasalization in (15) occurs if the vowel is followed by a nasal consonant in the syllable coda.

To take a somewhat more elaborate example, *SPE* develops the Main Stress Rule for English in the following manner, simplified somewhat here for the purpose of discussion. They observe that adjectives with a suffix consisting of a lax vowel followed by one or more consonants are stressed on the antepenultimate syllable if the penultimate syllable contains a lax vowel followed by at most one consonant (column I of 16); otherwise stress is on the penultimate syllable (columns II and III of 16, examples from *SPE*, 81).

(16)

I	II	III
pérsonal	anecdótal	dialéctal
máximal	adjectíval	incidéntal
medícinal	polyhédral	univérsal
ephémeral	mediaéval	abýsmal
magnánimous	desírous	moméntous
polýgamous	polyhédrous	polyándrous
vígilant	complaísant	repúgnant
signíficant	clairvóyant	obsérvant
díffident	antecédent	depéndent
benévolent	inhérent	contíngent

SPE defines a string consisting of a lax vowel followed by no more than one consonant as a WEAK CLUSTER. A string that consists of a tense vowel, as in column II, or a lax (or tense) vowel followed by two (or more) consonants, as in column III, is a STRONG CLUSTER (*SPE*, 29). However, not all strings of two consonants constitute a strong cluster, as the stress on the items in (17) demonstrates.

(17)   éloquent, recálcitrant, lúdicrous, vértebral, chívalrous

This leads *SPE* (83) to represent a weak cluster as in (18).[4]

(18) $\begin{bmatrix} -\text{tense} \\ V \end{bmatrix} C_0^1 \begin{bmatrix} \alpha\text{voc} \\ \alpha\text{cons} \\ -\text{ant} \end{bmatrix}_0$

---

[4] The subscript zero on the large bracket in (18) indicates zero or more of the category in question. *SPE* does not give examples of more than one consonant here.

As defined in (18), a weak cluster consists of a sequence of a lax vowel followed by at most one consonant followed optionally by a glide or [r]. This seems to be an overly complex way to represent the notion "weak cluster," which can be more straightforwardly characterized as a syllable that ends in a short (lax) vowel. Assuming, as we did above, that English syllables maximize the onset, we can syllabify the examples in (17) as *e.lo.quent, re.cal.ci.trant, lu.di.crous,* and *ver.te.bral.* In each case the penultimate syllable contains a weak cluster, and stress is placed on the antepenultimate syllable, following the pattern of column I of (16).[5] In these examples, the syllabic account offers a more elegant descriptive framework than the strictly linear account of *SPE.*

3.4 Internal structure of the syllable

There have been four different approaches to syllable structure in generative phonology since *SPE.* We can characterize these as the SYLLABLE BOUNDARY APPROACH, the AUTOSEGMENTAL APPROACH, the CONSTITUENT STRUCTURE APPROACH and the MORAIC APPROACH.

3.4.1 The syllable boundary approach
Hoard (1971), Stampe (1972), Hooper (1972), and Bailey (1978) represent the syllable boundary approach. Hooper proposes rules that insert syllable boundaries into a string of segments. She observes that a number of phonological processes in Spanish receive a much more insightful formulation when phonological rules can refer to syllable boundaries as well as segments and morphosyntactic boundaries such as word boundary and formative boundary (which were used in *SPE*). Hooper's approach is still basically linear, in that it conceives of the syllable boundary as one of the boundary symbols in the string of elements which phonological rules can refer to.

Stampe applies the same basic approach to English, especially to its faster and more reduced varieties. He discusses various, often subtle allophonic processes in terms of syllable boundaries. In this approach, stress determines syllabification, in that a stressed syllable attracts an onset from a following syllable into its own coda. For example, Stampe claimes that English *t* is flapped when syllable final (as in *wat.er*) and aspirated in syllable initial position (as in *a.ttack*), given his syllabifications.

---

[5] The case of *chivalrous* cited in (17) is problematic for the syllabic account, since *lr-* is not a possible syllable onset in English, although it would be allowed as an onset by the Sonority Sequencing Generalization (4). The reverse cluster is allowed in the coda of monosyllabic *Carl,* where it also conforms to the Sonority Sequencing Generalization.

Hoard carries Stampe's approach a step further. Hoard's syllabifications attach all intervocalic consonants to the preceding vowel if it is stressed, producing such syllabifications as *ampl.i.fy, atl.as, lingu.ist,* and *ostr.ich.* These syllabifications are contrary to the SSG (4) and to the onset maximization principle. Hoard also analyzes English stop allophones from this point of view.

Bailey's approach is similar, except that he argues for GRADIENT syllabifications, where some sequences can be syllabified differently depending on speech rate, style, dialect, etc. Bailey also assumes that stress affects syllabification, without, however, showing how stress is assigned. Given our argument in the preceding section that stress assignment depends on syllabification, these approaches that determine syllabification from stress are problematic. Selkirk (1984a) appears to resolve this dilemma by ordering syllabification before stress assignment, and then having stress-dependent resyllabification rules. As we argue in section 6.6, resyllabification is neither necessary nor desirable. In Chapter 5 we will show that all of the relevant allophonic rules can be adequately formulated in terms of syllabifications that conform to the SSG (4) and the onset maximization principle. To do this, we need higher prosodic constituents, which we demonstrate are needed independently.

3.4.2 The autosegmental approach

Kahn (1976) and Clements & Keyser (1983) represent the autosegmental approach to syllable structure. In this approach, syllables are built on strings of segments by a set of autosegmental associations. As we saw in Chapter 1, autosegmental associations link two or more tiers of elements, not necessarily on a one-to-one basis. Kahn, for example, proposes five rules for autosegmental association in English. His first rule associates a syllable to each [+syllabic] segment. His second rule then attaches the maximal permissible string of consonants as an onset to each syllable (his instantiation of the principle of onset maximization), and then attaches the maximal string of coda segments to each syllable. These first two rules are obligatory, and are assumed to be characteristic of slow speech, such as might be used for reading syllable by syllable.

For normal speech, Kahn proposes that some segments are AMBISYLLABIC, that is, that they belong to both the preceding and following syllables. In formalizing this, he makes use of the autosegmental provision for multiple linking between tiers. Kahn finds the *n* of *pony,* for example, to be *phonetically* ambisyllabic, although it is by no means clear that there is evidence for ambisyllabicity that is strictly phonetic. Kahn's rules make a single consonant between vowels ambisyllabic when the second vowel is unstressed; likewise the first consonant of a cluster in that same position. So, by his rules, the *s* of *Boston,* for example, is ambisyllabic. The stress of the vowel preceding an intervocalic consonant or cluster is not a factor in deciding whether the segment is ambisyllabic, in Kahn's framework. This means that the *t* of *capital* and the *m* of *enemy* would also be ambisyllabic. Since Kahn's ambisyllabification rule follows stress placement, this treatment is similar to Selkirk (1984a), and does not suffer from the apparent contradiction seen in the other syllable boundary approaches.

We question the need for ambisyllabicity from two angles. One is that such a construct is not needed when higher prosodic structure is taken into account. In Chapter 5, we show that aspiration of English voiceless stops can be predicted from their position in the foot: aspiration applies to voiceless stops in foot-initial position. Feet are needed independently to account for stress, as shown in Chapter 4. We shall see that all allophones of English segments can be predicted on the basis of their position in genuine prosodic units—the mora, the syllable, the foot, and the phonological word. Kahn's invoking of ambisyllabicity seems to stem from his failure to recognize higher levels of prosodic structure.

The other angle for questioning the need for ambisyllabicity arises when we consider the moraic structure of syllables in section 3.4.4. Kahn interprets an ambisyllabic segment as being simultaneously the coda of one syllable and (part of) the onset of the next. In moraic theory, a coda consonant contributes to the weight of a syllable, while an onset consonant does not. An intervocalic consonant that is simultaneously a coda and an onset can only be interpreted as a geminate in this theory, never as a single intervocalic consonant. Borowsky, Itô, & Mester (1984) attempt to link geminate and single intervocalic ambisyllabic consonants by giving them identical representations, claiming the differences are spelled out phonetically. But gemination, which constitutes a strengthening of intervocalic consonants, and ambisyllabicity, which constitutes a weakening (such as flapping in English and what Borowsky et al. refer to as consonant gradation in Danish), seem too incompatible to be represented in the same manner. Furthermore, since all the processes in Danish discussed by Borowsky et al. can be equally well formulated in prosodic terms, ambisyllabicity seems redundant there also. Since the notion of ambisyllabicity further leads to contradictions in moraic theory, we are led to abandon ambisyllabicity, since the arguments for moraic structure are quite compelling.

More recently, there have been other proposals for ambisyllabicity. Two of these are found in Hogg & McCully (1987) and in discussions of dependency phonology (see Anderson & Ewen 1987). Hogg & McCully initially adopt Kahn's approach to ambisyllabicity, then add some additional examples and analysis, primarily involving the aspiration of voiceless stops. In particular, they claim that the medial voiceless stop in *actress* is aspirated. They observe correctly that the following *r* is devoiced, which they regard as "an equivalent of aspiration" (Hogg & McCully 1987, 55). Their account of this goes well beyond Kahn's analysis in that they claim that the entire cluster *tr* becomes ambisyllabic. A look at the resulting structure in (19) shows why this account should be rejected.

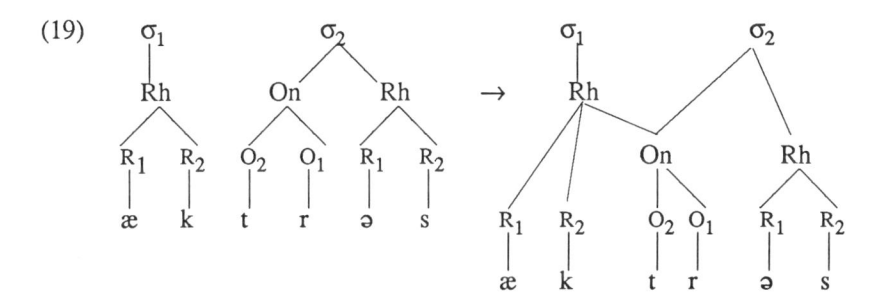

(19)

```
      σ₁              σ₂                      σ₁              σ₂
      |              / \                      |              / \
      Rh           On   Rh          →         Rh            /   \
     / \          / \   / \                  /|\          On     Rh
    R₁ R₂       O₂ O₁  R₁ R₂                / | \        / \     / \
    |  |         |  |  |  |                /  |  \      O₂ O₁   R₁ R₂
    æ  k         t  r  ə  s              R₁  R₂  \     |  |     |  |
                                          |   |         t  r     ə  s
                                          æ   k
```

As Vogel (1989, 224–5) points out, the rhyme of the first syllable in the derived structure "dominates not only R positions, but also an onset constituent. To my knowledge, this possibility has never been proposed elsewhere. Furthermore, since it would have rather far-reaching consequences for our understanding of the internal structure of syllables to allow a rhyme to dominate an onset, it seems rather hasty on the part of the authors to suggest such a solution without even mentioning some of its possible ramifications." Vogel also points out that, although in (19) *t* is literally "syllable initial and not syllable final"—Kahn's environment for aspiration (1976, 45)—Kahn's formal rule aspirates stops that are found only in onset position. Therefore, Hogg & McCully's treatment involves a misinterpretation of Kahn as well as a formally incoherent structure.

It seems to me that Hogg & McCully have confused two rules. It is not at all clear why the devoicing of a liquid after a voiceless stop should "be regarded as equivalent of aspiration." The *r* in *actress* is indeed devoiced, but there is no evidence for aspiration of *t* in this word. A word like *stress* further confirms this view: the *t* cannot be aspirated because of the preceding *s*, but the *r* is devoiced nevertheless. According to our formulation of this process in Chapter 5, section 5.2, Aspiration applies to voiceless stops that are foot initial, and no ambisyllabicity is needed. The rule that devoices sonorants after voiceless consonants is an entirely separate rule. In Chapter 5, section 5.2, we formulate this as a rule that devoices sonorants when they are preceded by a voiceless consonant in the same syllable. This rule devoices sonorants after any voiceless consonant, not only stops; for example, it devoices the *l* in *Islip*. Since these rules have distinct domains of application and distinct conditions, they must be separate rules. This result not only simplifies the statement of these processes but removes any need for structures such as that on the right of (19).

3.4.3 The constituent structure approach

In the constituent structure approach to the syllable, the syllable is divided into constituents. The first division is into an ONSET and RHYME, with the rhyme in turn further divided into a PEAK and CODA. This is illustrated in (20).

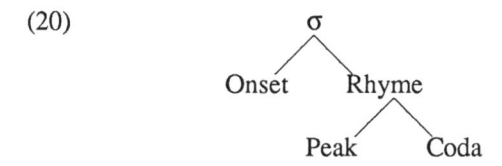

(20)
```
          σ
         / \
     Onset  Rhyme
            / \
          Peak  Coda
```

We use the Greek letter lower-case sigma (σ) to represent syllable. The division into onset and rhyme is justified by the fact that the rhyme is relevant to stress assignment in many languages, such as English, while the onset only rarely serves this function.[6] The distinction made in *SPE* between heavy and light clusters can now be seen as precisely a function of whether or not the rhyme contains a branching structure.[7] The rhyme is a unit of poetry in a number of languages. So in English we say that a group of monosyllables rhyme, such as *rhyme, time, lime, mime,* just in case they are identical in the rhyme component of the syllable. In addition, the units in (20) serve as the domain of PHONOTACTIC constraints. When we say that some group of consonants in English is a possible onset, we refer to this constituent. In the autosegmental approach, an onset cluster is not a single constituent.

3.4.4 The moraic approach

McCawley (1968, 58, fn. 39) defines the mora as "something of which a long syllable consists of two and a short syllable consists of one." Like the syllable, the mora is a unit which is convenient to use but difficult to define. It is perhaps easier to illustrate the concept by example than to define it explicitly. We will make

---

[6] See Davis (1988) for a few convincing cases of this type.

[7] This assumes that long vowels are represented as two syllabic positions. Notice, however, that saying that the rhyme contains a branching structure can either mean that the rhyme itself branches into a peak and a coda consonant (or cluster), or that the rhyme dominates a branching peak. The moraic approach allows a further simplification: a heavy syllable is one that contains two moras (i.e., that branches). The moraic approach does not allow reference to the onset and rhyme as constituents; however, the required phonotactic constraints are still expressible.

considerable use of moras in our discussion of English stress in Chapter 4. The mora concept also plays an important role in prosodic morphology (McCarthy & Prince 1986; 1990). We will use the terms HEAVY and LIGHT in reference to syllables instead of McCawley's long and short, reserving the latter terms for segment length.

There are two approaches to moraic structure currently in vogue. In this book, we will follow the theory presented in Hyman (1985), with slight amendments. In Hyman's theory the mora is a subconstituent of the syllable. The mora organizes segments into constituents, which are somewhat different from the constituents described in section 3.4.3 on the constituent structure approach. In Hyman's theory, the mora can be considered a true prosodic unit in the sense that all segments belong to moras. This is part of a more general principle of prosodic structure, formalized by Itô (1986, 2; 1989, 230) as the principle of PROSODIC LICENSING (21).

(21) *Prosodic Licensing*:
All phonological units must be prosodically licensed, i.e., belong to higher prosodic structure.

This requires that all segments must belong to moras,[8] all moras must belong to syllables, all syllables must belong to feet, and all feet must belong to phonological words.

Hyman assumes that each segment of an underlying representation is provided initially with a weight unit, which he represents by 'x' but which we will refer to as 'm' for mora. Whenever a [+consonantal] segment is followed by a [−consonantal] segment, the first segment loses its weight and is attached to the following segment by the Onset Creation Rule (22). We assume that this rule applies as part of the syllabification process on stratum 1 of the lexical phonology.

(22) *Onset Creation Rule*

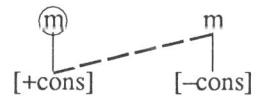

```
    ⓜ         m
    |        ╱
    |    ╱
[+cons]   [−cons]
```

The circle around the first *m* symbolizes that it is deleted by the rule, which simultaneously forms a link from the [+cons] segment to the second *m*. This

---

[8] Itô does not specifically include the mora in her treatment of the syllable, but the mora is considered a prosodic unit in most treatments.

creates a CV mora, which is equivalent to the core CV syllable discussed in section 3.1. Additional material is incorporated into this mora in a language like English, which allows fairly complex syllable onsets (see section 3.5.1). It should be noted that the Onset Creation Rule expresses the same claim as Itô's Onset Principle (2), which is that syllables have onsets if possible.

We will adopt a slightly different version of moraic theory here. Hyman defines the feature [+consonantal] somewhat differently than usual. In particular, he has glides as [+consonantal]. This makes it more difficult to capture the set of vowels and glides as a natural class [−consonantal] in the usual characterization of this feature. It also makes it more difficult to describe vowel-glide alternations, of which we will see some English examples in Chapter 7.

A syllable may consist of at most two moras in English. Languages differ as to what may count as a mora.[9] In English, a light syllable is one which ends in a short, lax vowel while a heavy syllable is anything else—a heavy syllable can contain a tense (or long) vowel or it can be closed by a consonant. In (23) we propose the rules for the assignment of moras in English.

(23) 1. Assign a mora to the string C_0V, where V is a local sonority maximum according to the Sonority Hierarchy (3) and C_0 is a possible (maximal) onset according to the sonority hierarchy and the restrictions and dispensations on onsets.

2. If V in 1. is tense, assign a second mora to it.[10]

3. A string C_1 which does not belong to an onset must be a coda. Adjoin such a string to the second mora of a bimoraic vowel; assign it a mora on its own after a monomoraic vowel.

The examples in (24) (opposite) illustrate the operation of these rules on some of the words we considered in (16) of section 3.3.[11] We can now state the generalization for the stress of words such as those in (16) even more simply. These words receive penultimate stress just in case the penultimate syllable contains two moras.

---

[9] In Chapter 4, section 4.2.2, we will discuss the stress system of Eastern Cheremis, which has a different characterization of the mora than English.

[10] We might alternatively assume that tense vowels have a single mora in underlying representation, to which rule 1 assigns a second mora.

[11] We will not consider word-final consonants to be moraic, since, as we argue in Chapter 4, these consonants are extrametrical, meaning that they are ignored by the rules for syllabification and stress. We will also argue that the final suffix is extrametrical in the words of (16), a point we are disregarding for the moment.

(24) I personal   magnanimous   vigilant

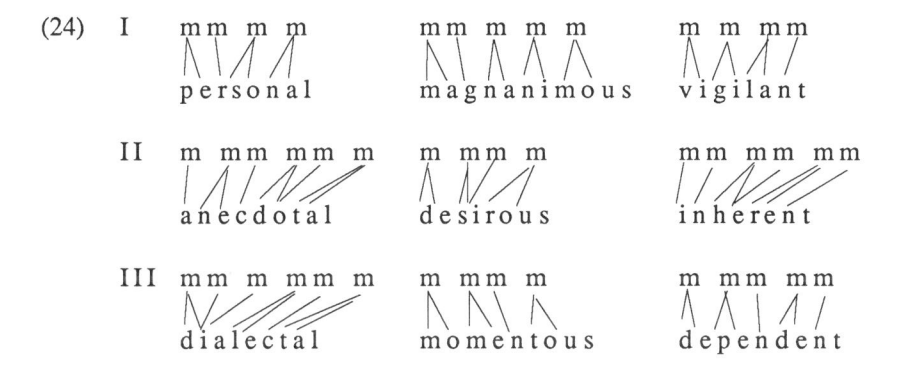

II anecdotal   desirous   inherent

III dialectal   momentous   dependent

3.5 The syllable in English

In this section we will catalogue the possible syllables of English by looking at possible onsets at the beginning of words and possible codas at the end of words. We will then turn to sequences of syllables within the word.

3.5.1 *The onset*
Syllable onsets may consist of from zero to three consonants in English. Vowel-initial words have zero onset. Any single consonant from the inventory of English consonants (Table 1 of Chapter 2) can begin a syllable, phonetically. Two apparent exceptions are *ž* and *ŋ*, which cannot begin a word, but may be said to begin word-medial stressless syllables as in *pleasure* and *singer*, respectively. In Chapter 2, section 2.2.5, we explained the absence of word-initial *ŋ* as the result of its being always derived from an underlying representation consisting of *n* plus a velar consonant or *h*. There is no comparable explanation for the lack of word-initial *ž*, which seems to result from accidental historical changes. Word internally *ž* seems to be completely parallel to its voiceless partner *š*, as in *pressure*, which does occur word initially.

In Table 1 (overleaf) we list possible two-segment onset clusters in English. In (25) we list some words that illustrate the clusters in Table 1.

(25) play, pray, pueblo, pure
blade, braid, bwana, beauty
trim, twin, tune
dry, dwell, dune
clan, cry, quick, cute
glow, green, Guam, gules

(continued overleaf)

	p	t	k	f	m	n	l	r	w	y
p							pl	pr	(pw)	py
b							bl	br	(bw)	by
t								tr	tw	ty
d								dr	dw	dy
k							kl	kr	kw	ky
g							gl	gr	gw	gy
f							fl	fr		fy
v							(vl)	(vr)		vy
θ								θr	θw	θy
s	sp	st	sk	sf	sm	sn	sl		sw	sy
š	(šp)				(šm)		(šl)	šr	(šw)	
h										hy
m										my
n										ny
l										ly

Table 1. Two-consonant onsets in English (based on Bauer et al. 1980).

fly, fry, few
Vladimir, vroom, view
three, thwart, thulium
speak, steak, scan, Sphinx, smile, snow, slow, swarm, suit
spiel, schmalz, schlep, shrink, schwa
hue
mute
new
lute

In presenting Table 1, we have made a few additions. We have added the clusters *Cw-, vl-,* and *kr-* (*pueblo, bwana, Guam, Vladimir,* and *vroom*). While foreign in origin or unusual, we consider these clusters to be integrated into the phonotactics of English, since they do not present any difficulty to English speakers. We have added *gules* and *view* for a somewhat different reason. A quick survey of (25) is enough to conclude that the only English onsets consisting of a consonant followed by *y* are ones in which *y* is followed by the vowel /u/. This is a skewed distribution. No other onset cluster in English is restricted in terms of the vowel that follows.[12] In Chapter 7 we shall suggest an explanation for this skewness: the

---
[12] Words like *William* are not a problem for this claim, since C and *y* are in different syllables.

y is inserted by a phonological rule. We will claim that *y* never participates in onset clusters at all, in the initial syllabification. We can capture this by proposing a constraint on syllabification, similar to the constraints we saw in (6), (7), (8), and (9), which prohibits onset clusters ending in *y* at stratum 1 syllabification, as in (26).

(26) $*[_\sigma C_1^2 \, y$

This constraint will be important in our discussion of certain segmental processes in Chapter 7.

In Table 1 we have also added the clusters represented by the examples *tune, dune, thulium, suit, new,* and *lute*. Since these are clusters involving *y*, our remarks about the skewness of the distribution of such clusters with the following vowel apply here also. In particular, we assume that the *y* here is not present at stratum 1 syllabification, but it is inserted by rule. Because Bauer et al. were describing *American* English pronunciation, they did not include clusters of a [+coronal] consonant followed by *y*. Now, it is true that many North American English speakers do not produce such clusters, but we felt that it was safer to include these clusters, since they are produced by many speakers, including many North Americans.

We have also added five clusters beginning with *š*. These clusters appear only in borrowed words, but they are not particularly difficult for English speakers and they fit well with the regularities of English syllable structure.

Three-consonant onsets are limited to those listed in (27).

(27)   a.   spl   splice   b.   spy   spew
            spr   sprite   sty   stew
            str   stray   sky   skew
            skl   sclera
            skr   scream
            skw   squeak

These three-consonant onsets are what one would expect. The three-consonant onsets are those whose first two consonants form a possible two-consonant onset, and whose last two consonants form another possible two-consonant onset. The sonorants *l, r, w* and *y* appear frequently as the second member of a two-consonant cluster, but do not appear as first members of such clusters (except for *ly*, which we explain in terms of *y*-Insertion). Two-consonant onsets beginning with nonsonorants are limited to *s* plus a voiceless stop, and so we are left with clusters whose first member is *s*, second member is a voiceless stop, and final member is a sonorant, with *stl* excluded because *tl* is not a possible onset. The lack of *spw-* and *stw-* appears to be accidental. The impossibility of *sfl-*, *sfr-*, and *sfy-* may simply be a result of the rarity of *sf-* initial clusters in English. It should be possible to get *smy-* and *sny-*, but these are excluded also; *sly-* may be attested in *sluice*. Once again, three-consonant clusters whose last member is *y* (27b) appear only before *u*, and we consider this *y* to be inserted, with these clusters excluded at stratum 1 syllabification.

3.5.2 The coda

The coda is problematic, given the complexity of possible structures that may appear there. A number of inflectional suffixes can appear at the ends of words, giving rise to quite complex coda clusters, as in *sixths* [sɪksθs], which also includes the derivational suffix *-th*. Codas can contain clusters of two stops or two sonorants. We noted in section 3.5.1 that such clusters are excluded from onsets. Finally, the most complex codas appear after a short nucleus but not after a long nucleus. This implies that we have to consider the structure of the rhyme as a whole, not the coda alone, in determining the possible combinations in these positions.

First, we will catalogue the possible two-consonant codas in Table 2 (opposite) as we did with onsets in Table 1. In (28), we list words containing these clusters as codas. The final clusters represented in italics are found only where the final consonant is inflectional.

(28) apt, depth, copse
robed, robes
eighth
width, adze
act, ax
sagged, sags
watched
judged
soft, fifth, *laughs*
loved, loves
pithed, deaths
smoothed, smooths
rasp, last, bask
gazed
wished
rouged   *(continued opposite)*

	p	b	t	d	k	g	č	ǰ	f	v	θ	s	z	š	m	n	l
p			pt								pθ	ps					
b				bd									bz				
t											tθ						
d											dθ		dz				
k			kt									ks					
g				gd									gz				
č			čt														
ǰ				ǰd													
f			ft								fθ	fs					
v				vd									vz				
θ			θt									θs					
ð				ðd									ðz				
s	sp		st		sk												
z				zd													
š			št														
ž				žd													
m	mp		mt						mf				mz				
n			nt	nd			nč	nǰ			nθ	ns	nz				
ŋ				ŋd	ŋk						ŋθ		ŋz				
l	lp	lb	lt	ld	lk		lč	lǰ	lf	lv	lθ	ls	lz	lš	lm	ln	
r	rp	rb	rt	rd	rk	rg	rč	rǰ	rf	rv	rθ	rs	rz	rš	rm	rn	rl

Table 2. Two-consonant codas in English (based on Bauer et al. 1980).

lamp, *dreamt,* lymph, *reams*

paint, hint, *pained,* hand, lunch, lunge, tenth, flounce, tense, lens, Haines, *ringed,* rink, length, *rings*

gulp, bulb, bolt, fold, bulk, mulch, bulge, elf, twelve, health, pulse, Wells, Welsh, helm, kiln

harp, herb, heart, hard, bark, pygarg, arch, gorge, surf, carve, hearth, farce, Mars, marsh, torm, barn, snarl

Three-consonant codas are more limited. The list in (29) is probably exhaustive.

(29) /dst/ midst /lpt/ sculpt
/kst/ next /lkt/ mulct
/ksθ/ sixth /lks/ calx
/mpt/ tempt /lfθ/ twelfth
/mps/ mumps /rkt/ infarct

/nst/	against	/rmθ/	warmth
/ŋst/	amongst	/rpt/	excerpt
/ŋkt/	instinct	/rps/	corpse
/ŋks/	lynx		

Four-consonant codas appear to be limited to cases where the three-consonant codas in (29) are followed by an inflectional suffix: *sixths, instincts, sculpts, excerpts.*

It should be noted that the last consonant in all the examples of (29) is a voiceless coronal obstruent *t, s,* or *θ*. In (28) also, two-consonant codas mostly end in coronals. With few exceptions, the words in (28) and (29) have short, lax vowels. A long vowel may occur before a two-consonant cluster if the cluster contains only coronals but not otherwise: *paint* but not *paimp. Long vowels do not occur before three-consonant clusters at all. These facts suggest that we have a closer look at the structure of words and the possible syllables within words.

3.5.3 The Coda Condition

One striking fact about the codas investigated so far is that they are all *word final*. When we look at codas *internal* to the word, we find that they are considerably more limited. If the vowel of a nonfinal syllable is long (i.e., tense or a diphthong), it tends to be an open syllable. The examples in (30) are typical.

(30) me.te.or, fi.nal, li.brary, foi.ble, vo.cal, au.thor, pow.der

If a nonfinal syllable is closed, it tends to have a short vowel. In (31) we give examples where two consonants appear between vowels. Where these two consonants cannot form an onset to the second syllable, the two consonants are divided between the two syllables, the first consonant forming the coda of the first syllable and the second consonant forming the onset of the second syllable. As a result the first syllable is closed.

(31) in.ter.nal, cap.tain, tem.per, pan.ther, sel.dom

In cases where the first syllable is closed and contains a long vowel, its closing consonant is most frequently a sonorant HOMORGANIC (i.e., sharing its point of articulation) with a following consonant. The examples in (32) illustrate this.[13]

---

[13] Data from Borowsky (1989), who presents an apparently exhaustive list of examples of this type. Notice that in *ointment* the homorganic obstruent is in the same syllable as the sonorant; in the other examples, the obstruent begins the following syllable.

(32)   chamber, angel, dainty, launder, mountain, ointment

Examples with a long vowel followed by a nonhomorganic consonant in nonfinal position are extremely rare, the list in (33) being exhaustive (from Borowsky 1989, 153).

(33)   deictic, deixis, seismic, peascod, fo'c'sle

We find numerous cases of two consonants between vowels where both consonants belong to the following syllable. These are cases where the two consonants make a well-formed onset. In these cases, both long and short vowels are found in the first syllable.

(34)   *stress on first syllable*   *stress on second syllable*

   whi.sper, A.pril, ci.trus,   de.spair, di.sturb, e.scape,
   sa.cred, aw.kward   su.blime, se.crete, re.quire

Likewise, if three consonants form a possible onset, they belong to the second syllable. These all begin with /s/, as we saw in (27), and the vowel of the first syllable may be long or short.[14]

(35)   mi.stress, di.stress, pa.stry, pa.strami, boi.strous, texture [tɛk.styur]

If the three consonants cannot form an onset, the last two form an onset if they can. Here again, the vowel of the first syllable is typically short.

(36)   pam.phlet, coun.try, pil.grim, an.thrax, in.stant, textile [tɛk.stɑɪl]

Long vowels are found in this environment in (37), apparently the only examples, according to Borowsky (1989).

---

[14] Hayes (1980, 147–149; 1982, 247, fn. 9) suggests that the unmarked syllabification of the sequence Vs.C(L)V is as indicated by the period, claiming that this is an exception to the principle of onset maximization. He cites the stress of words like *Alaska,* where his syllabification would be Alas.ka, making the second syllable closed and so able to attract stress. In this case, we might say that the marked character of *s*-stop clusters, requiring a special dispensation (10), takes precedence over the principle of onset maximization. On this view, words like *orchestra* need to have a specially marked syllabification in the lexicon.

(37)   Cam.bridge, laun.dry, scoun.drel, foun.dry, wain.scot

The syllable division is after the second of three consonants when the last two cannot form an onset (and the first two *can* form a coda). The first vowel is usually short here too, and the coda consonants are homorganic.

(38)   ant.ler, emp.ty, func.tion, pump.kin, part.ner, vint.ner

Long vowels in this position appear to be limited to words in *-ment*.

(39)   oint.ment, appoint.ment

Four consonants between vowels are limited to cases where the second consonant is /s/, and the last three consonants form the onset of the second syllable. The first vowel is always short in these cases.

(40)   in.strument, ob.struct, express [εk.sprεs], exclaim [εk.skleym], extra [εk.strə]

To summarize the results of this section so far, when a sequence of consonants appears between vowels, the consonants are divided between syllables so that the maximal group of consonants forms the onset of the second syllable, with the remaining consonants, if any, constituting the coda of the first syllable. This much follows from the principle of onset maximalization.

Borowsky explains the limited possibilities in the rhyme by representing the rhyme in English not as the complex structures we saw in (28) and (29), but the simpler structures in (41), where X can represent either C or V and VV is interpreted as a long (tense) vowel.

(41)   a. medial   Rhyme   b.   final   Rhyme
                    /\   /|\
                   V X   V X C

Word-medial heavy rhymes (41a) are a tense (long) vowel with no coda or a single short lax vowel followed by a single consonant. Word finally, more complex rhymes can arise in two ways. One is that a single word-final consonant can be considered EXTRAMETRICAL (i.e., unsyllabified), and as such does not count in the calculation of possible rhymes. We will use extrametricality quite extensively in Chapter 4 when we discuss English stress. The second is that one or two coronal consonants at the end of a word can form an APPENDIX, which is outside the rhyme proper. Therefore, Borowsky considers that words like *kee(p), lea(ve), lar(k), el(k), har(p)* have the final consonant extrametrical (indicated here by parentheses), and so are not a violation of the rhyme structure in (41a). Similarly, words like *sixth* (see 29) have the permissible rhyme [ɪk] followed by the appendix [sθ] of coronals. For words like *tempt*, we must reckon a permissible rhyme [ɛm] followed by the extrametrical [p] followed by the appendix [t]. Because of extrametricality and the appendix, all rhymes can be considered to have the structure in (41a), with one exception that we will get to very shortly. Borowsky proposes a Coda Condition which can be stated in moraic terms as in (42).

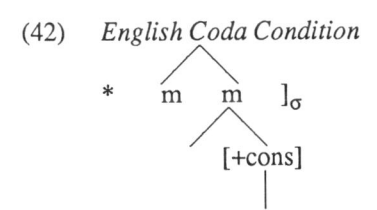

(42) *English Coda Condition*

$$* \quad \underset{[+\text{cons}]}{\hat{m} \ \hat{m}} \ ]_\sigma$$

i.e., the second mora of a syllable may not dominate a nonbranching consonantal segment if the moras are linked.

The intended interpretation of (42) is that the second mora of a syllable cannot dominate a sequence of two segments, either the second half of a tense vowel plus a consonant or a sequence of two consonants. It may be a bit of a misnomer to call this a Coda Condition since the coda is that part of the syllable that follows the nucleus, be it long or short. The moraic notation does not explicitly include a coda constituent. Nonbranching second moras are permitted whether they dominate a consonant as in *captain* (31) or the second half of a tense long vowel, as in *final* (30).

We now have to explain cases like *antler* and *Cambridge*, which seem to violate the Coda Condition. In *antler*, the second mora of the first syllable dominates two consonants: *nt*. In *Cambridge*, the second mora of the first syllable dominates the second half of a tense vowel plus the consonant *m*.

The key to the problem is the fact that both words have adjacent homorganic consonants: the sequence *mb* in *Cambridge* and the sequence *nt* in *antler*. In autosegmental phonology it is common to assume that segments that share an articulation actually share the feature matrix that defines that articulation. This is known as LINKING. Linked segments often behave differently than unlinked segments. For example, in Tigrinya there is a rule that makes a back obstruent (such as *k*) into a fricative when it follows a vowel. Hayes (1986, 336) formulates this rule as in (43).

(43)   V   C
         |
$\begin{bmatrix} -son \\ +back \end{bmatrix}$ → [+cont] / ___

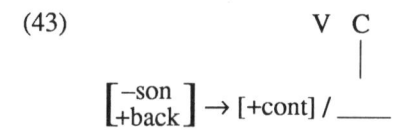

In (44a) we give the underlying and surface forms for 'dogs' to illustrate the operation of the rule. In (44b) we give the underlying and surface forms for 'he boasted,' which does not undergo the rule.

(44) a.   /ʔakaləb/   →   [ʔaxaləb]   'dogs'

      b.   /fäkkär-ä/   →   [fäkkärä]   'he boasted'
                               *[fäxxärä]
                               *[fäxkärä]

While a single velar stop becomes a fricative in (44a), the geminate velar stop in (44b) fails to spirantize in whole or in part. Hayes explains this in terms of the LINKING CONSTRAINT, which we cite as (45).

(45) *Linking Constraint* (Hayes 1986, 331)
      Association lines in structural descriptions are interpreted as exhaustive.

Because the geminate k in Tigrinya *fäkkär-a* has a structure like that in (46), where two consonant slots are linked to a single articulation [k], and because rule (43) requires only a *single* link between one consonant and an articulation, the Linking Condition prevents the application of spirantization to this form.

(46)   C   C
             \   /
              \ /
               k

Itô (1986, 27) proposed that the Linking Condition could constrain passive conditions (such as the English Coda Condition) as well as active rules (such as Tigrinya Spirantization). She illustrated this effect with coda conditions for Japanese, Italian, and Finnish. In the case of the English Coda Condition, we assume that adjacent consonants with the same point of articulation are linked to a common place node (part of the feature hierarchy given as (13) in Chapter 1). The explanation for cases like *antler* (38) is now as follows: because [n] and [t] are both coronal, they share their place node. Because of the Linking Constraint (45), the English Coda Condition (42) rules out a branching second mora whose second member is an *unlinked* matrix, but does not rule out cases with linked matrices, i.e., with a shared place specification. This allows *empty* but not, e.g., **emkty*. It also allows *Cambridge* but not **Camkridge* (with a long vowel in the first syllable). To make this clearer, we show the domain of the English Coda Constraint in both types of examples in (47).

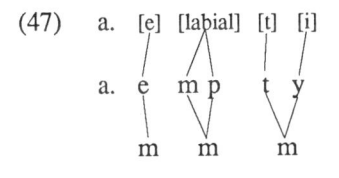

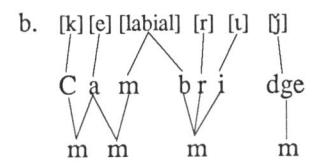

(47) a. [e] [labial] [t] [i]

     a. e m p t y
          m   m   m

    b. [k] [e] [labial] [r] [t] [j]

        C a m b r i dge
        m m   m   m

There remains a residue of cases which cannot be explained by this analysis so far. In addition to word edges, rhymes with branching second moras, ruled out by (42), are found inside compounds and before certain suffixes, which we will refer to as stratum 2 suffixes, a concept to be developed at greater length in Chapter 6. If the basic principles governing syllabification (and, as we argue in Chapter 4, stress) apply only to underived lexical items and items derived with stratum 1 affixes, then compounds and stratum 2 affixes are no longer a problem. Some examples of both appear in (48).

(48) a. *Compounds*
       worldwide, bandsman, helmsman, tribesman

    b. *Stratum 2 suffixes*
       childhood, apartment, cowardly, eventful, tasteless, worldly

Genuine counterexamples appear to be rather rare. With a long vowel, the words of (33) are a problem. With a short vowel, words like *arctic* are a problem. Borowsky gives a list of fifteen items of this type, that is, with word medial CCC clusters with a syllable division after the second C where no adjacent pairs can have linked place features. Many of these items are rare. We should also note the common pronunciation [ɑrrɪk] for *arctic*. In short, the English Coda Condition (42) appears to put just the right conditions on intervocalic clusters in English. If rhymes are limited to two positions after the first vowel position, with onsets unrestricted (beyond 27), we explain why intervocalic clusters are limited to four.[15]

3.7 Exercises

1. Divide the words of exercise 1 of Chapter 2 into syllables. Show the structure of each syllable in terms of a metrical structure dominated by σ with moras as in (23) of this chapter. Save the results for a further exercise in Chapter 4.

2. Repeat exercise 1 using:
    a. your name
    b. your birthplace
    c. your favourite singer, actor, or whatever.

3. Which of the following hypothetical English words are impossible, and why?

    a. blick
    b. bnick
    c. warmk
    d. creenst
    e. faypk
    f. streenk
    g. streelts

4. Make up three more impossible English words, and show why they are so.

5. See how close you can come to writing your name in the Japanese, Eskimo, and Cherokee syllabaries given in Figures 1, 2, and 3. Discuss the types of difficulties you encounter, if any.

---

[15] It would seem that these constraints allow a five-consonant intervocalic cluster if the first two could be linked for place, as in the hypothetical *antstral*. No examples of this sort have been found, to my knowledge. Philip Hamilton (personal communication) suggests *angstrom* [æŋkstrəm], although the [k] may be epenthetic here.

4 English stress

4.1 Preliminaries

English stress has been the topic of wide-ranging discussion, from the standard marking of stress in dictionaries to technical discussion in books and articles. There is a fair degree of agreement on the facts, including stress differences between dialects, although a strict definition of the term STRESS itself is difficult to provide. Linguists generally distinguish SENTENCE STRESS, picking out the most prominent word in a sentence, from WORD STRESS, picking out the prominent syllables within a word. We will be primarily concerned with word stress in this chapter. A word can have one or more stressed syllables, one of which is considered the primary stress. Stressed syllables can contain FULL VOWELS and DIPHTHONGS; unstressed syllables generally contain REDUCED VOWELS. We will return to the distribution of vowels in Chapter 7. We will describe stress in terms of stress FEET, which organize the syllables of a word. The foot can be defined as a grouping of syllables that contains exactly one stressed syllable (Leben 1982, 182). The analysis will proceed in terms of rules that assign feet to sequences of syllables, plus some rules that remove feet under certain circumstances (destressing rules).

From the taxonomic point of view, English stress is "phonemic." This means that the position of primary stress can distinguish utterances, as for example the noun *ímport* and the verb *impórt*. From this point of view, stress has to be listed as an idiosyncratic aspect of every word (or lexical item). But to do this is to miss important regularities. For example, the majority of examples adduced to demonstrate the phonemic nature of stress are noun-verb pairs of the sort just cited, where the noun has stress one syllable further left than the corresponding verb. Furthermore, the noun and the verb are closely related in meaning in all such cases. There are only a handful of pairs of words that differ only in the location of primary stress but have no meaning relationship whatever. MacKay (1987,

188) suggests *défect* (noun) and *deféct* (verb). Kreidler (1989, 197) suggests *bíllow* and *belów, réefer* and *refér;* Ladefoged (1972, 105) suggests *díffer* and *defér*. Another is *ábess* and *abýss*. Pairs of words that differ just in the position of primary stress are therefore to be distinguished from segmental differences, such as the distinction between *pit* and *bit,* which demonstrates the phonemic value of voicing in obstruents. Such pairs are generally totally unrelated semantically. Even when it is possible to find items in the same lexical class, say two verbs, which differ by stress only, it is generally possible to find a meaning relation between them and also to find a noun which shares some meaning with the verb that is stressed like the noun. A concrete example is the verb *protést* 'to complain' and the verb *prótèst* 'to demonstrate.' The verbs are related in meaning—people *prótest* when they want to complain (i.e., *protést*) about the actions of governments or other groups. Furthermore, a *prótèst* is the manifestation of such complaints. These examples suggest that there is a relation between parts of speech and stress. In this chapter, we will seek to develop rules that govern the location of stress in English. Of course, we will still encounter a certain degree of idiosyncrasy, but certain patterns emerge, such as the tendency for heavy syllables to be stressed in certain environments, the general tendency toward alternating stresses, and the tendency for primary stress to be the last stress in a word which is not on the final syllable.

4.2 A parametric approach to stress

Much recent work in generative grammar has been based on the idea that Universal Grammar determines the basic form of the grammars of individual languages, and that variation among grammars results from the setting of PARAMETERS, each of which generally allows a binary choice. In syntax there is a parameter which determines the position of the HEAD of a phrase. Some languages, like English and Italian, have the head at the left end of a phrase, and are called HEAD-FIRST languages. Other languages, like Japanese and Korean, have the head at the right end of the phrase, and are called HEAD-LAST languages. Fixing this one parameter has wide implications for the word order in these languages.

Hayes (1980) develops a parametric approach to stress, and describes the stress patterns of a number of languages, including English, in these terms. Universal Grammar provides for stress feet, which are binary branching trees (i.e., each node can dominate at most two other nodes). A branching node dominates two positions, one labelled strong (s) and the other labelled weak (w). The strong node is the HEAD of the foot. Such a branching node can be considered analogous to a magnet. Every magnet has both a north and a south pole. If you break the magnet in half, each half still has a north and a south pole; you cannot break a magnet in such a way as to isolate the north and south poles from each other. Similarly, every strong node in a metrical tree has a corresponding weak sister, and vice versa.

4.2.1 *Quantity insensitive systems*

We will first consider quantity insensitive systems, where syllable weight plays no role in stress assignment. In order to constrain the types of stress feet that can appear in languages, Hayes assumes the constraint in (1) on basic foot construction.[1]

(1)   *Constraint on foot construction*
        Within the foot only strong nodes may branch.

Constraint (1) permits feet of the type given in (2). The strongest syllable in each foot (labelled *s* and dominated only by strong nodes) is interpreted as stressed; the rest are unstressed.

(2)   a.   Left nodes labelled strong

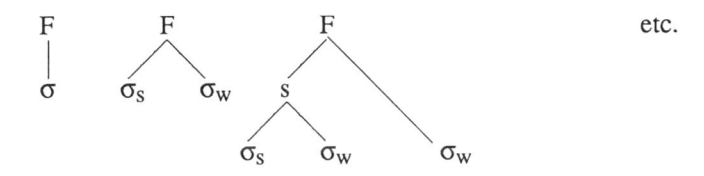

             F   F   F   etc.
             | / \   / \
             σ   σ_s σ_w   s   \
                             / \   \
                            σ_s σ_w σ_w

        b.   Right nodes labelled strong

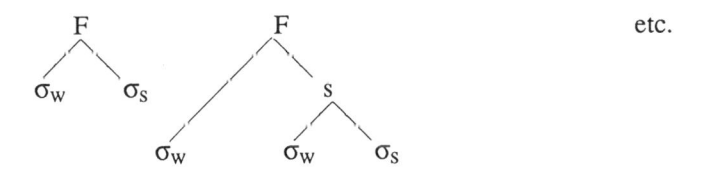

             F   F   etc.
            / \   / \
           σ_w σ_s   /   s
                       /   / \
                     σ_w σ_w σ_s

The first stress foot in (2a) has no branching (and hence no *s-w* labelling). Such a foot, containing a single syllable, is known as a DEGENERATE foot. The *etc.* after

---
[1] Hayes actually formulates (1) using the term *dominant* instead of strong, and he defines dominant in a technical sense slightly different from the term *strong*. This difference is not relevant to our discussion here.

both (2a) and (2b) indicates that larger feet are possible within each set, as long as only strong nodes are branching. The terminals are labelled as syllables and would dominate syllable trees like those we saw in Chapter 3.

Once feet have been constructed, they are gathered together into a word tree. Word trees are also labelled with s-w nodes. Just as the strong syllable within a foot is interpreted as stressed, the strongest foot in a word is interpreted as containing the primary word stress. However, constraint (1) does not constrain the word tree. Word trees are labelled by different principles than those that apply to labelling within the foot, as discussed in section 4.4.

We can now exemplify some of Hayes's parameters. The first is given in (3).

(3) *Parameter 1*
Stress feet are either MAXIMALLY BINARY or UNBOUNDED.

A foot is maximally binary if it can be no longer than two syllables. This allows for the possibility of a degenerate (one-syllable) foot within a binary system. A foot is unbounded if it contains the maximum number of syllables consistent with the constraint in (1). In the simplest case, a single foot is constructed over an entire word. In Latvian (Halle & Vergnaud 1987) stress appears on the initial syllable of each word. This can be accounted for in Hayes's theory by constructing a left-headed unbounded foot over the word, which is then the only foot in the word tree. Feet will look like those in (2a), and the first syllable of each word will be stressed. We appeal to parameter 2 here, which is given in (4).

(4) *Parameter 2*
Stress feet are either LEFT DOMINANT or RIGHT DOMINANT.

A foot is left dominant if its left branches are labelled strong, and right dominant if its right branches are labelled strong. We can use the terms left headed and left dominant interchangeably.

For languages that have maximally binary feet, and also for cases where unbounded feet can be constructed that do not cover the whole word, we need two additional parameters. Parameter 3 specifies the direction of stress foot construction.

(5) *Parameter 3*
Stress feet are constructed either right to left or left to right.

Parameter 4 specifies the dominance of the word tree.

(6) *Parameter 4*
The word tree that groups the feet of a word together is either left dominant or right dominant.

We assume that word trees are always unbounded and cannot be maximally binary.[2]

As an example of these four parameters, Hayes gives the example of Maranungku (data from Tryon 1970), which has primary stress on the initial syllables of words, with secondary stresses falling on alternate syllables after that, as shown in (7).

(7) a. tíralk   'saliva'
    b. mérepèt   'beard'
    c. yángarmàta   'the Pleiades'
    d. lángkaràtetì   'prawn'
    e. wélepènemànta   'kind of duck'

Hayes accounts for this stress system by constructing left dominant binary feet from left to right, and organizing the stress feet into a left dominant word tree. Here, the notion of degenerate foot is illustrated by a word like (7b). We give the complete tree for this word in (8) (adapted from Hayes using our notation); the word-final foot is degenerate. (The symbol ω refers to the phonological word. We will discuss this concept further in Chapter 5.)

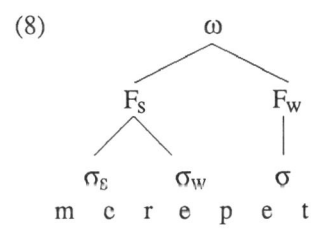

(8)
```
              ω
           /     \
         F_s      F_w
        /   \      |
       σ_s   σ_w   σ
       m  e  r  e  p  e  t
```

As one more example of this type, consider the structure of (7e) in (9) (overleaf).

---

[2] Hayes (1980, 55) suggests that Passamaquoddy organizes feet into binary intermediate structures which are then organized into an unbounded word tree. This accounts for the alternating prominence of feet (not just of syllables). However, English has alternating prominence of feet without such intermediate structures. Their status is therefore not clear.

(9)

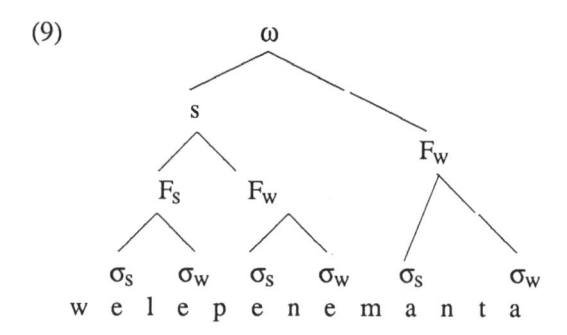

```
                    ω
              _____|_____
             s             \
          __/ \__           Fw
         Fs     Fw         /  \
        / \   /  \        /    \
       σs σw σs  σw      σs    σw
       w  e  l  e  p  e  n  e  m  a  n  t  a
```

Hayes does not discuss the relative prominence of the secondary stresses in longer words such as (7d, e). He simply marks all the secondary stresses the same, with the grave accent mark. We might expect there to be some variation in the degree of stress on secondary stressed syllables, given the geometry of tree structure provided by the theory and the tendency for relative degrees of prominence to alternate. In a fairly clear intuitive sense, the primary stress is the syllable dominated only by strong nodes. Nonprimary stresses are strong syllables in their feet, but the feet themselves have a weak labelling. In (9), for example, we might expect a difference between the relative strength of the second and third stressed syllables, based on the fact that the second stress foot is more deeply embedded in the word tree than the third. In their discussion of English stress, Liberman & Prince (1977, 259) propose a formal algorithm for converting stress trees of this type to *SPE* stress numbers. We paraphrase this algorithm in (10).[3]

(10) a. If a foot is labelled *s*, its stress number is equal to the number of nodes dominating the first *w* node dominating the foot, plus one.

b. If a foot is labelled *w*, its stress number is equal to the number of nodes dominating it, plus one.

In practice, the first clause of Liberman & Prince's algorithm assigns primary stress to the strongest syllable of a foot labelled *s*, since only one foot can be labelled *s*, given the logic of binary branching trees. The second clause of this algorithm assigns lower degrees of stress to the strong syllables of feet depending on their degree of embedding. This implies a stress pattern 132 for *wélepènemànta*.

---

[3] Liberman & Prince stated this algorithm in terms of terminal nodes, rather than feet. It seems that this procedure would assign stress numbers to unstressed syllables also. We have therefore restated it in terms of feet.

It remains to investigate the language further to see if this pattern indeed obtains. For English, as we will see, there is a clear differentiation between nonprimary stresses within long words. For example, *hamamelidanthemum* (with stress numbers 2, 3, 1 over the 1st, 3rd, and 5th stressed syllables) has a greater degree of nonprimary stress on the first syllable than on the third, as indicated by the *SPE* stress numbers. Another way to visualize this is to make use of metrical grids, an alternative device which Liberman & Prince introduced to account for the Rhythm Rule. Since we will account for the Rhythm Rule entirely with trees, we will not use grids as a formal device, but merely as a way of illustrating relative prominence. The grid makes use of marks over syllables, where the higher the column of marks, the greater the stress on that syllable. *Hamamelidanthemum* is represented as in (11) using grids.[4]

(11)
```
                    x
     x              x
     x      x       x
     x  x   x x     x   x
     h a m a m e l i d a n t h e m u m
```

In the grid, each syllable is assigned a mark on the first line. Each *stressed* syllable is assigned a mark on the second line, here on alternating syllables starting from the first (but ignoring the last). The third line has a mark for those stressed syllables that have greater prominence, and the fourth line has a mark on the primary stressed syllable. The tree representation for *hamamelidanthemum* is given in (12, overleaf). We will show how such trees are constructed for English in section 4.3.

Liberman & Prince's algorithm (10) for constructing the *SPE* stress numbers runs as follows. The first foot is labelled weak, so its stress number is equal to one more than the number of nodes dominating it (10b). The only node dominating it is the word node, so its stress number is 2. The second foot is also labelled weak, but it is dominated by two nodes, so its stress number is 3. The final foot is labelled strong, so its stress number is one more than the number of nodes dominating the

---

[4] Whereas Liberman & Prince introduced both the tree and the grid as formal devices, subsequent development concentrated on trees. Prince (1983) developed a metrical theory using grids only, but the lack of constituents caused difficulties for phonologies in which stressed vowels can be deleted. In these languages, stress shifts to an adjacent vowel within the same constituent (a foot) when a stressed vowel is deleted. A compromise notation sometimes used today is the constituentized grid: a grid with constituents indicated. It is not our intention to discuss the intricacies of all these systems here, except to note that grids, including constituentized ones, are unable to express certain regularities that we want to capture. We will therefore use only trees as the formal representation of stress.

(12)

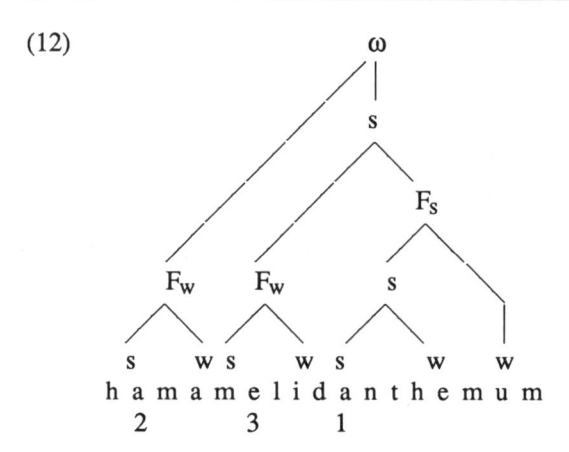

```
                    ω
                   / |
                  /  s
                 /  / \
                /  /   Fs
               /  /   / \
             Fw  Fw  s   \
            / \ / \ / \   \
            s w s w s  w   w
            h a m a m e l i d a n t h e m u m
            2   3   1
```

lowest weak node dominating it (10a). There are no weak nodes dominating it, so its stress number is 1.

As a second illustration of Hayes's parameters, consider the stress pattern of Warao (data from Osborn 1966).

(13) a. yàpurùkitàneháse   'verily to climb'
     b. nàhoròahàkutái   'the one who ate'
     c. yiwàranáe   'he finished it'
     d. enàhoròahàkutái   'the one who caused him to eat'

Hayes analyzes this system as one involving the construction of binary left dominant feet from right to left, with a right branching word tree. However, this is not quite sufficient, since it would imply that the initial syllables of (13c, d) would be stressed, since degenerate feet would be constructed on these syllables. There seems to be a general tendency for languages to avoid stresses on adjacent syllables, a situation known as STRESS CLASH. In Warao, Hayes proposes a destressing rule, which we will write as in (14).

(14) $F_w \to \emptyset$
        $|$

In this somewhat opaque notation, the subscript w on the foot indicates that it is a weak foot (which is our usual notation). The vertical line below the foot indicates that it is nonbranching. So the rule means "delete a nonbranching weak foot." It is clear from the data in (13) that the syllable dominated by the foot remains when the foot is deleted.

An example of a derivation involving (14) is *yiwàranáe*. The structure in (15a) results from the application of the parameters. Rule (14) converts this to (15b) under Hayes's assumption that the defooted syllable is incorporated directly into the word tree.

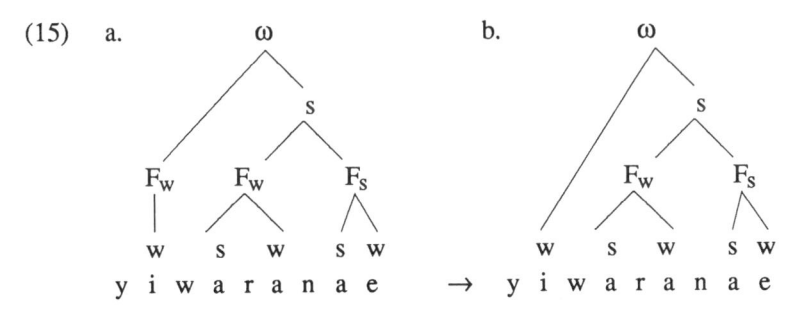

(15) a.

```
            ω
          /   \
         /     s
        /    /   \
       Fw   Fw    Fs
       |   / \   / \
       w  s   w s   w
       y  i w a r a n a e
```

b.

```
            ω
          /   \
         /     s
        /    /   \
            Fw    Fs
           / \   / \
          w   s w   s w
    →    y i w a r a n a e
```

However, this structure violates the principle of PROSODIC LICENSING which we cited as (21) in Chapter 3, according to which all syllables must belong to feet. In order to derive a structure that conforms to this principle, we must incorporate the first syllable of (15) into a foot, in this case, necessarily to the foot on its right. We will adopt a generalized version of Hayes's STRAY SYLLABLE ADJUNCTION. Hayes's rule adjoined a stray syllable (any syllable not incorporated into any foot) only to a foot to its left. Our version adjoins a stray syllable to an adjacent foot in either direction (Jensen 1990).

(16)   *Stray Syllable Adjunction*
       Adjoin a stray syllable by Chomsky Adjunction as a weak member of an adjacent foot.

Chomsky Adjunction is a term borrowed from syntax. In the context of metrical phonology, this refers to duplicating the foot node to which adjunction is to take place so that the new foot node dominates the formerly stray syllable and the old foot node (Jensen 1990). Adjunction of the first syllable to the foot to its right in (15) produces (17b) from (17a) (overleaf). This solution conforms to Prosodic Licensing without violating the fundamental definition of the foot as a prosodic unit containing exactly one stressed syllable. The embedded foot contains exactly one stressed syllable, *wa*. The foot that dominates it also contains exactly one stressed syllable, the same *wa*. Without Chomsky Adjunction we are unable to maintain this generalization. Another possible way to maintain prosodic licensing is to turn the first unstressed syllable into a foot on its own. This is proposed

(17) a.

```
            ω
          /    \
        Fw      Fs
       /  \    /  \
      σ   σs  σw  σs  σw
      y   i   w   a   r   a   n   a   e
```

→

b.

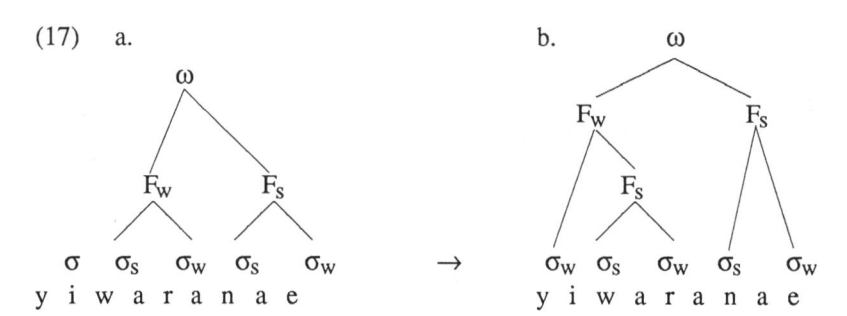

```
              ω
            /    \
          Fw      Fs
         /  \    /  \
             Fs
            /  \
      σw  σs  σw  σs  σw
      y   i   w   a   r   a   n   a   e
```

in Kiparsky (1979) and by Nespor & Vogel (1986), although they did not use the term prosodic licensing. But this stressless foot is contrary to our definition of the foot. The Chomsky Adjoined foot maintains both requirements. It also allows us to account for certain aspects of the English stress system in more satisfactory way than Hayes's (see the discussion of *abracadabra* in section 4.5.2).

We will not illustrate all the possible combinations of Hayes's four parameters given as (3), (4), (5), and (6). One further combination is given for you to work out in the exercises. Instead, we will turn now to a fifth parameter, Quantity Sensitivity.

4.2.2 *Quantity sensitive systems*

Up to this point we have been examining stress systems in which syllable weight plays no role. As discussed in section 3.4.4, a light syllable is one which contains a single mora; a heavy syllable is one which contains two moras. In all quantity sensitive systems, a syllable containing an onset followed only by a short, lax vowel is light (18a), and a syllable containing an onset followed by a long or tense vowel (whether or not it has a closing consonant) is heavy (18b, c).

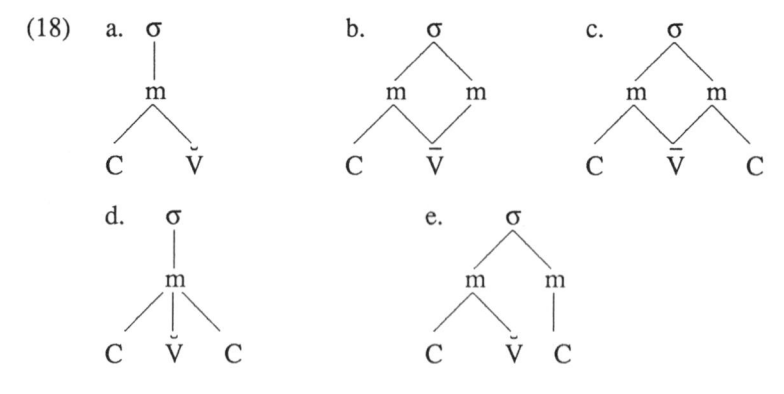

(18) a. σ — m — C V̆

b. σ — m m — C V̄

c. σ — m m — C V̄ C

d. σ — m — C V̆ C

e. σ — m m — C V̆ C

A closed syllable whose vowel is short and lax is treated differently in different languages. Such a syllable is monomoraic in Eastern Cheremis and Khalkha Mongolian, for example, and has the syllable representation (18d). In Latin and English, such syllables are bimoraic and have the syllable representation (18e). Let us look at stress in Eastern Cheremis.

In Eastern Cheremis, stress falls on the last full vowel of a word, or on the initial syllable if the word contains only reduced vowels. Hayes interprets the term "reduced vowel" to mean short, or, in our terms, monomoraic, while "full vowels" are long or bimoraic. With the rules in (19) to assign moras (cf. the rules in (23) of Chapter 3 for assigning moras in English), rule (20) will correctly assign stress in Eastern Cheremis.

(19) 1. Assign a mora to the string C_0V, where C_0 is a possible (maximal) onset according to the sonority hierarchy and the restrictions and dispensations on onsets.

2. Assign a second mora to a long (full) vowel and any following consonants that are not already part of a mora.

(20) a. Form left dominant, unbounded feet from right to left, where a weak node may not dominate a branching (bimoraic) syllable.

b. Form a right dominant word tree.

If feet are unbounded, they may dominate any number of syllables. Unlike the Latvian example we saw earlier, this does not mean that feet will always dominate the entire word. Because of the second clause in (20a), foot construction stops when a heavy syllable is encountered. Otherwise, a weak branch would come to dominate a branching syllable. This can best be seen by examining a few examples.

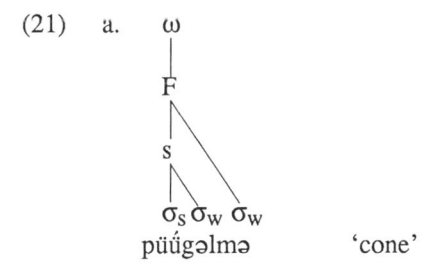

(21) a.   ω
            |
            F
           /\
          s \
         /\   \
        σₛ σw σw
        püügəlmə   'cone'

b. ω
    |
    F
   /|\
  s \
  | \
  s   \
  /\   \
 σ_s σ_w σ_w σ_w
 kiidəštəžə   'in his hand'

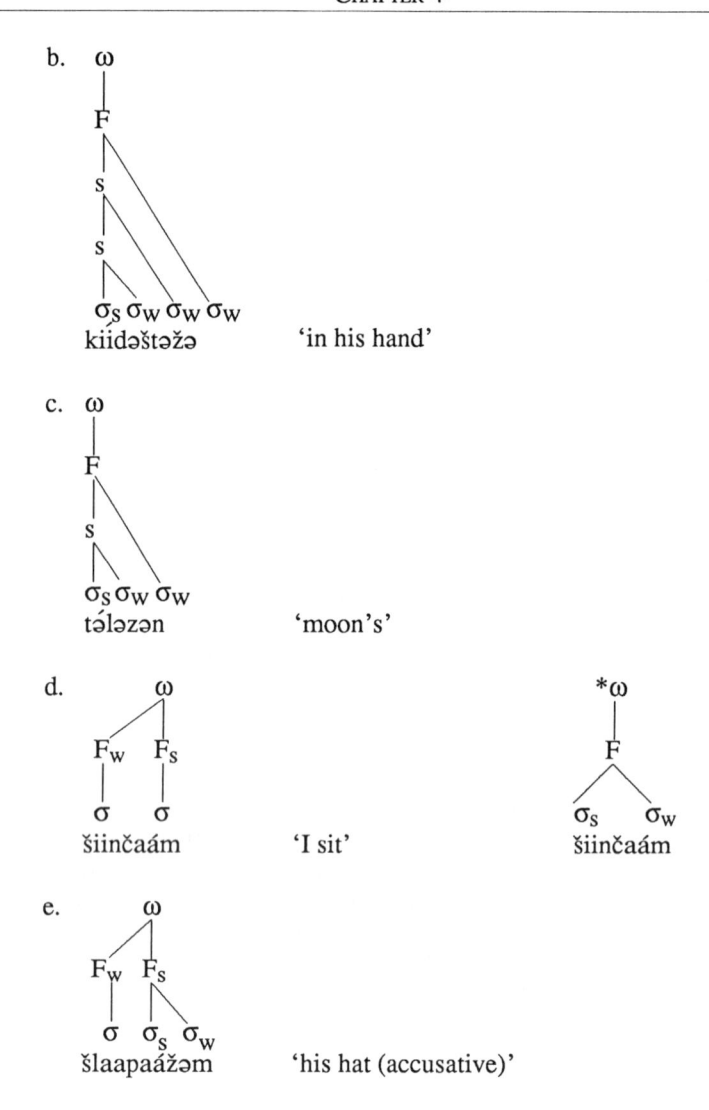

c. ω
    |
    F
   /\
  s \
  /\ \
 σ_s σ_w σ_w
 tələzən   'moon's'

d.   ω   *ω
      / \ |
     F_w F_s   F
     | | / \
     σ   σ   σ_s σ_w
    šiinčaám   'I sit'   šiinčaám

e.   ω
      / \
     F_w F_s
     | /\
     σ σ_s σ_w
    šlaapaážəm   'his hat (accusative)'

In (21a, b), a foot is constructed over the entire word. The first syllable is the only one with two moras, and it is the only strong syllable in the foot. Thus, no weak node in the foot dominates a branching syllable. In (21c), there are no branching syllables in the word, so again a foot can be constructed over the entire word. In (21d), however, both syllables are branching. The tree on the right of (21d) is disallowed because the weak right branch of the foot dominates a heavy syllable. Therefore, two feet are constructed, as on the left of (21d). Labelling the right branch strong by (20b) gives us main stress on the last syllable. Likewise in (21e), there are two heavy syllables. Two feet are again constructed, of which only the right can be branching.

Our analysis differs from Hayes's in one respect. Rather than construct feet from right to left, Hayes's rule constructs a single foot at the right edge of a word. Evidence is somewhat scanty on the question of secondary stresses in Eastern Cheremis. However, there is indirect evidence that multiple feet are constructed in words containing more than one full vowel. This evidence is from a vowel harmony process that assimilates reduced vowels in backness and roundness to the nearest preceding full vowel. As Hayes notes, this can be stated more perspicuously by saying that vowel harmony operates within the domain of the foot.

A second example of a quantity sensitive stress system is Classical Latin. Latin stress falls on the penult (next-to-last syllable) if it is heavy and in disyllables, otherwise the antepenult is stressed. In Latin, a heavy syllable is one which either contains a long vowel or is closed by a consonant. One way to describe this would be to construct maximally ternary feet, of which the middle node must not branch (dominate two moras). This would account for the stresses observed in (22)—the macron indicates a long vowel).

(22) a. reféctus 'restored (masc. sg. participle)'
     b. refēcit 'restored (perfect 3rd sing.)'
     c. réficit 'restores (present 3rd. sing)'

But Hayes's theory allows only maximally binary or unbounded feet and cannot accommodate such a system. There are two approaches we could take. One is to expand our inventory of feet to accommodate maximally ternary feet of the required type for Latin. Another would be to find some way to account for the Latin case using only the feet provided by Hayes's theory. Hayes provides some evidence for this latter approach. One particularly interesting example concerns the stress system of Winnebago. In this language, primary stress falls on the third mora from the beginning of the word, a relatively unusual pattern. What is more interesting is that secondary stresses in Winnebago fall on every second mora after the main stress, not on every third mora. If we expanded our foot inventory to include ternary feet, we would have to construct a right dominant ternary foot on the first three moras and binary feet thereafter. Hayes adopts Liberman & Prince's (1977) suggestion that certain elements can be marked EXTRAMETRICAL.

For Winnebago, he proposes that the first mora be marked extrametrical, i.e., invisible to the stress rule. The stress rule then constructs right dominant binary feet over the remaining moras. This correctly achieves primary stress on the third syllable and secondary stresses on alternating syllables thereafter.

This analysis provides a more insightful way of dealing with Winnebago, and it can be extended in a natural way to account for Latin, and in turn, English. In Hayes's discussion, there can be rules that mark certain items extrametrical, and any extrametrical elements are ignored by the stress rules. Not just anything can be marked extrametrical, however. The item to be made extrametrical must be a linguistic unit of some sort—generally syllables or moras in the case of stress rules. Furthermore, it must be at the edge of some domain: either the right or left (more often the right). For Latin, we must mark word-final syllables extrametrical,[5] then construct a left-dominant, quantity-sensitive foot at the right edge of the word. Of course, the syllable left extrametrical before the stress rules apply must be rejoined to the word before the phonology is finished, since it is actually pronounced. Once again we can appeal to Hayes's universal convention of Stray Syllable Adjunction, according to which a stray (in this case, extrametrical)[6] syllable is adjoined as a weak member of an adjacent foot.[7] We simply assume that the foot (23a), derived by rule on *refi,* for example, is converted to the foot (23b) by Stray Syllable Adjunction.

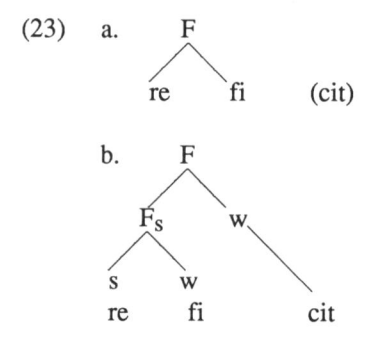

(23) a. F
         / \
        re fi   (cit)

    b.   F
        / \
       Fs   w
      / \   \
     s   w   \
     re fi   cit

---

[5] Words of one syllable (excepting clitics) are stressed on their only syllable. Hayes assumes a constraint that prevents marking the entire domain extrametrical, in this case the last and only syllable of the word.

[6] We will see later that there are other ways for syllables and other units to become stray. This formulation is sufficient for present purposes.

[7] We continue to assume Chomsky adjunction in this case, even though the additional structure is not needed here for prosodic licensing. Prince (1980, 545) suggests that Chomsky adjunction is useful in the description of gradation in Estonian. He further suggests that the

This shows that extrametricality allows us to retain a maximally constrained system of stress foot construction in the face of apparently recalcitrant data. In the next section we will explore the stress system of English, which seems to present some challenges to Hayes's constrained stress foot framework, and shows that it, too, is amenable to description in terms of a maximally constrained theory of the foot.

4.3 Stress assignment in English

4.3.1 The English Stress Rule

English stress initially appears to pose considerable challenges to Hayes's stress theory. For one thing, there are a considerable number of ternary feet in various positions in the word, as in Hayes's examples in (24).

(24) a. *Ternary feet in word-final position*
América, lábyrinth

  b. *Ternary feet in nonfinal position*
detérioràte, Nèbuchadnézzar, héterodòx, pàraphernália

Despite such examples, there is a considerable degree of regularity to English stress. Liberman & Prince (1977) point to the nonexistence of such nonsense forms as *pódectal* and *pónitode* [pánĭrôwd], which are systematically absent from English. Hayes points out that Russian words like *Nínotchka* and *bábushka* are borrowed into English with penultimate stress. While Kahn (1976, 85) points to exceptions like *cháracter,* the basic regularity seems to be that nouns whose penults are heavy (i.e., are closed or have a long vowel) are stressed there; otherwise, they are stressed one syllable further left. Selkirk (1980b) proposed to account for English stress with a maximal foot template, as in (25). In Selkirk's view, stress is marked on all lexical items, but stress markings cannot violate (25).

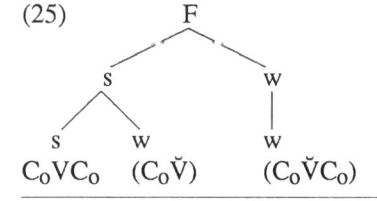

(25)   F
           / \
          s   w
         / \ |
        s   w w
     C₀VC₀ (C₀V̆) (C₀V̆C₀)

---

notion MINIMAL FOOT (i.e., the embedded foot after adjunction) is universally the domain for weakening processes, citing the obligatory flapping of *t* in *pity* vs the optional flapping of *t* in *unity*. This idea deserves further development.

Hayes argues against Selkirk's claim that stress is represented only by a template. He notes that both absolute numbers and historical change indicate that stress feet are maximal when possible. However, Selkirk's approach would allow minimal stress feet to be marked lexically anywhere. (Kahn disputes this by citing the Massachusetts town name *Pòpponésset,* presumably stressed as marked. Such names are presumably exceptional and will have to be treated as such in Hayes's framework.) However, Hayes appears to accept the possibility that stress is stored along with lexical entries as well as being derived by rule (p. 146). This paradox is resolved by the theory of lexical phonology, where phonological rules can operate within the lexicon. In this theory it is no longer necessary to assume that underlying lexical items actually carry an indication of stress, outside of certain exceptional cases.

We can set the parameters for English as follows.

(26) 1. Stress feet in English are maximally binary.
2. Stress feet in English are left dominant and quantity sensitive at the right edge of the word only.
3. Stress feet in English are constructed from right to left.
4. The word tree in English is right branching, and right nodes are labelled strong if and only if branching (to be revised in section 4.4).

The simplest case where the basic regularity of English stress appears is in verbs and unsuffixed adjectives. They are stressed on the final syllable if this has a long vowel or ends in a string of at least two consonants; otherwise the penultimate is stressed. Hayes gives the forms in (27).

(27)   *long vowel in*   *two or more*
              final syllable   *final consonants*   *other*

  a. verbs   obéy   molést   astónish
              atóne   usúrp   devélop
  b. adjectives divíne   robúst   cómmon
              discreét   overt   illícit

This pattern is evidently quantity sensitive, but it is remarkable that final stress occurs with *two* final consonants, as in the second column of (27), not with only one, where stress occurs on the penult, as in the last column of (27). Hayes proposes that word-final consonants are extrametrical, by a rule called Consonant Extrametricality (28), and that stress is assigned by the English Stress Rule (ESR, 29).

(28)   *Consonant Extrametricality*[8]
        C → [+ex] / ___]

(29)   *English Stress Rule*[9]
        Form left dominant maximally binary feet from right to left. The rightmost foot is quantity sensitive.

We will begin our discussion of the examples in (27) with the first (rightmost) application of the ESR. Consider the derivations in (30).[10]

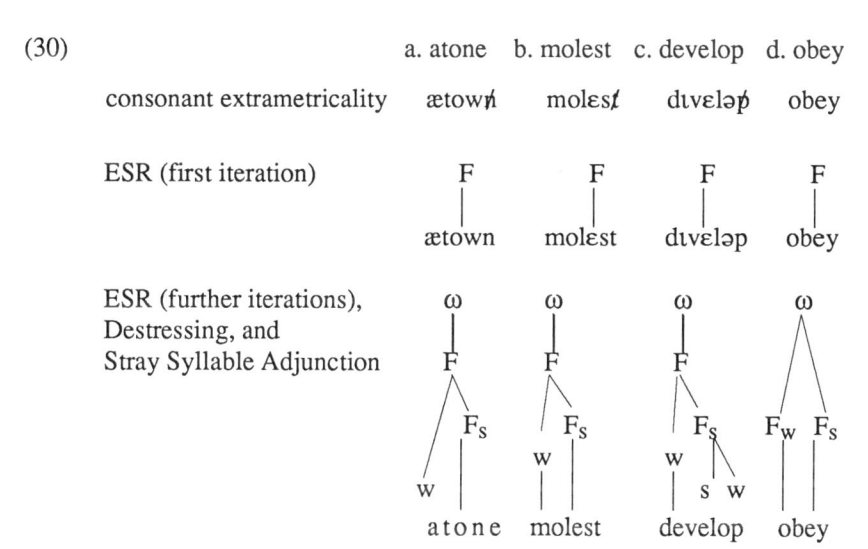

(30)   a. atone   b. molest   c. develop   d. obey

        consonant extrametricality   ætown̸   molest̸   dɪvɛləp̸   obey

        ESR (first iteration)   F   F   F   F
                                        | | | |
                                      ætown   molɛst   dɪvɛləp   obey

        ESR (further iterations),   ω   ω   ω   ω
        Destressing, and | | | / \
        Stray Syllable Adjunction   F   F   F   Fw Fs
                                      / \   / \   / \ | |
                                     / Fs   Fs   Fs
                                    / | w | w / \
                                   w | | / s w
                                   a t o n e   molest   develop   obey

With nouns, the most regular cases have stress one syllable to the left of where it appears in verbs and unsuffixed adjectives. That is, a heavy penult is generally stressed; the antepenultimate is stressed if the penult is light. Hayes gives the examples in (31).

---

[8] The feature [+ex] for 'extrametrical' appears somewhat ad hoc, but, as no suitable replacement has occurred to me, I retain it here.

[9] We will give the rules for forming the word tree in section 4.4, since it seems that a destressing rule (Sonorant Destressing, section 4.5.4) must intervene between the ESR and word tree construction in English. This exposition differs from Hayes's in that his rule provided just one quantity-sensitive foot at the right edge of words, assigning other stresses by a different rule. Kiparsky (1982a, 52) showed that the two rules are one and the same.

[10] These derivations are shown as beginning with the phonetic transcription of the words. The stress rules operate on the underlying representations, whose vowels are often quite different. Chapter 7 explores the rules that derive the phonetic forms of the vowels.

(31)   *light penult*   *long vowel in penult*   *consonant-final*
                                                        penult
       América   Arizóna   agénda
       díscipline   factótum   appéndix
       lábyrinth   elítist   amálgam

Here the situation is very much like the Latin examples in (22) we discussed earlier. Hayes appeals to the same mechanism: extrametricality. For English, the extrametricality of a final syllable is restricted to nouns, so Hayes refers to the rule in (32) as Noun Extrametricality.

(32) Noun Extrametricality
      σ → [+ex] / ____]$_N$

With Noun Extrametricality, the nouns in (31) can be stressed using the same rule we used for the verbs and unsuffixed adjectives in (27). We can demonstrate this with the derivations in (33).

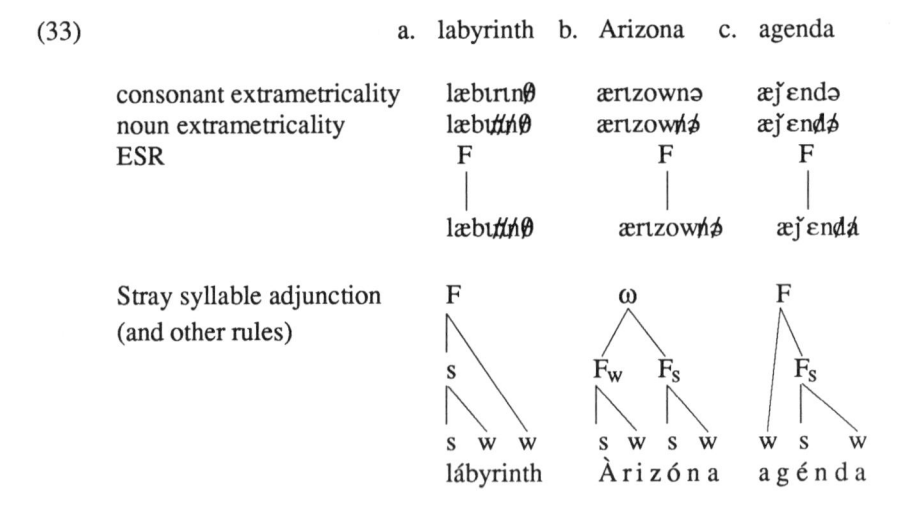

(33)   a. labyrinth   b. Arizona   c. agenda

      consonant extrametricality   læbɪrɪnθ̸   ærɪzownə   æǰɛndə
      noun extrametricality   læbʉ̸ɾɪ̸n̸θ̸   ærɪzow̸n̸ə̸   æǰɛn̸d̸ə̸
      ESR   F   F   F
                                    | | |
                                    læbʉ̸ɾɪ̸n̸θ̸   ærɪzow̸ń̸ə̸   æǰɛńd̸ə̸

      Stray syllable adjunction   F   ω   F
      (and other rules)   /\   / \   /\
                                  s \   F_w F_s   / F_s
                                 /\   \   /\   /\   /   /\
                                s w   w   s w s w   w   s w
                                lábyrinth   À r i z ó n a a g é n d a

This analysis cannot capture the stress patterns of nouns whose final syllables are stressed. Hayes observes that, if the final syllable of a noun contains a long vowel, it receives stress, either secondary (34a) or primary (34b).

(34)   a.   Mánitòu   cálvalcàde   mísanthròpe   vétò
       b.   mònsóon   ènginéer   sèrenáde   trùstée

Hayes accounts for these by assuming a rule of Long Vowel Stressing, before the extrametricality rules. This rule stresses long vowels in the final syllable of words. We can give this rule a moraic formulation as in (35).

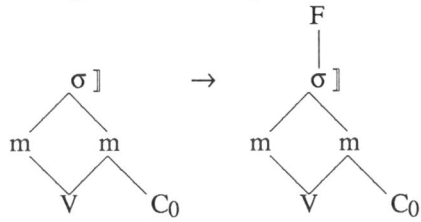

(35) *Long Vowel Stressing*

$$\begin{array}{c} \sigma\,] \\ /\backslash \\ m \quad m \\ \backslash / \\ V \quad C_0 \end{array} \rightarrow \begin{array}{c} F \\ | \\ \sigma\,] \\ /\backslash \\ m \quad m \\ \backslash / \\ V \quad C_0 \end{array}$$

Each of the examples in (34) has an additional stress on a syllable other than the last. We will discuss these in section 4.4 when we consider further iterations of the ESR and the question of word tree construction.

The last case to be considered of the rightmost application of the ESR is that of suffixed adjectives. These pattern like the nouns in (31), as shown in (36). These contrast with unsuffixed adjectives, which pattern like verbs (27a).

(36) | light penult | long vowel in penult | consonant-final penult |
|---|---|---|
| munícipal | adjectíval | fratérnal |
| magnánimous | desírous | treméndous |
| signíficant | clairvóyant | relúctant |
| ínnocent | complácent | depéndent |
| prímitive | condúcive | expénsive |

Hayes proposes a rule of Adjective Extrametricality, which marks a suffix extrametrical at the end of an adjective.

(37) [X]$_{\text{Suffix}}$ → [+ex] / ____]$_A$

Once again, we can illustrate this with some derivations in (38) (overleaf).

(38)   a. magnanimous   b. reluctant

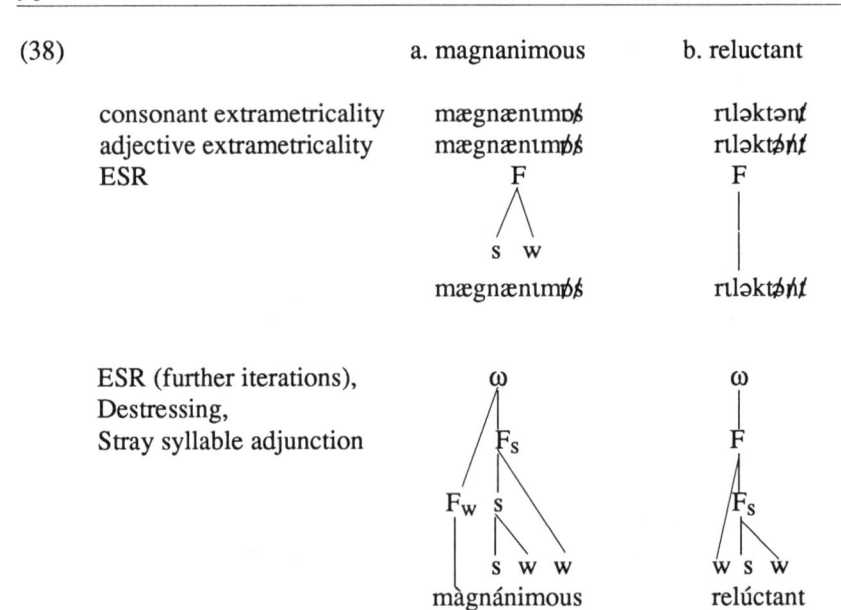

	a. magnanimous	b. reluctant
consonant extrametricality	mægnænɪmə⟨s⟩	rɪləktən⟨t⟩
adjective extrametricality	mægnænɪm⟨əs⟩	rɪləkt⟨ənt⟩
ESR	F ╱╲ s w mægnænɪm⟨əs⟩	F │ │ rɪləkt⟨ənt⟩
ESR (further iterations), Destressing, Stray syllable adjunction	ω ╱╲ F_w F_s │ ╱╲ s s w w màgnánimous	ω │ F ╱╲ F_s ╱╲ w s w relúctant

4.3.2 Stress retraction

So far we have discussed the assignment of stress at the right edge of English words. However, we formulated the parameters for English in (26) in such a way that maximally binary feet are constructed from right to left, so that in long words multiple stresses are assigned. Hayes considers the assignment of additional stresses to be a separate rule from the one that assigns stress at the right edge of words. He refers to this rule as STRESS RETRACTION, although stress is not literally retracted. Previously assigned stresses remain and additional stresses are assigned in a leftward direction. The term retraction is taken from Liberman & Prince (1977), where three modes of retraction are identified. One of these is STRONG RETRACTION, which constructs binary, left-dominant, quantity insensitive feet from right to left from a stress assigned at the right edge of the word. This is built into our English stress rule (29), which stipulates that English stress is quantity sensitive only at the right edge of words. Liberman and Prince developed two other modes of retraction, but Hayes shows that the effects of these other two modes can be produced in other ways. Liberman & Prince's WEAK RETRACTION places stress two syllables before the adjective suffix *-oid* if the syllable before *-oid* is light (39a, b); otherwise, it places stress on the syllable immediately before *-oid* if it is heavy (39c) or the only remaining syllable in the word (39d).

(39) a. pyrámidòid   b. hóminòid   c. ellípsòid   d. líthòid
       encéphalòid   crýstallòid   mollúscòid   óvòid
       tentáculòid   ánthropòid   cylíndròid   théròid
       cartiláginòid   sólenòid   salamándròid   céntròid

This mode of retraction is quantity sensitive in the same way as the English Stress Rule, and so Hayes achieves the same effect with Adjective Extrametricality, as we have already seen in (38).

Liberman & Prince's Strong Retraction is a separate rule for Hayes but is built into our English Stress Rule, as suggested by Kiparsky (1982b, 166). This produces the regular pattern of alternating stresses in long monomorphemic English words. This can be illustrated by the derivations in (40).

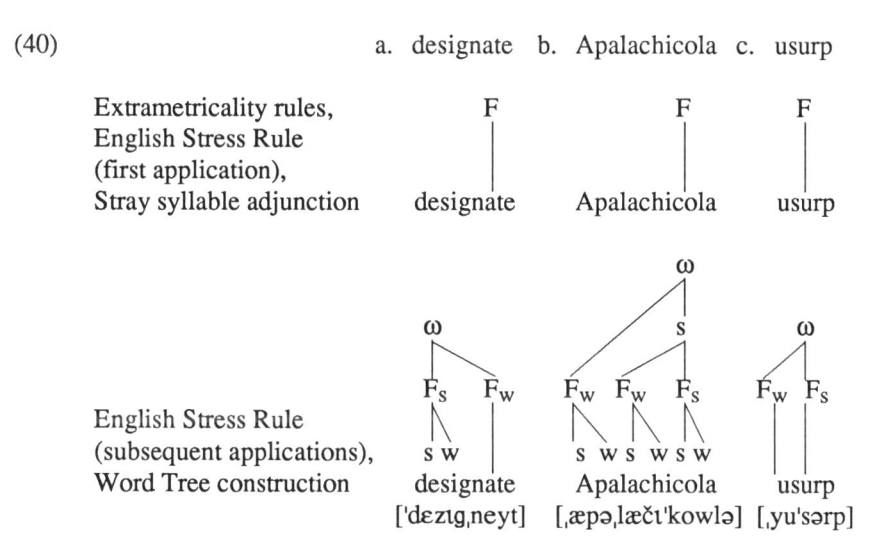

(40)   a. designate b. Apalachicola c. usurp

Extrametricality rules,   F   F   F
English Stress Rule | | |
(first application),
Stray syllable adjunction   designate   Apalachicola   usurp

                                                   ω
                                                  /|
                                   ω   / s   ω
                                  /\   / /\   /\
                                 F_s F_w   F_w F_w F_s   F_w F_s
English Stress Rule   /\ | /\ /\ /\ | |
(subsequent applications),   s w | s w s w s w | |
Word Tree construction   designate   Apalachicola   usurp
                             ['dɛzɪgˌneyt] [ˌæpəˌlæčɪ'kowlə]   [ˌyu'sərp]

Liberman & Prince recognize a third mode of retraction, LONG RETRACTION, which places stress three syllables before an existing stress. This is exemplified by certain monomorphemic words like *rigamarole* and includes certain place names like *Kalamazoo*, cases with a sequence of two short vowels like *deteriorate*, certain forms with Greek prefixes like *heterodox*, words in *-atory* like *halucinatory*, and miscellaneous words like *disciplinary*. Since long retraction involves constructing ternary feet, it is not permitted in Hayes's framework. Hayes proposes a different explanation for each of these cases. For *rigamarole* and *Kalamazoo*, Hayes proposes a destressing rule, Poststress Destressing, which is discussed in section 4.5.2. For Greek prefixes, Hayes proposes an analysis as compounds: [hetero]$_N$ [dox]$_N$. Each part undergoes the stress rules separately at stratum 1 and they are combined into a compound at stratum 2, where the Compound Stress rule makes the first more prominent, the normal rule for compound nouns (cf. $\overset{1}{fire}\overset{2}{engine}$). For sequences of two vowels (*deteriorate*) Hayes observes that the first is always *i*, and proposes underlying representations with /y/ and a rule that converts this to [i] after the stress rules have applied. Finally, cases like *hallucinatory* and *disciplinary* may be handled with irregular stratum 2 affixation, as suggested by Liberman and Prince (1977, 277).

To conclude this section, stress retraction is accomplished by a non–quantity sensitive version of the English stress rule. In the most usual case, this builds binary feet from right to left across the word, producing a pattern of alternating stress. When this procedure finds only the initial syllable unfooted, a degenerate foot is built on that syllable. Other patterns are produced by destressing and Stray Syllable Adjunction.

4.4 Word Tree Construction

Once the feet have been established, it is necessary to construct a word tree. Our word tree construction parameter for English (26, 4) states that word trees are right branching and that right nodes are labelled strong if and only if they are branching. This produces the tree (12), repeated as (41), for *hamamelidanthemum*, which we gave in grid format in (11).

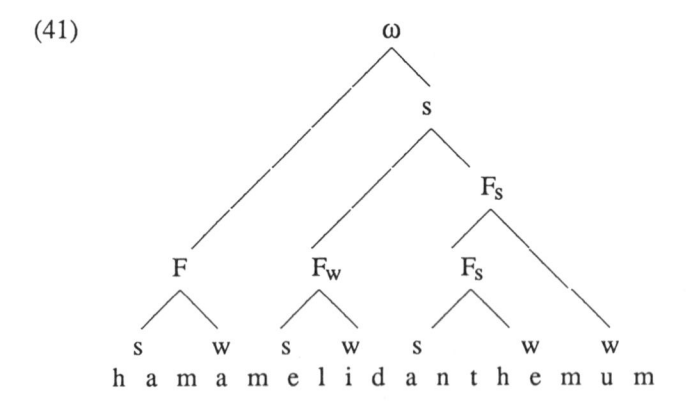

(41)

The word tree labelling rule, right strong if and only if branching, accounts for the stress patterns of a great many English words. For example, it predicts the common observation that the main stress of a word is its last stressed syllable that is not the last syllable of a word. Two names illustrate this basic pattern. $\overset{1}{I}s\overset{2}{i}dore$ has two feet and the rightmost is labelled weak because it is nonbranching. But $\overset{2}{I}s\overset{1}{i}dora$ has a branching right foot, labelled strong, and so a stress pattern opposite to that of $\overset{1}{I}s\overset{2}{i}dore$.

Liberman & Prince identify a number of other environments where right feet are labelled strong, even when nonbranching. One case concerns a number of endings (not necessarily actually suffixes), largely of French origin, that have final main stress. We give these in (42). We can follow the essentials of Liberman & Prince's analysis by assuming that word tree labelling is sensitive to these endings, and assigns them the label strong.

(42)   -ier, -eer   engineer, frontier, veneer, cavalier, chandelier
            -oon   pantaloon, octoroon, tycoon, baboon, poltroon
            -ique   unique, antique, bezique, Mozambique
            -oo   tattoo, kazoo, shampoo, bamboo, canoe
            -ise   chemise, valise, expertise
            -ade   serenade, cascade, grenade, stockade, blockade
            -ette   novelette, cigarette, vignette, corvette
            -ee   deportee, addressee, trustee, absentee, Tennessee
            -elle   bagatelle, moselle, villanelle
            -air   affair, corsair, debonair
            -che   cartouche, pastiche, brioche, panache
            -esce   acquiesce, recrudesce, incandesce, effervesce
            -ane   mundane, transpadane, ultramontane, chicane
            -ar   guitar, bizarre, cigar, bazaar
            -eau   flambeau, tableau, chateau, portmanteau
            -esque   picturesque, grotesque, statuesque, romanesque

Another case where Liberman & Prince identify unexpected nonbranching strong right branches is with certain words of two syllables with light initial syllables such as those in (43).

(43) July, manure, attire, patrol, lament, obey

There is a certain amount of lexical idiosyncrasy in this class of items: the more regular case (right node weak if nonbranching) is shown by cases like those in (44).

(44)   satire, essay, rabbi

The right weak labelling of the words in (39) is predicted by the regular rule that the right node is weak if nonbranching. This is quite regular for suffixes of this type.[11] Therefore, this can be built directly into the word tree labelling rule.

A third case of unexpected strong labelling of nonbranching right nodes includes disyllabic verbs and adjectives such as those in (45).

(45)   maintain, caress, harass, advance, bombard, torment, discourse, infer, rotund, overt, august, robust

For this class of cases the first syllable need not be light, as was the case in (43). This case has very few exceptions *(comment, ribald)* and includes a number of verb-noun pairs in which the noun is stressed differently from the verb. We give a few of these in (46).

(46)   *verbs*   *nouns*
        survéy   súrvèy
        detáil   détàil
        transfér   tránsfèr
        permít   pérmìt
        expórt   éxpòrt
        protést   prótèst

For the verbs we can say that the right node is marked strong in spite of being nonbranching. In North American English this provision does not apply in the case of the suffixes *-ize* and *-ate,* though these do receive primary stress in British English. The nouns in (46) will be derived cyclically from the corresponding verbs. The notion of cyclic derivation will be detailed in section 4.7 and in Chapter 6.

---

[11] While Liberman & Prince build this fact into their word tree labelling rule, Hayes (1982, 272) suggests a more ingenious way to deal with this case. Since the last syllable of the words in (39) is extrametrical, if we assume that extrametricality markings persist (unless they are removed from elements that are no longer peripheral), then these elements are not eligible to be labelled strong and so will ultimately emerge as weak by Stray Foot Adjunction, an extension of Stray Syllable Adjunction. This solution extends to the case of *Isidore* and *Isidora* discussed above, as long as the word tree rule is generalized to make right nodes strong regardless of branching.

The fourth and final case of nonbranching right strong labelling occurs in verbs that contain a latinate stem. (The meaning of the Latin stem is not always transparent.) We give some of these cases in (47).

(47)   intervéne, interséct, interspérse, interpóse, intercépt, superpóse, comprehénd, supervéne, circumvént.

There are occasional exceptions such as *súpervìse, círcumcìse*. This case does not apply to adjectives, as seen in cases like *círcumspèct, dérelìct*.

We can now summarize the rules for word tree construction in (48).

(48)   *Word Tree Construction*
Construct a right-branching word tree over the feet of a word.
Within the word tree the right branches are labelled strong if any of the following conditions is met:
a. the right node branches.
b. the right node immediately dominates one of the endings in (42) (*engineer*).
c. in disyllables where the first syllable is light and the right node does not dominate a suffix (*July, lithoid*).
d. in verbs and adjectives (and specially marked nouns) of two syllables, where the right node does not dominate *-ize, -ate* (North American English) (*omit, advance*)
e. in verbs where the right node dominates a latinate stem (*intervene*).
Otherwise, right nodes are labelled weak.

This will account for the majority of cases. Exceptions can be marked as not undergoing individual clauses of (48). For example, *Ládefòged* can be marked as [–48a]. Some specially marked nouns observe the verb pattern of (18d), such as *advance, delay, accord*. Liberman & Prince mark these nouns with the diacritic [+R].

So far we have assumed that stress rules apply to complete words, either monomorphemic or stems concatenated with affixes. This is the case with the affixes we have considered so far, technically known as stratum one affixes. We argue in Chapters 6 and 7 that there are two strata of morphology and phonology in English, with stratum one ordered before stratum two. Affixes added at stratum two do not affect the stress of the stems they are attached to, since we assume that the stress rules apply only at stratum one. However, some stratum two affixes are stressed, such as *-ship* in *kingship*, *-like* in *lifelike*, *-hood* in *childhood*, and *un-* in *unnatural*. Opposed to these are stratum two suffixes that are entirely stressless, as *-less* of *stressless*, *-ness* in *happiness*, and *-dom* in *kingdom*. Mohanan (1986, 19–20) proposes that such affixes can be assigned stress on stratum one before being attached to stems on stratum two. Stressless stratum two affixes are simply exceptions to the stress rules.

4.5 Destressing rules

4.5.1 Prestress Destressing

Given that the English Stress Rule ensures that every syllable belongs to a foot, by proceeding leftward across the domain of the entire word, there will inevitably be certain syllables that receive stress during the derivation even though they are phonetically unstressed. In particular, the ESR will always stress the initial syllable of a word. But word-initial light syllables are unstressed in a large number of common words, such as those in (49a). Word-initial syllables are stressed if they are heavy, either by virtue of having a long (tense) vowel (49b) or by being closed (49c) (from Liberman & Prince 1977, 284).

(49) a. *light*   b. *heavy (long vowel)*   c. *heavy (closed)*
       banana   psychology   bandana
       Monongahela   totality   lactation
       balloon   Daytona   pontoon
       asparagus   neutrality   sectarian
       mosquito   tisane   Cartesian
       astronomy   maintain   technique

The generalization is that a light syllable is destressed immediately before another stress (which need not be the main word stress, as shown by examples like *Monongahela*). We can express this rule as in (50), called Prestress Destressing.

(50) *Prestress Destressing (postcyclic, preliminary version)*

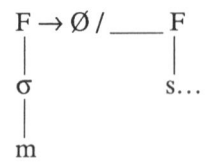

$$F \rightarrow \emptyset\ /\ \underline{}\ F$$
$$||$$
$$\sigmas\ldots$$
$$|$$
$$m$$

This formulation states that a foot that dominates a single mora is deleted before another foot whose leftmost branch is strong.[12] This rule, and in fact all destressing rules, are subject to a constraint that Hayes (1982, 257) states as (51).

(51)   No foot in strong metrical position may be deleted.

The constraint in (51) ensures that the initial syllable of *essay*, for example, is not destressed even though it otherwise meets the requirements of (50).

Some words with closed initial syllables are also destressed. In particular those of (52) appear to present problems for this analysis.

(52)   Kentucky, Vermont, Berlin.

However, these are not a problem if we regard their initial syllables as containing a syllabic sonorant at the stage when Initial Destressing takes place: [kn̩'təki], [vr̩'mɒnt]. Then the initial syllables in (52) are monomoraic and meet the requirements of (50).

Somewhat more serious is the destressing of initial latinate prefixes in (53b).

(53)   a. *stressed*   b. *unstressed*   c. *stressed*
          condensation   condense   contemplate
          advantageous   advance   adulate
          abnormality   absurd   abnegate
          proclamation   proclaim   promulgate
          relaxation   relax   replicate

The generalization in (53) is that prefixes, whether heavy or light, are destressed when immediately followed by a stronger stress. We can build this into the Prestress Destressing rule (50) by generalizing it as in (54).[13]

---

[12] This rule has a number of exceptions, such as *raccoon* (in North American English), *tattoo*, *settee*. In a few other cases, destressing takes place despite an underlying long vowel: *phŏnology* (cf. *phōnate*), *schĕmatic* (cf. *schēma*), *bănality* (cf. *bānal*), and *lĕgality* (cf. *lēgal*). Liberman & Prince (1977, 284) assume that these words undergo a minor shortening rule which feeds initial destressing.

[13] While all the examples in this section show the destressing of initial syllables, Prestress Destressing can affect some medial syllables, such as the second syllable of *migratory*. Because of the complexity of the ordering relations involving this rule, we defer discussion of this case until Chapter 6, section 6.7.

(54) *Prestress Destressing (postcyclic, final version)*

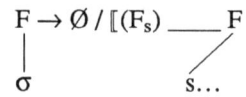

$$F \rightarrow \emptyset / [(F_s) \underline{\quad} F$$
$$|/$$
$$\sigmas...$$

where the syllable of the foot to be deleted dominates either a single mora or a latinate prefix, or is open when medial.

Prestress destressing must be postcyclic on the basis of words like *expect* and *expectation*. The prefix *ex-* is destressed in *expect* but not in *expectation*. To anticipate section 4.7, complex words like *expectation* are derived by first applying all the cyclic rules (those of stratum 1) to the base form *expect*, then adding the suffix *-ation* and applying all the cyclic rules again to the entire derived word. If Prestress Destressing were a cyclic rule, the stress on *ex-* of *expect* would be removed on the first cycle, and would remain so after the addition of the suffix. Thus, the prefix *ex-* would be unable to receive secondary stress on the second cycle by other rules that will be more fully discussed in section 4.7. Therefore we assume that the stress on *ex-* remains until all the cyclic rules have been applied. Then, postcyclically, *ex-* in *expect* can be destressed, but not in *expectation*, where it is followed by a weaker stress.

4.5.2 Poststress Destressing

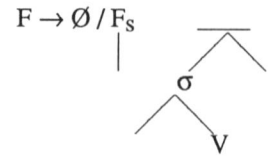

A second destressing rule removes stress from a metrically weak open syllable between a stressed and an unstressed syllable. This is motivated on the basis of data such as that in (55), from Kiparsky (1982a, 42).

(55) a. tránsitòry   b. advísory
         prómissòry   cúrsory
         plánetàry   plénary

This shows that the suffixes *-ary* and *-ory* retain their secondary stress (55a) when they follow an unstressed syllable but are destressed following another stress. Hayes (1982, 258) proposes the rule of Poststress Destressing (56) to account for this.

(56) *Poststress Destressing*

$$F \rightarrow \emptyset / F_s \underline{\quad}$$
$$|\wedge$$
$$\sigma$$
$$\wedge$$
$$V$$

This rule deletes a binary foot whose first syllable is open when it is immediately preceded by a nonbranching strong foot. Like all destressing rules, it is governed by the condition in (51) that disallows deleting a metrically strong foot. This accounts directly for the lack of stress on the suffixes *-ary* and *-ory* in (55b) but does not affect these suffixes in (55a), where they are preceded by a branching foot.

In order to get stress on the suffixes *-ary* and *-ory* in the first place, we adopt the analysis first given by Liberman & Prince and continued by Hayes. Notice that these are adjective suffixes, and so are extrametrical by Adjective Extrametricality at the time that the stress rules apply. They must therefore be stressed by a rule that precedes Adjective Extrametricality, which can only be Long Vowel Stressing (35). But recall that Long Vowel Stressing can apply only to the final syllable of a word. Liberman & Prince (1977, 293) suggest that the suffixes *-ary* and *-ory* are in fact underlyingly monosyllabic, having the glide /y/ as their final segment. This analysis allows these suffixes to be stressed by Long Vowel Stressing. It also accounts for their weak labelling, since they are monosyllabic at the time Word Tree Construction (48) takes place. This analysis requires a rule to syllabify final glides following consonants, which we give here as (57).[14]

(57) *Sonorant Syllabification*

$$[+son] \rightarrow [+son]^{\sigma} / C\_\_\_\_ \ ]$$

Hayes shows that Poststress Destressing in fact applies more generally, and accounts for certain cases of ternary feet in nonfinal position. This eliminates many of the cases of Liberman & Prince's long retraction, and allows us to maintain a more restricted theory of metrical structure. Consider the derivation of *abracadabra*. As an interjection, this word is not subject to Noun Extrametricality or Adjective Extrametricality, and, since there is no final consonant, it is not subject to Consonant Extrametricality either. ESR and Word Tree Construction produce the structure in (58).

---

[14] There are other cases where final orthographic *y* is best treated as nonsyllabic. Morris Halle (class lectures) notes the contrast between *Lómbardy* and *Lombárdi* and several words like *gálaxy* can be correctly stressed under this assumption.

(58)

```
            ω
           /|
          / s
         /  |
        Fw Fw Fs
        |  /\ /\
        s  w s w
     abracadabra
```

Poststress Destressing is applicable in this structure, which produces (59).

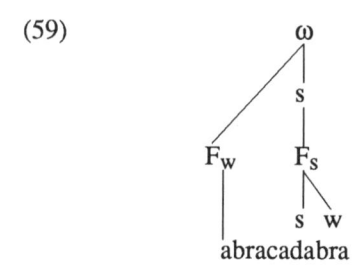

(59)

```
            ω
           /|
          / s
         /  |
        Fw  Fs
        |   /\
        s   s w
     abracadabra
```

In order for a well-formed structure to result from this representation, the stray syllables have to be adjoined into feet. Here, we part company from Hayes. On his account, the two stray syllables are both adjoined to the foot on the left. This is at least partly due to Hayes's claim that Stray Syllable Adjunction is STRUCTURE PRESERVING, in that it preferentially produces feet that would be produced by the stress rules, which in English are primarily left branching. Hayes discusses another possibility, that of attaching both stray syllables to the right, which would allow the further possibility of wiping out the initial stress as well, by Prestress Destressing. He does not discuss a third possibility, advocated by Withgott (1982, 146), which splits the two stray syllables between the surrounding feet, adding one to the left and one to the right. We will adopt this version here. This produces the structure in (60).

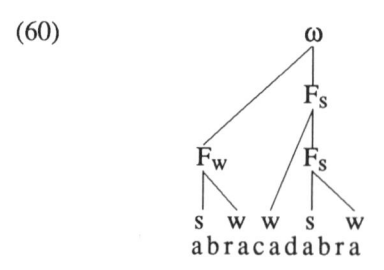

(60)

```
              ω
             /|
            / Fs
           /  /|
          Fw / Fs
          /\ / /\
         s w w s w
       abracadabra
```

Some evidence that this is the correct structure comes from the fact that the [k] at the beginning of the third syllable is aspirated. In Chapter 5, we argue that Aspiration is a rule that affects voiceless stops in foot-initial position. If this is true, then our rules should make this [k] foot initial in (60), which seems correct.

The alert reader will have noticed that Prestress Destressing could also apply to (58). We will assume that Poststress Destressing is ordered before Prestress Destressing and therefore takes precedence over the latter. We can assume that both rules are postcyclic. None of the cases we used to motivate Prestress Destressing are subject to Poststress Destressing. In most cases (e.g., *banana*), the second foot is marked strong, and therefore by (51) not subject to deletion. In the case of *Monongahela,* the first syllable of the second foot is closed, and therefore does not undergo Poststress Destressing.[15]

4.5.3 Medial Destressing

A third destressing rule is known as Medial Destressing. It destresses the second of three stressed syllables, where the second and third are consecutive and the rightmost foot in the sequence is labelled strong. It is motivated by cases like *fràternizátion*. At the end of the first cycle we have *fráternìze*. The suffix *-ation* is added during the second cycle, and the ESR applies to it, producing the structure in (61) after the word tree is formed.

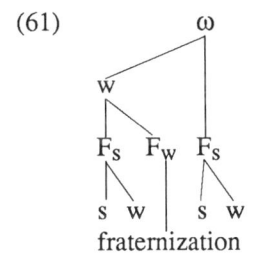

(61)

```
           ω
         /   \
        w     \
       / \     \
      Fs  Fw   Fs
      /\   |   /\
     s  w  s  s  w
     fraternization
```

---

[15] Words like *emànuénsis* are stressed like *Monòngahéla* despite having an open second syllable, which would entail a derivation exactly like that for *àbracadábra*. Hayes (1982, 261) suggests that *emanuensis* irregularly has a left-branching word tree, as in (i).

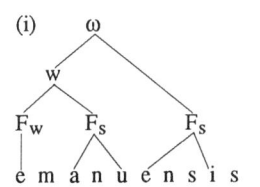

(i)
```
         ω
        / \
       w   \
      / \   \
     Fw  Fs  Fs
     |   /\  /\
     e  m a n u e n s i s
```

(footnote continued overleaf)

Medial destressing removes the middle foot. We formulate the rule as in (62).

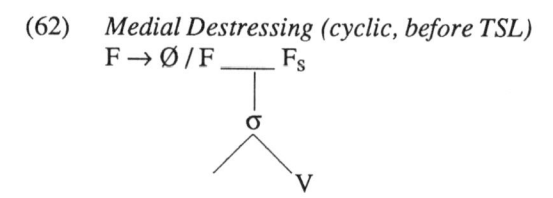

(62) *Medial Destressing (cyclic, before TSL)*
$$F \rightarrow \emptyset\ /\ F \underline{\quad} F_s$$
with structural condition: the destressed F dominates a σ branching to V.

The result of applying (62) to (61) is (63) after the stray medial syllable has been Chomsky adjoined to the preceding foot.

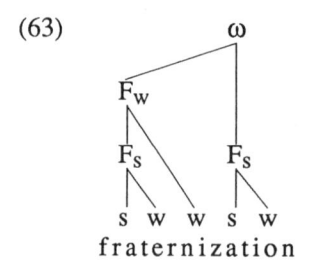

(63)

                ω
         F_w
     F_s   F_s
   s w w s w
   f r a t e r n i z a t i o n

Hayes proposes that Medial Destressing is just a medial application of Initial Destressing (he calls the two rules together Prestress Destressing). There are two difficulties with this. First, there are segmental differences between the rules. Initial Destressing destresses light or prefixal syllables while Medial Destressing destresses open syllables whether heavy or light. More seriously, Initial Destressing must be postcyclic, as we have seen, while Medial Destressing must be cyclic since it precedes the cyclic rule Trisyllabic Laxing. We will discuss cyclicity at greater length in Chapter 6.

4.5.4 Sonorant Destressing

Our final destressing rule is Sonorant Destressing. We return to words with the suffixes *-ary* and *-ory* to develop this rule. Kiparsky (1979, 428 ff.) observes that words with these suffixes generally have stress on the syllable preceding the suffix if that syllable is heavy (64a) but two syllables before the suffix if the syllable preceding the suffix is light (64b).

In this structure Poststress Destressing is inapplicable because the second foot is labelled strong. Therefore Prestress Destressing will produce the correct results. The whole question of lexical exceptionality will be taken up again in sections 4.7–8.

(64) a. òlfáctory   b. prelíminàry   c. dýsentèry
       trajéctory   líteràry   vóluntàry
       perfúnctory   premónitòry   désultòry

    d. légendàry   e. èleméntary   f. infírmary
       mómentàry   còmpliméntary   dispénsary
       frágmentàry   rùdiméntary   respónsory

Curiously, this pattern is interrupted if the syllable preceding the suffix ends in a sororant (64c), where stress is two syllables before the suffix despite the fact that the syllable preceding the suffix is closed by the sonorant. Kiparsky (1979, 428) proposed that they are stressed in the normal way, but then destressed by a rule of Sonorant Destressing, which Hayes (1982, 253) gives as (65).

(65) *Sonorant Destressing*

$$F \rightarrow \emptyset \,/\, F \underline{\quad} F$$

with inner structure: σ dominating m m, where the second m is $\begin{bmatrix} +\text{son} \\ +\text{cons} \end{bmatrix}$

This rule removes a nonbranching foot whose syllable dominates a vowel followed by a sonorant when it is between two other feet, the first of which is nonbranching. This will correctly remove the medial foot in (64c), with this syllable adjoined to the preceding foot by Stray Syllable Adjunction.

Let us illustrate the rule with the derivation of *desultory*. Recall from section 4.5.2 that the suffixes *-ory* and *-ary* are underlyingly monosyllabic and end in a glide *y*. The *o* of the suffix *-ory* receives a foot by Long Vowel Stressing. The suffix then becomes extrametrical by Adjective Extrametricality. At this point the English Stress Rule places a foot on the syllable *-sul-* because it is heavy. The English Stress Rule then iterates and places a third foot on the initial syllable. At this point the structure looks like (66a). Note that Word Tree Construction has not yet applied: we assume crucially that Sonorant Destressing is ordered before Word Tree Construction. Stray Syllable Adjunction and Word Tree Construction produce the final result in (66b).

(66) a.

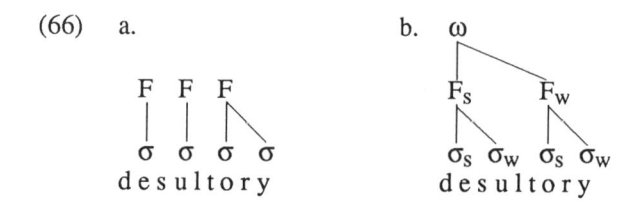

$$\begin{array}{cccc} F & F & F \\ | & | & \wedge \\ \sigma & \sigma & \sigma\ \sigma \end{array}$$
d e s u l t o r y

b.
$$\omega$$
$$F_s \qquad F_w$$
$$\sigma_s\ \sigma_w\ \sigma_s\ \sigma_w$$
d e s u l t o r y

Derivations of (64a) differ in that sonorant destressing is not applicable. The second syllable of *olfactory*, for example, is closed by an obstruent, not a sonorant. The result is that Poststress Destressing applies postcyclically to destress the suffix instead, as explained in section 4.5.2.

The cases in (64a, b, c) all illustrate noncyclic (monomorphemic) derivations. When we examine cyclic cases, the situation becomes slightly more complicated. In (64d), *légend* is stressed as shown on the first cycle. On the second cycle the stress rules apply again stressing the suffix *-ary* (by Long Vowel Stressing), which then becomes extrametrical. The syllable *-gend-* is then stressed by the English Stress Rule. No further iterations occur, since the first syllable has been stressed on the first cycle. The result is analogous to (66a), except that there is internal structure. At this point, Sonorant Destressing can remove the stress on the middle syllable.

In (64e), stress is assigned to *élement* on the first cycle. Adding the suffix *-ary* induces a second cycle, with the suffix stressed as before. The English Stress Rule stresses the syllable *-ment-*. Sonorant Destressing is not applicable here, because the foot preceding *-ment-* is branching. The derivation is completed by Poststress Destressing postcyclically.

The cases in (64f) have a different stress on the first cycle, e.g., *infírm*. There is also a stress on the first syllable of *infirm*, by the iteration of the English Stress Rule, but this remains until it is removed on stratum two by Prestress Destressing. The two feet are labelled right strong by Word Tree Construction on the first cycle because the second foot is a stem. The addition of the suffix induces a second cycle. After the stressing of the suffix, we again have a structure to which Sonorant Destressing (65) is potentially applicable. However, Sonorant Destressing is inapplicable here because the foot with the sonorant, *-fir-* is metrically strong, and such feet cannot be deleted because of (51).[16]

---

[16] The Strict Cycle Condition, developed in section 4.7 and in Chapter 6, section 6.5, permits the stress rules to change existing foot structure in derived environments in cases like (64d, e). Here, the stress rules on the second cycle apply stress to a syllable that was a weak member of a foot on the preceding cycle (e.g., the *ment* of *elementary*). Apparently the stress rules do not completely replace an existing foot, as would happen if the ESR could place a foot on *firm* of *infirmary* on the second cycle.

4.6 Summary of the stress rules

In this section we give a summary of the stress rules developed so far, along with their ordering. Following the standard convention of generative phonology, an arc joining two rules indicates that the top rule is crucially ordered before the lower one.

(67) a. Cyclic rules (stratum 1)

   (Re)syllabification (Chapter 3)
   Long Vowel Stressing (35)
   Extrametricality
      Consonant (28)
      Noun (32)
      Adjective (37)
   English Stress Rule (29, iterative)
   Sonorant Destressing (65)
   Word Tree Construction (48)
   Rhythm Rule (section 4.7)
   Medial Destressing (62)

   b. Postcyclic rules (stratum 2)

   Sonorant Syllabification (57)
   Poststress Destressing (56)
   Prestress Destressing (54)

4.7 The cyclicity of stress rules

We follow *SPE* in assuming that stress rules apply cyclically. This means that the stress rules (and in fact all rules on stratum 1) apply first to underived stems, then reapply after each layer of derivation on stratum 1. This cyclicity is built into the model of lexical phonology developed in Chapter 6, as indicated by the back-and-forth arrows connecting the morphology and the phonology on stratum 1 (see figure 1 in Chapter 6). We claim that stratum 2 is noncyclic (or postcyclic, since it follows the cyclic stratum).[17]

---

[17] The designation of lexical strata appears to be a language particular matter. Mohanan (1986) claims that none of the four lexical levels he posits for Malayalam is cyclic.

In Chapter 1, section 1.2, we briefly illustrated the concept of the cyclic assignment of stress using the word *theatricality*. A further illustration is possible using the contrasts in (68).

(68)   a. òbjèctívity   b. ànecdótal
          èlàstícity   dèsignátion
          èxpèctátion   ìndignátion
          syntàctícian

The words in (68a) have a reduced level of stress on their second syllables, while the words in (68b) have no stress in that position. This is explained in a cyclic model of phonology by applying stress first to the underived items *objective, elastic, expect,* and *syntax*. The reapplication of stress rules after the addition of the affixes alters the stress pattern, but the stress assigned on the earlier cycle is retained. In (68b), the first cycle processes *anecdote* and *designate*. The second syllables of these words are not stressed on the first cycle,[18] and consequently have no stress there to retain when the second cycle operates.

The derivation of words like *expectation* illustrates a further rule which plays an important role in the system of English stress and intonation: the RHYTHM RULE (Kiparsky 1979, 424).[19] This rule reverses the prominence of two sister feet labelled weak-strong if followed by a strong node. It can be given as in (69).

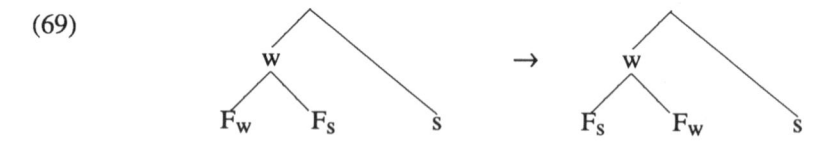

(69)

       w   →   w

F_w F_s s F_s F_w s

In the derivation of *expectation*, we first assign stress to *expect*. After Consonant extrametricality the final syllable is still closed, and so the ESR assigns stress to the final syllable and also to the first syllable in its second iteration. The right foot is labelled strong because it dominates a latinate stem. On the second cycle the stress rules operate again, assigning stress to the suffix. At this point, we have the structure in (70a) (opposite), after Word Tree Construction. This is precisely the type of structure that the Rhythm Rule applies to, reversing the labelling of the first two feet (boxed) to produce (70b). Intuitively, the Rhythm Rule applies to resolve a clash of stresses that results when a strong stress is followed by a

---

[18] *Ánecdòte* is apparently an exception to Noun Extrametricality, compared to the more regularly stressed *staláctìte* (North American English).

[19] Nespor & Vogel (1986) refer to this rule as IAMBIC REVERSAL.

(70) a.

```
           ω
          /|
         w  \
        /|   \
      Fw  Fs  Fs
      |   |   |\
      σ   σ   σs σw
      e x p e c t a t i o n
```

b.

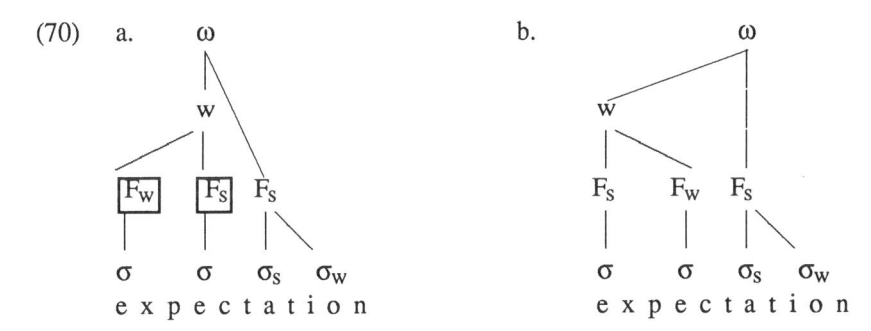

```
              ω
             /|
            w  \
           /|\  \
          Fs Fw Fs
          |  |  |\
          σ  σ  σs σw
          e x p e c t a t i o n
```

stronger stress within the same domain. The strong stress on the final syllable of *expect* clashes with the stronger stress on the suffix added on the second cycle. The Rhythm Rule resolves this clash by reversing the labelling of the first two feet. The stresses are not removed, unlike the case with destressing rules, merely reversed in prominence. Not all stress clashes can be resolved. If there is no destressing rule that can apply and if the Rhythm Rule is inapplicable, a clash of stresses simply remains in the form.

Kiparsky shows that the Rhythm Rule is subject to the restriction in (71).

(71) The Rhythm Rule (usually) does not apply when it would create a word-internal metrical structure of the form (i), where the first *s* is nonbranching.

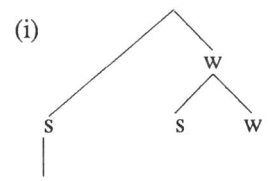

(i)
```
         /\
        /  w
       /  /\
      s  s  w
      |
```

The intuitive idea here is that the Rhythm Rule does not apply to relieve one stress clash only to produce another. Consider the structures in (72, overleaf), which involve potential phrasal applications of the Rhythm Rule.[20] The symbol ω represents the phonological word and the symbol φ represents the phonological phrase. These concepts are further developed in Chapter 5. The Rhythm Rule does not apply in (72) because its application would produce the configuration in (71i) word internally in *sensational* and *Montana* respectively.

The situation is similar in cyclically derived complex words. An example is the derivation of *sensationality*. *Sènsátion* is so stressed by our rules. There is no

---

[20] We will consider phrasal application of the Rhythm Rule further in Chapter 5, section 5.4.

(72) a.

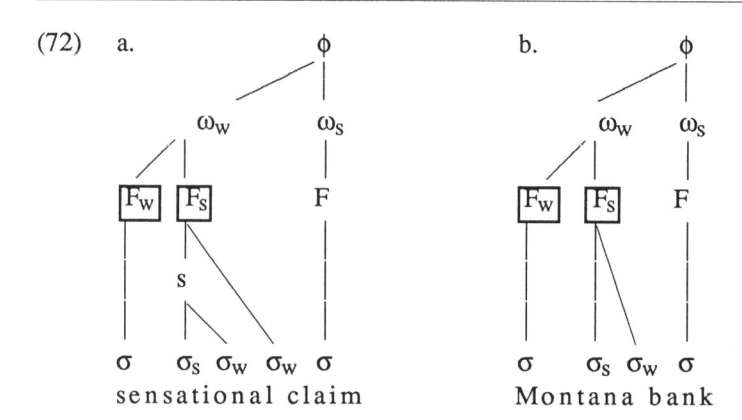

```
              φ
           ╱  │
         ωw    ωs
        ╱ │     │
      [Fw][Fs]  F
        │  ╱╲   │
        s ╱  ╲  │
        │╱    ╲ │
        σ  σs σw σw σ
        sensational claim
```

b.
```
              φ
           ╱  │
         ωw    ωs
        ╱ │     │
      [Fw][Fs]  F
        │  ╱╲   │
        │ ╱  ╲  │
        σ  σs σw σ
        Montana bank
```

change in stress with the addition of the suffix -*al*, which is subject to Adjective Extrametricality, and the right foot is already strong, since it branches. At this point we add the noun suffix -*ity*. The metrical structure looks like (73) once we have applied the rules applicable to nouns.

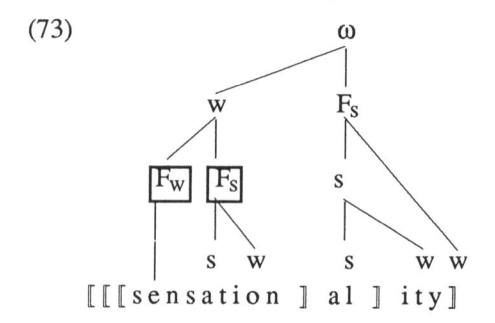

(73)
```
              ω
           ╱  │
          w    Fs
        ╱ │    ╱╲
      [Fw][Fs] s
        │  ╱╲  ╱╲
        s  w  s  w w
     [[[sensation ] al ] ity]
```

It appears that the Rhythm Rule is applicable to this structure, since the boxed foot nodes meet the requirements of (69) for reversal. But this would produce the prohibited structure of (71i) within the subpart of the tree that dominates *sensation*. Therefore, the Rhythm Rule is blocked. The effect here is somewhat more subtle than in the case of *expectation*. There, the Rhythm Rule reversed two nonprimary stresses to produce a more euphonious alternation of prominences. In *sensationality*, the clash remains so that a word-internal clash is not produced.

We assume that stress rules, as cyclic rules, are subject to a constraint known as the STRICT CYCLE CONDITION. This can be stated as in (74), roughly following Kiparsky (1982a, 41). We will present a more formal version in Chapter 6, section 6.5, example (18).

(74) *Strict Cycle Condition*
Cyclic rules may not change structure except in derived environments.

We consider an environment DERIVED if it results from the concatenation of morphemes on a given morphological stratum or if it has been changed by a phonological rule on a given phonological stratum. If a form is underlying, or if it has been derived by phonological or morphological changes on a previous stratum, we consider it UNDERIVED. On the morphological side, this distinction is ensured by BRACKET ERASURE (see Chapter 6, section 6.3). The Strict Cycle Condition does not prevent rules from *adding* structure in underived environments, as we have assumed to be the normal case for stress rules. See Chapter 6, section 6.5 for more discussion of rule cyclicity and the effects of the Strict Cycle Condition.

4.8 On the treatment of exceptions

Although our stress rules are generally quite successful in predicting the stressing of English words, there are a number of exceptional cases. The exceptions are not totally aberrant in terms of the rules. Even the exceptions conform to the basic tendencies that we noted in section 4.1: the tendency for heavy syllables to be stressed in certain environments, the tendency toward alternating stress, and the tendency for the primary stress to be the last stress in a word which is not on the final syllable.

One type of exception is represented by words like *vanílla, Attíla,*[21] which have penultimate stress, although our rules predict initial stress in these words, as in the more regularly stressed *Pámela*. Three types of explanation have been given for these stresses.

SPE proposed that words like *vanilla* had an underlying form with a geminate /ll/: /vanılla/ (with a remarkable similarity to the orthographic representation of this word). With this underlying form, the penultimate syllable is heavy (because it is closed), and will be stressed regularly by our rules. A subsequent rule of degemination is required to reduce the geminate [ll] to a single [l]. This rule is needed independently for words like *in+nocuous*. Notice that geminate consonants can be produced in stratum 2 (in *unnatural,* with geminate [nn]), but not on stratum 1. While this gives the right results, it relies on a rather abstract underlying representation. In particular, we can say that there is no INDEPENDENT MOTIVATION for a geminate /ll/ in *vanilla:* its only purpose is to predict the stress correctly. We

---

[21] The British English pronunciation *Átilla* represents a regularization of this word.

have argued that abstract underlying representations are justified to the extent that they have independent motivation; that is, that they account for a variety of phenomena or allow a significant simplification of the grammar. That is not the case here.

Kiparsky (1982a, 50) proposed a different solution, one which more directly expressed the exceptional nature of such words. Kiparsky gave the underlying form in (75), with a foot present in the underlying representation.

(75)

```
        F
       / \
  v a n i l l a
```

Because the foot is present in underlying form, it cannot be overridden by the stress rules, which would initially place a foot over the first two syllables *vani*. This is a consequence of the strict cycle condition (74): the stress rules cannot override the foot that is present in the underlying form, since this form constitutes a nonderived environment.

A third possible answer is to say that *vanilla* is an exception to Noun Extrametricality. This implies that the final syllable of *vanilla* will not be marked extrametrical, and that foot construction will initially construct the foot shown in (75), with identical consequences to marking that foot underlyingly.

Assuming that we do not wish to adopt the *SPE* solution on the grounds that it contains unmotivated abstractness, we are faced with a choice between Kiparsky's solution, using underlying stress (i.e., a foot), and marking some items exceptions to Noun Extrametricality. How do we choose between these alternatives?

We might start by determining which mechanism is more CONSTRAINED, assuming that both are adequate to deal with the facts. It is clear that Kiparsky's solution is fairly unconstrained, in that it allows, in principle, any arbitrary foot structure to be part of underlying representations, for example, a foot of five syllables, of which only the third is stressed. As we have observed, no such foot can be constructed by Hayes's rules. Nor do we find exceptional stress patterns of this sort. *Vanilla,* although stressed irregularly, has a foot structure independently attested in *potato*. If we try to build the information about what can be a possible foot in English into the kinds of exceptional stresses that we find, we will be duplicating the information about regular foot patterns that is already contained in the regular foot construction rules of English. In this respect, the marking of *vanilla* as exceptional to Noun Extrametricality is more constrained. First, notice that the notion of exceptions to rules is needed anyway. We have observed that such forms as *obese* are exceptions to Trisyllabic Laxing (when they appear in derived forms like *obesity*). Exceptions to extrametricality rules are constrained by the nature of extrametricality itself: because only *single units* can be subject to extrametricality, we cannot achieve the five-syllable foot discussed above (stressed on the third syllable only) by extrametricality, since the first *and* last syllables would have to be extrametrical. Nor could we mark even two adjacent syllables extrametrical, since they would have to be joined into a unit, say a foot, but, at this stage, they could not be such a unit, since the feet have not yet been formed. With respect to forms like *vanilla,* then, the approach using exceptions to Extrametricality seems to be more constrained, yet equally able to handle the facts, and therefore to be preferred. Further examples of exceptions to Noun Extrametricality include *ánecdòte, Tènnessée* (Hayes 1982, 256; 274).

A second type of exception includes nouns with final stress even though their final syllable contains no long vowel, as in (76a), contrasting with similar words with no final stress (76b).

(76) a. mániàc, pársnìp, prótòn, ínsèct, gýmnàst, nárthèx, pálimpsèst
     b. Ísaac, kétchup, ápron, súbject, témpest, hélix

Ross (1972, 242–254) discusses a number of loose regularities governing these cases. Roughly, nouns that end in (most) clusters and in noncoronal obstruents require stress on the last syllable, with certain exceptions both ways (as seen in 76). Hayes appeals to underlyingly marked stresses to account for (76a). A better approach is to consider these nouns exceptions to both Noun Extrametricality and Consonant Extrametricality. In this way, the ESR puts a stress on the final syllable because it is heavy, if no part of the word is extrametrical. Iteration of ESR places stress on the initial syllable (a branching foot in *maniac,* nonbranching feet in the other examples of (76a).

Exceptions to Consonant Extrametricality are needed for some other cases. Some adjectives and verbs are stressed in a way that suggests that their final consonants are not extrametrical: adjectives like *parallel, agog,* and verbs like *begin, attack, caress.* We can therefore say that these adjectives and verbs are exceptions to Consonant Extrametricality.

The adjective suffix *-ic* as in *acídic, artístic, telegráphic* generally requires that main stress fall on the syllable immediately preceding the suffix. We can capture this by saying that this suffix is an exception to Adjective Extrametricality.[22]

---

[22] As exceptions to the exception we have *Árabic* and *chóleric*.

We have now seen four types of exceptionality to the English stress rules, all of which involve exceptions to extrametricality rules. We can summarize these in (77).[23]

(77) a. Exceptions to Noun Extrametricality
vanilla, Attila, palimpsest, Arbuthnot, anecdote, Tennessee; all the nouns with the endings in (42) (*engineer, tycoon,* etc.)
b. Exceptions to Consonant Extrametricality
parallel, agog, begin, attack, caress
c. Exceptions to Noun Extrametricality and Consonant Extrametricality
maniac, parsnip, proton; nouns in (42) with endings consisting of a single short vowel followed by a single consonant (*novelette, bagatelle*)
d. Exceptions to Adjective Extrametricality
-ic; all adjectives having the endings of (42) (*unique, picturesque,* etc.)

There are other stress idiosyncrasies of a less systematic nature. Certain words, like òdóntòid, Trìdéntìne, amálgam are exceptions to Sonorant Destressing (Hayes 1982, 254). In some cases, nonmaximal feet are constructed, as in chìmpànzée, ìncàntátion (Hayes 1982, 274). Certain Greek derived words behave as compounds, such as those in (78).

(78) hélicogràph, síderoscòpe, héteronỳm, eléctrogràph, larỳngoscòpe, kaléidoscòpe, hómonỳm

Hayes (1982, 265) suggests treating these words as compounds, with structures like [[helico]$_\omega$ [graph]$_\omega$]. If each part is stressed separately, the right results are obtained, as long as the first part is subject to noun extrametricality. The correct word tree labelling is obtained by the postcyclic rule of Compound Stress, which labels right nodes strong if and only if they are branching. The ω on the right branch counts as nonbranching in the examples of (78).

There are two correct consequences of this move, which seem to indicate that it is on the right track. First the final *o* of prefixes like *helico-* is often tensed, as is the final *o* of simple words like *buffalo*. We give the rule involved here, Stem-

---

[23] This is not to say that lexically marked stresses are never needed. The stress pattern of the place name Àdiróndàck would seem to be derivable only under the assumption that there is an underlying foot on the final syllable (Hayes 1982, 272–3).

final Tensing, as (50) of Chapter 7. Second, as observed by Siegel (1974), conjunction reduction is possible with some of these words, e.g., *hyper-* and *hypothyroid,* like *apple and cherry pie.*

4.9 Further reading

Because English stress has inspired such a large amount of literature, we can only list the most salient references here. Fudge (1984) provides a largely nontechnical analysis designed primarily for those who are teaching or learning English as a foreign language, and provides extremely useful lists of data illustrating rules and their exceptions. Hogg & McCully (1987) provide a useful summary of the development of metrical phonology, although with somewhat different emphases than we have given. It should be read in conjunction with Vogel's (1989) review. Halle & Vergnaud (1987) give a highly formalized treatment of a somewhat different approach to stress than we have given here, with a final chapter devoted to stress in English. Goldsmith (1990) devotes a chapter to metrical phonology. Finally, the sources on which this chapter has relied heavily provide further background to the issues, namely Liberman & Prince (1977), Kiparsky (1979; 1982a), and Hayes (1982). When consulting these primary sources, you should beware of some terminological inconsistencies, which I have tried to standardize here.

4.10 Exercises

1. In Garawa, main stress falls on the initial syllable, secondary stress falls on the penultimate, and tertiary stresses appear on alternate syllables preceding the penult. However, nonprimary stress never appears on a syllable directly following the main stress. The following forms are suggestive (Furby 1974). Set the parameters so that the correct stress patterns are produced. Also state a destressing rule needed to complete the analysis. (Cited in Hayes 1980, 54.)

yámi	'eye'
púnjala	'white'
wátjimpàŋu	'armpit'
náṟiŋinmùkunjìnamìṟa	'at your own many'

2. Show how the stress pattern of each of the following words is derived using the rules of this chapter. Assume that the word tree rule labels right nodes strong when they are branching; otherwise, the left branch is strong. Tense

vowels are marked with a macron, e.g., ā; lax vowels are marked with a breve where this is important, e.g., ă. Note that no cyclic derivations are involved in this exercise.

a. màgnánim + ous (A)
b. cónfiscăte (V)
c. stăláctìte (N)
d. Tīcònderóga (N)
e. còmpurgătion (N)
f. rĕlúct + ant (A)
g. désignăte (V)
h. mérchandĭse (N)
i. ŏsténs + ible (A)
j. àrchimándrĭte (N)

3. Show that a cyclic derivation of this word is necessary to get the correct stress pattern; i.e., that a noncyclic derivation produces incorrect results.

   [[fraterniz]V ation]N

4. Discuss the role of the Rhythm Rule (69) in the cyclic derivation of the following words.

   a. expectation
   b. extrametricality

5. Using the words you transcribed in exercise 2.1 and syllabified in exercise 3.1, show how their stress patterns are derived. Note: some of these stress patterns are very difficult to derive without recourse to some of the primary literature, especially Kiparsky (1982a). State explicitly any additional assumptions you need to get the derivations correct.

5 Prosodic phonology

5.1 Prosodic constituents in phonology

5.1.1 Why prosodic constituents?
As we mentioned in Chapter 1, section 1.2, the phonological theory of *SPE* had all phonological rules operating on the output of the syntax, mediated by a set of readjustment rules. In the theory of lexical phonology, which we assume in this book, a significant portion of the phonological rules operate in the lexicon, before syntactic concatenation. However, any phonological rule that refers to more than one word must necessarily apply after the syntax. This class includes all rules that supply intonational structure, rules that affect a word-final consonant before a vowel-initial word, and others that we will explore in this chapter. *SPE* acknowledges that such rules do not necessarily apply to the syntactic surface structure in their discussion of the intonational structure of (1).

(1) This is [NP the cat that caught [NP the rat that stole [NP the cheese]]]

SPE comments:

> Clearly the intonational structure of the utterance does not correspond to the surface structure. Rather, the major breaks are after *cat* and *rat;* that is, the sentence is spoken as the three-part structure this is the cat—that caught the rat—that stole the cheese (*SPE*, 372).

SPE proposes to derive the correct intonation contour by means of a readjustment rule. This rule would convert (1), "with its multiply embedded sentences, into a structure where each embedded sentence is sister-adjoined to the sentence dominating it." They do not provide any explicit structures or rules for achieving this. But they claim that

> it can certainly be plausibly argued that this "flattening" of the surface structure is simply a performance factor, related to the difficulty of producing right branching structures...Hence it can certainly be argued that these problems do not belong to grammar—to the theory of competence—at all (*SPE*, 372).

However, in discussing such structures, Chomsky (1965, 10–15) stresses that it is repeated nesting, and especially self-embedding, that contributes to unacceptability whereas left branching and right branching structures can be recognized by "an optimal perceptual device, even with a bounded memory," suggesting that right branching is not a problem at all in (1). Thus it seems undesirable, even within the context of *SPE* theory, to attribute the discrepancy between the syntactic structure and the intonation structure of (1) to performance factors alone.

A second reason for rejecting the performance explanation for the intonation of (1) is the robustness of the intonation that *SPE* observes. The sentence in (1) would be virtually unrecognizable as an English utterance with the intonation breaks at the left NP brackets in (1) rather than after *cat* and *rat*. For this reason, we must recognize the placement of intonation breaks as part of grammar, that is, competence, after all, and not attribute it to vague performance factors.

The theory of prosodic phonology brings the study of intonation, and many other prosodic phenomena as well, back into the theory of competence by eliminating the category of readjustment rules altogether. Many of the explicit readjustment rules in *SPE* are of a largely morphological nature, and are assigned to the lexical morphology in the theory of lexical phonology and morphology, not to the phonology. For truly prosodic processes, prosodic phonology (Nespor & Vogel 1986) proposes prosodic categories. These include the word-internal categories we have already discussed: the mora, the syllable, the foot, and the phonological word. Above the phonological word the prosodic categories are derived from syntactic structure but are not identical to it. The evidence for this is twofold. On the one hand, Nespor & Vogel describe a number of phonological processes whose domain cannot be stated in a general way in terms of syntactic categories, but which can be easily stated in prosodic terms. This is true of the prosodic categories from the clitic group up to the intonation phrase. On the other hand, Nespor & Vogel describe certain phonological processes whose domain is larger than the sentence. Since the sentence is the largest syntactic category, there is no syntactic category available to serve as the domain for these processes.

These rules, which include Flapping in English, will be described in terms of the phonological utterance, which under certain conditions can contain more than one sentence.

5.1.2 The prosodic hierarchy

The essential proposal of prosodic phonology is a hierarchy of prosodic units. The idea of the hierarchy is that each unit is made up of some number of units from the next lower level. Nespor & Vogel propose a hierarchy of seven prosodic constituents. By now it is clear that the mora also constitutes a prosodic unit, so we add it to their hierarchy, giving the eight units in (2), along with the symbols we will use for each.

(2) *The prosodic hierarchy*
    a. mora   m
    b. syllable   σ
    c. foot   F
    d. phonological word   ω
    e. clitic group   C
    f. phonological phrase   φ
    g. intonation phrase   I
    h. phonological utterance   U

The requirement that each prosodic unit belong to a constituent of the next higher rank in the hierarchy is simply the requirement of prosodic licensing, which we introduced as (21) in Chapter 3.

Nespor & Vogel in fact impose a somewhat more restrictive version of prosodic licensing, which they refer to as the STRICT LAYER HYPOTHESIS.[1] We give their formulation in (3).

(3)   *Principle 1.* A given nonterminal unit of the prosodic hierarchy, X^p, is composed of one or more units of the immediately lower category, X^{p-1}.

      Principle 2. A unit of a given level of the hierarchy is exhaustively contained in the superordinate unit of which it is a part.

The strict layer hypothesis in effect imposes prosodic licensing in both directions: every unit must belong to the next higher unit (moras to syllables, syllables to feet,

---
[1] The term is from Selkirk (1984b), where it is defined somewhat differently.

etc.) but also each unit must exhaustively contain units of the next lower rank (phonological words contain only feet, feet contain only syllables, etc.) Hayes's analysis of English stress violated Principles 1 and 2 by attaching stray syllables directly to the word tree (see Chapter 4, section 4.2.1). Our analysis involving Chomsky Adjunction of stray syllables to an adjacent foot violates Principle 1 in a different way by allowing a foot to dominate another foot. In this chapter we will see an application of this type of derived structure in the determination of the allophones of English stops. We will not therefore impose the strict layer hypothesis, although we respect it in spirit, in that we allow it to be violated only in the case of structures derived by rule, not in basic structures. The only case where this occurs is in the Chomsky Adjunction of a syllable to a foot. We do not find cases where an intonation phrase dominates another intonation phrase, for instance.[2] We will impose prosodic licensing. As already noted in Chapter 4, section 4.2.1, structures with nested feet conform to the principle of prosodic licensing.

Nespor & Vogel impose two additional conditions on prosodic structures, which they refer to as Principles 3 and 4.

(4) *Principle 3.* The hierarchical structures of prosodic phonology are n-ary branching.

Principle 4. The relative prominence relation defined for sister nodes is such that one node is assigned the value strong (s) and all the other nodes are assigned the value weak (w).

Principle 3 contrasts with earlier work in metrical and prosodic phonology that permitted only binary branching. If some prosodic unit Y comprises three (say) of the next lower category X, an n-ary branching structure will look like (5a), while a binary structure will look like (5b).

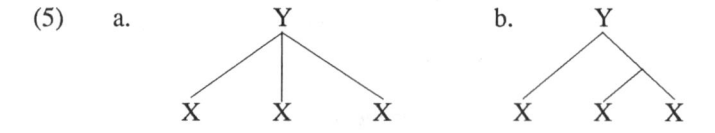

(5) a.   Y   b.   Y
           /|\   / \
          X X X   X   X
                                             / \
                                            X   X

Nespor & Vogel argue that n-ary branching structures are simpler than binary branching structures because they do not require the additional intermediate

---

[2] In Chapter 8, section 8.2, we consider the possibility of nested phonological words in a somewhat different analysis of certain affixes.

nodes that the limitation to binary branching entails. These intermediate nodes do not correspond to any phonological constituent. So we will accept the conclusion that prosodic structures are n-ary branching, while admitting that this is still controversial. Principle 4 is required as a labelling convention for n-ary branching structures. It allows only one daughter of a given prosodic category to be strong, while all others must be weak. This replaces the original metrical requirement that strong and weak must occur in pairs. This does not appear to play havoc with any of the metrical structures we have discussed so far.

Nespor & Vogel follow Selkirk (1980a) in distinguishing three types of prosodic rules. Domain span rules affect a segment in the context of other segments, where every part of the rule is contained within the domain of a particular prosodic unit, as in (6).

(6) *domain span:*
$A \to B / [\ldots X \underline{\quad} Y \ldots]_{D_i}$

Domain juncture rules apply to a segment in the context of other segments at the juncture of two prosodic units of the same type, where these two units are adjacent within the next larger prosodic unit, as in (7).

(7) *domain juncture:*
 a. $A \to B / [\ldots [\ldots X \underline{\quad} Y]_{D_j} [Z \ldots]_{D_j} \ldots]_{D_i}$
 b. $A \to B / [\ldots [\ldots X]_{D_j} [Y \underline{\quad} Z \ldots]_{D_j} \ldots]_{D_i}$

Finally, domain limit rules apply at the right or left edge of a prosodic constituent, as in (8).

(8) *domain limit:*
 a. $A \to B / [\ldots X \underline{\quad} Y]_{D_i}$
 b. $A \to B / [X \quad Y \ldots]_{D_i}$

We will see examples of rules of these various types as we examine a number of rules of English phonology that apply within prosodic domains.

5.2 The syllable (σ) and the foot (F)

Kahn (1976) argues that a number of allophonic rules in English have the syllable as their domain. Kiparsky (1979) reanalyzed several of Kahn's rules as foot domain rules, thereby making Kahn's appeal to ambisyllabicity unnecessary. However, the rule of Diphthong Shortening is incorrectly characterized as a foot domain rule by Kiparsky. In the next section we will show that the domain of Diphthong Shortening is in fact the phonological word. In this section we will consider phonological rules with the syllable or the foot as their domains.

Our first example of a syllabically conditioned rule is Glottalization. Expressed in segmental terms, the environments for the glottalization of voiceless stops in North American English appear quite varied. In each case the glottalized segment is preceded by a [–consonantal] segment. In addition, it must be final, followed within a (phonological) word by a consonant other than *r*, or by a syllabic *n*, or followed by a word that begins with a consonant or glide. The examples in (9) are based on Nespor & Vogel (1986, 77).

(9)   a. great   [ɡreit^ʔ]
       b. quart   [kwɒrt^ʔ]
       c. pliant   [plaiənt^ʔ]
       d. butler   [bət^{ʔ}lər]
       e. witness   [wɪt^{ʔ}nɪs]
       f. button   [bət^{ʔ}n̩]
       g. great party   [ɡreit^ʔ parri]
       h. great reunion   [ɡreit^ʔ rɪyunyən]
       i. great wonder   [ɡreit^ʔ wəndər]

We have illustrated Glottalization with the voiceless alveolar stop, which shows the effect of the rule most clearly. In many cases in (9), the symbol [t^ʔ] could easily be replaced by [ʔ]. The other voiceless stops are also glottalized in the same environments, but in these cases the result is actually a simultaneous glottal and labial or velar closure, never a simple glottal stop. What all these environments have in common is that the voiceless stop appears in syllable-final position. Therefore, Nespor & Vogel formulate a domain limit rule to glottalize voiceless stops in syllable-final position following a nonconsonantal segment, as in (10).

(10)   *Glottalization*
$$\begin{bmatrix} -\text{cont} \\ -\text{voice} \end{bmatrix} \rightarrow [+\text{constr}] \, / \, [\ldots[+\text{son}] \underline{\quad}]_\sigma$$

The one problematic case here is (9f), where *t* does not appear to be in syllable-final position, and yet is glottalized. According to the rules of syllabification that we developed for English in Chapter 3, *t* should form an onset to a following syllabic sonorant, as indeed it does with other nasals and liquids, producing flapping, not glottalization, in words like *bottom, bottle, water*. This is especially true if syllabic [n̩] is derived from the sequence V*n*, which seems plausible, since syllabic [n̩] can trigger Sonorant Destressing in forms such as *mackintosh*. (Cf. Chapter 4, section 4.5.4). Withgott (1982, 165ff) assumes that *t* should be analyzed as being in syllable-final position in such cases as (9f), observing that *t* is not generally glottalized after a consonant, before a syllabic [n̩], as in the examples of (11).

(11) a. assistant [əsɪstn̩t]
     b. clandestine [klændɛstn̩]
     c. pectin [pɛktn̩]
     d. intestine [ɪntɛstn̩]

Withgott assumes that the sequence V*n* is reduced to syllabic [n̩] by a rule when it follows V*t*, and that *t* is resyllabified as a coda before syllabic [n̩]. If true, this is a curious solution. While it is true that *tn* cannot begin a syllable, this is also true of *tl* and *tm*, and yet *t* is not glottalized before syllabic *l* and *m*.

Another process that appears to operate within the syllable is the one that determines the allophones of the lateral [l] in some dialects of English. In the dialect described by Halle & Mohanan (1985), /l/ is "dark" or velarized in the rhyme, otherwise it is light, as in (12).

(12) a. *light [l]*   b. *dark [ɫ]*
     let, lie, blow   milk, belt, dull

Halle & Mohanan give a rule that adds the feature [+back] to [l] when it is dominated by R (rhyme). In the prosodic framework, such a rule is not allowed, because it does not fall into the types of prosodic rules discussed in section 5.1.2, namely domain span, domain juncture, and domain limit. It can easily be reformulated as a domain limit rule, however. Nespor & Vogel (1986, 73–74) discuss a similar case, where the nasal [n] is velarized to [ŋ] in the rhyme in certain dialects of Spanish, as in the examples in (13).

(13) a. cantan   ca[ŋ]ta[ŋ]
     b. instituto   i[ŋ]stituto
     c. constante   co[ŋ]sta[ŋ]te

Following their discussion, we can reformulate *l*-Velarization in English as in (14).

(14) l-*Velarization*
 l → [+back] / ____ C₀]σ

The distribution of light and dark *l* is quite variable in various English dialects. According to Wells (1982, 43), in RP, light [l] occurs before a vowel or /y/, as in *let, blow, valley, million, fall off*, while dark [ɫ] occurs before a consonant, /w/, or pause, as in *milk, meals, always, feel*. In Irish English (Wells 1982, 74), [l] is light in all environments. In many North American dialects, [l] is light only at the beginning of a foot, so that [l] is velarized in *valley, silly, yellow*, as well as in the types of words illustrated in (12b). We can give rule (15) for these dialects.

(15) l-*Velarization*
 l → [+back] / [F X ____   (X ≠ ∅)

Another class of examples concerns words like *alarm, velocity*. If light [l] is found in these words, it follows the generalization stated in (15). But many speakers have dark [ɫ] in these words. For these speakers, we can say that [l] is dark except at the beginning of a *maximal* foot. According to our procedure in Chapter 4, word-initial stray syllables are Chomsky adjoined to a following foot. Therefore, the word *velocity* has the structure of (16).

(16) [F ve[F locity]]

With this structure, [l] will be velarized by rule (15) if we add the requirement that F be maximal. These examples show that the foot, which we constructed originally to determine the distribution of stressed syllables, serves as the domain of certain segmental processes as well.

Notice that a theory that recognizes the syllable, but no higher levels of prosodic structure, would have difficulty accounting for dialects in which *velocity* has a dark [ɫ]. For the dialects where *valley* has dark [ɫ] but *velocity* has light [l], such theories can simply say that syllable final [ɫ] is dark, assuming that the *l* in *valley* is ambisyllabic. But there is no way for the *l* of *velocity* to be ambisyllabic, since the following syllable is stressed. Therefore, to account for dark [ɫ] in *velocity*, reference to the foot, and nested feet, is required.

To account for the distribution of light and dark [l], we made reference to both the syllable and the foot. Another rule that has the foot as its domain is Aspiration of stops. Kahn (1976) argued that stops are aspirated when they are syllable initial but not syllable final. This basically affects stops at the beginning of words and at the beginning of stressed syllables, such as the first two syllables of *potato*. It correctly excludes stops such as the *t* of *butter*, since this is ambisyllabic in Kahn's system. However, it also affects stops such as the *t* of *Washington*, since there is no way for this stop to be ambisyllabic.[3] Given our assumption that stray syllables are Chomsky adjoined to a following foot, we correctly predict aspiration of the two voiceless stops of *potato*, since these are both at the beginning of a foot. (We do not require foot maximality here.) The voiceless stops of *butter* and *Washington* are not foot initial, and so remain unaspirated. We can formulate Aspiration as in (17).

(17) Aspiration
$$\begin{bmatrix} -\text{cont} \\ -\text{voice} \end{bmatrix} \rightarrow [+\text{spread glottis}] / [_F \underline{\quad} \ldots]$$

As a further demonstration of the correctness of (17) for Aspiration, we can cite some examples from Withgott (1982, 157–8). The contrast in (18) is particularly instructive.

(18) a. mili*t*aristic   [t^h]
     b. capi*t*alistic   [ɾ]

These two words have a very similar superficial structure, and, in particular, the *t* in each appears in the same segmental environment at the beginning of a stressless syllable. Yet the *t*s have sharply contrasting realizations, being aspirated in (18a) and flapped in (18b). The explanation lies in the cyclic nature of stress assignment (i.e., foot construction). On the first cycle, feet are constructed on [$_F$ mili][$_F$ tary] and [$_F$ capital] respectively. On the second cycle, the suffixes are added, and Prestress Destressing removes the foot on [tary] in *militaristic,* so that the metrical structure is now [$_F$ mili] ta [$_F$ ristic] and [$_F$ capita][$_F$ listic]. The stray syllable *ta* is now adjoined to its right, giving [$_F$ mili][$_F$ taristic]. Therefore, the *t* in *militaristic* is aspirated, since it begins a foot, even though its syllable is unstressed. The *t* in *capitalistic,* on the other hand, is not foot initial at any stage of the derivation, and so remains unaspirated. It is flapped by the Flapping rule, which applies after Aspiration.[4]

---

[3] Kahn (1976, 47) claims that [t] is aspirated in *Washington,* as required in his system, since [t] must be syllable initial and can't be syllable final. But aspiration of [t] in *Washington* must be a peculiarity of Kahn's dialect; I find aspiration here extremely unnatural (contrast the clear aspiration of *t* in *Washingtonian*). This shows that reference to foot structure is necessary to predict correctly that [t] is unaspirated in *Washington.* Syllable structure alone, even with ambisyllabicity, is unable to capture these facts.

[4] The weak point in this argument is the question of why the destressed syllable *ta* is Chomsky adjoined to its right rather than to its left. In the cases we examined in Chapter 4, there was

Kiparsky (1979) discusses a number of other rules of English that have the foot as their domain. One is the obligatory assimilation of *n* to a following velar, as in *ink*. The fact that assimilation is obligatory in *increment* also shows that it is not the syllable that forms the domain for this assimilation. Notice that assimilation of *n* is optional in cases like *incréase* (V), *íncrèase* (N), where the nasal and the following velar are in separate feet.

Several other processes that Kiparsky treats as foot bounded appear to be better treated syllabically. One is the devoicing of sonorants after voiceless consonants. This affects the italicized sonorants in (19a) but not those in (19b).

(19) a. c*r*y
  p*l*ay
  st*r*ay
  matt*r*ess
  app*l*y
  Is*l*ip
  eye s*l*ip
 b. At*l*as
  ice *l*ip

We therefore state the rule as in (20).

(20) *Sonorant Devoicing*
  [+son] → [−voice] / [...[−voice] ___ ...]$_\sigma$

If this rule were stated on the foot domain, as suggested by Nespor & Vogel (1986, 93), it would incorrectly devoice the *l* in *Atlas* (19b).

Another rule that Kiparsky states with a foot domain is what he refers to as "mutual assimilation" of [k] and [r] to what he writes as KR. This should be transcribed phonetically as [k̟r̥], where [k̟] indicates a fronted variety of [k] and the circle under the *r* denotes devoicing. The assimilation of [r] in this case is just the sonorant devoicing we have just discussed (rule 20). The data in (21a) illustrate this mutual assimilation, with no such assimilation in (21b). The velar stop under consideration is italicized. The fronting of velar stops can be given as a syllable span rule (22).[5]

no ambiguity since each stray syllable had only one foot adjacent to it that it could adjoin to. The direction of adjunction of a single stray syllable between two feet is a problem for further research.

[5] This rule is given a more general formulation which affects voiced [g] as well as [k], since I assume that it would affect [g] in *grew, ingratiate*, etc., in the same way as in (21a).

(21) a. *cr*ew   [k̯r̥]
        in*cr*éase_V
        ín*cr*èase_N
        in*cr*ement
    b. ba*ck* rub   [kr]
        co*ckr*oach

(22) *Velar Fronting*

$$\begin{bmatrix} -\text{son} \\ -\text{cont} \\ -\text{cor} \\ -\text{ant} \end{bmatrix} \rightarrow [-\text{back}] / [\ldots \underline{\quad} \text{ r} \ldots]_\sigma$$

This fronting of [k] has a lot in common with a rule that Nespor & Vogel refer to as Alveopalatalization, which affects the alveolar stops, and which Nespor & Vogel formulate as a syllable span rule, as in (23) (slightly modified).

(23) *Alveopalatalization*

$$\begin{bmatrix} -\text{cont} \\ +\text{cor} \end{bmatrix} \rightarrow [-\text{ant}] / [\ldots \underline{\quad} \text{ r} \ldots]_\sigma \quad \text{(phonetic symbols ṱ, ḓ)}$$

This rule is motivated by data like that in (24). The rule applies in (24a) but not in (24b). The alveolars in question are italicized.

(24) a. *t*reat   [ṱ]   b. nigh*t* rate   [t']
       s*t*reet   ra*t* race
       re*t*rieve   cu*t* rate
       ci*t*rus   tigh*t* rope
       des*t*roy
       ni*t*rate

Sonorant Devoicing (20), Velar Fronting (22), and Alveopalatalization (23) are not crucially ordered with respect to each other or to any other rule.

A final process that Kiparsky attributed to foot conditioning is Diphthong Shortening. As Nespor & Vogel (1986, 108) note, this is part of a more general

---

     Obviously [r] is not devoiced in this environment.

        Kiparsky formulates mutual assimilation as a foot span rule. In this case and in the case of Alveopalatalization (23), it is not clear whether it is the syllable or the foot that is relevant, since a stop followed by *r* will always be syllabified together unless they are in different phonological words, as they are in (21b). We will choose the syllable in these two rules for concreteness.

process that shortens vowels before voiceless consonants. In the case of the diphthongs [ay, aw], this process noticeably affects the quality of the first part of the diphthong, making it more central. Diphthong Shortening shortens the italicized diphthongs in (25a) but not those in (25b).

(25) a. *I*slip
        *i*ce lip
        n*i*ght rate
        n*i*trate
    b. *eye* slip
        N*ye* trait

Kiparsky correctly argued that Diphthong Shortening cannot be a syllable-based process, since it affects diphthongs followed by a voiceless consonant in another syllable in examples like *I.slip* and *ni.trate*. But, for the same reason, it cannot be foot based. The word *nitrate* has two feet (each syllable is stressed and so constitutes a foot), yet Diphthong Shortening applies in the first syllable. Note also that ambisyllabicity would not help here. The *t* in *nitrate* cannot be ambisyllabic, because of the stress on the following syllable. The correct characterization of this rule is that it has the next higher prosodic unit as its domain, the phonological word. It is to this unit that we now turn.

5.3 The phonological word (ω) and the clitic group (C)

5.3.1 The phonological word and Diphthong Shortening

Nespor & Vogel give no illustrations of the Phonological Word from English, since they accept Kiparsky's characterization of Diphthong Shortening as a foot domain rule. In their discussion there are two possible ways to define the phonological word for any given language. On the one hand, the phonological word may be equal to the terminal elements of the syntactic tree (roughly any syntactic element dominated by a lexical category node, and quite intuitively equal to what we normally call a "word"). They argue that this is the case of Demotic Greek and Classical Latin. On the other hand, it may be smaller than what is normally considered a word. Two processes in Turkish illustrate this possibility. Monomorphemic and derived words in Turkish are normally stressed on the final syllable, as shown by the examples in (26).

(26) a. çocúk   'child'
    b. çocuklár   'children'
    c. çocuklarımíz   'our children'
    d. çocuklarımızín 'of our children'

In compounds, however, the main stress is on the last syllable of the first member of the compound, with secondary stress on the last syllable of the last member of the compound. This is illustrated in (27) (examples from Nespor & Vogel 1986, 120).

(27) a. düğünçiçeği   'buttercup'
        'of yesterday flower'

    b. çáy evì   'tea house'
        'tea house'

This implies that each member of a compound must be considered separately for stress purposes. A second process that treats compound elements separately is vowel harmony. We will illustrate this with data from Hungarian, where the facts of vowel harmony are similar to Turkish. Normally, a monomorphemic word has only back vowels or only front vowels. A compound can be made of two words with opposite harmonic properties, each of which retains its individual harmony within the compound. Each element of a compound is therefore a separate domain for vowel harmony also. Any suffix attached to the compound harmonizes to the last member of the compound. This is illustrated in (28).

(28) a. főváros   'capital (city)'
        'head city'
        fővárosunk   'our capital city'

    b. látkép   'view'
        'see picture'
        látképünk   'our view'

This implies that, in Hungarian as in Turkish, the phonological word includes a stem and any associated affixes. The affix belongs semantically with the com pound as a whole, however. This shows that the phonological word is not coextensive with any morphosyntactic category in these languages.

For languages like Turkish, Hungarian, and English, Nespor & Vogel define the phonological word as in (29).

(29) ω domain
    a. The domain of ω consists of a stem and any linearly adjacent string of affixes.
    b. Any unattached element forms a ω on its own.

In English we can consider the phonological word as the domain of Diphthong Shortening, as mentioned at the end of the last section. We noted that this rule cannot have either the syllable or the foot as its domain of application, because of examples like *nitrate*. This word has two feet, and the diphthong in the first syllable shortens. We can capture this by stating Diphthong Shortening as a domain span rule operating within the phonological word, as in (30).[6]

(30) *Diphthong Shortening*

$$V \rightarrow \begin{bmatrix} -\text{low} \\ -\text{tense} \end{bmatrix} / [\ldots \underline{\quad} [-\text{cons}] [-\text{voice}] \ldots]_\omega$$

Note, however, that Diphthong Shortening does not operate within a compound such as *Nye trait,* where the diphthong is final within the first element of the compound and the voiceless consonant is found in the second element of the compound. This shows that the phonological word should be defined for English in a way similar to its definition in Turkish and Hungarian. That is, each element of a compound word (along with associated affixes) is a separate phonological word. Diphthong Shortening does of course apply in a compound like *night rate,* where the requirements of (30) are met entirely within the first element of the compound.

As we discussed in Chapter 1, section 1.1, Diphthong Shortening is crucially ordered before Flapping. In section 5.7 we will return to some questions involving the ordering of the rules discussed in this chapter.

5.3.2 *The clitic group (C)*

The next higher prosodic category in Nespor & Vogel's hierarchy is the Clitic Group. In a number of ways, this is a problematic category. One problem is that the clitic group is necessarily composed of phonological words, which in turn are composed of feet. Because each foot contains a stress, this implies that clitics ought to bear stress, although one of the principal defining characteristics of clitics is their stresslessness. For this reason one is tempted to eliminate this category and to consider clitics as unstressed members of phonological words.

Hayes (1989, 207) defines the clitic group "roughly as a single content word together with all contiguous grammatical words in the same syntactic constituent." He gives a more precise definition which adjoins grammatical words (clitics) right or left to a content word (host) with which it is most closely bound syntactically. For the purpose of applying this definition, we can take content

---

[6] Although this rule laxes a vowel, the result is not subject to Vowel Reduction (section 7.6), since these vowels are stressed. Furthermore, Diphthong Shortening is postlexical and Vowel Reduction is postcyclic (i.e., stratum 2 of the lexicon).

words to include nouns, verbs, adjectives, and adverbs, while grammatical words include pronouns, articles, auxiliaries, and prepositions. For the syntactic structure (31a) Hayes assigns the division into clitic groups (31b).

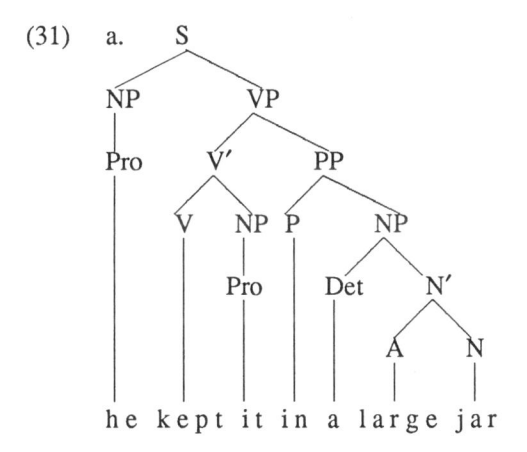

(31) a.

```
                    S
              ┌─────┴─────┐
             NP           VP
              │        ┌───┴───┐
             Pro       V'      PP
                    ┌──┴──┐  ┌──┴──┐
                    V    NP  P    NP
                         │        │
                        Pro      Det   N'
                                      ┌─┴─┐
                                      A   N
                                      │   │
                    he  kept  it  in  a large jar
```

b.   [C he kept it] [C in a large] [C jar]

The clitic group is somewhat more difficult to exemplify in English than the other prosodic categories we have looked at, although Nespor & Vogel give a number of examples from Italian and Modern Greek. Hayes does give two phonological processes that seem to depend on this category, which were originally discussed by Selkirk (1972). The first of these deletes a word-final [v] before a consonant-initial word in certain lexical items. This is exemplified in the examples of (32), where clitic groups are bracketed.

(32) a. [C Please][C leave them][C alone]
         [liː]
      b. [C Will you save me][C a seat?]
         [sey]
      c. [C John][C would have left]
         [wʊdə]
      d. [C a piece][C of pie]
         [ə]

But where the triggering consonant occurs in a separate clitic group, [v] cannot be deleted, as shown in (33).

(33) a. [c Please][c leave][c Maureen][c alone]
         [liːv]
     b. [c Will you save][c those people][c a seat]
         [seyv]
     c. I can't do it this week, [c but I would have][c last][c week]
                                                    [hæv]
     d. [c It was thought of][c constantly]
         [əv]

There is no way to reanalyze this rule using the syllable, whether or not ambisyllabicity is invoked, since the [v] to be deleted and the consonant that triggers deletion will always be in separate syllables.

A second rule that applies within the clitic group is a rule of palatalization that converts [s] or [z] to [š] or [ž] respectively before [š] or [ž]. At normal rates of speech this rule applies only within the clitic group, as in (34). At faster rates or in sloppy speech, it can also apply across clitic groups. This is exemplified in (35).

(34) a. [c his shadow]
         [ž]
     b. [c is Sheila][c coming?]
         [ž]
     c. [c as shallow][c as Sheila}
         [ž]   [ž]
(35) a. [c Laura's][c shadow]
             [ž] (fast or sloppy speech only)
     b. [c he sees][c Sheila]
         [ž]   (fast or sloppy speech only)
     c. [c those boys][c shun him]
             [ž]   (fast or sloppy speech only)

In these examples Hayes's characterization of clitics as a unit attached to a host with which it is most closely bound syntactically seems to hold. However, Klavans (1982; 1985) provides a number of examples where the syntactic host for a clitic is not the same as its phonological host. To take just one example from English, it is well known that auxiliary contraction does not take place if a syntactic gap appears to the right of the auxiliary. (Example 36 is from Klavans 1985, 110.) But phonologically, auxiliary contraction is clearly to the left, as shown by voicing assimilation in (37) (Klavans's examples).

(36)　This won't have the effect on us $\begin{cases} \text{a. that it will have on you} \\ \text{b. that it will \_\_\_\_ on you} \\ \text{c. that it'll have on you} \\ \text{d. *that it'll \_\_\_\_ on you} \end{cases}$

(37)　Jack's a fool ([ʤæks], *[ʤækz])

Klavans suggests the partial structure in (38) to account for the dual clitic nature of the contracted auxiliary in (36c).

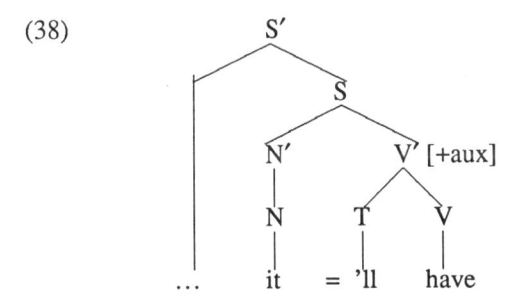

(38)

```
            S'
           /  \
              S
            /   \
          N'     V' [+aux]
          |     /  \
          N    T    V
          |    |    |
         ...  it = 'll  have
```

In this structure, the equal sign (=) shows phonological cliticization to the left. Syntactically, however, the clitic 'll is placed initially in the V', before the verb. This shows that phonological cliticization need not always follow the direction of syntactic cliticization.

5.4　The phonological phrase (φ)

Nespor & Vogel motivate the phonological phrase primarily with evidence from Italian, but it serves as the domain for several rules of English also. The phonological phrase is defined with reference to syntactic structure, but is not coextensive with any morphosyntactic unit. We will quote Nespor & Vogel's (1986, 168) principle of phonological phrase formation in full.

(39)　*Phonological phrase formation*
　　I.　φ *domain*
　　　　The domain of φ consists of a C which contains a lexical head (X) and all Cs on its nonrecursive side up to the C that contains another head outside the maximal projection of X.
　　II.　φ *construction*
　　　　Join into an n-ary branching φ all Cs included in a string delimited by the definition of the domain of φ.

III. φ *relative prominence*
   In languages whose syntactic trees are right branching, the rightmost node of φ is labelled *s;* in languages whose syntactic trees are left branching, the leftmost node of φ is labelled *s*. All sister nodes of *s* are labelled *w*.

We will try to be more precise about the terms in these definitions. The lexical head in (39I) is intended as ranging over N, V, and A and Adv. That is, prepositions do not count as lexical heads for the purposes of phonology. We also assume that the direction of recursion is a parameter (in the sense defined in Chapter 4, section 4.2). Languages like English and Italian are right recursive; that is, their syntactic trees are right branching and new phrases are introduced productively to the right of phrasal heads. In contrast, languages like Japanese are left branching. So the phrase "nonrecursive side" in (39I) means the left side in English and Italian, the right side in Japanese. Roughly, then, (39I) creates phonological phrases by grouping a lexical head with all syntactic material to its left, up to but not including the next lexical head, which begins a new phonological phrase. Let us consider a simple example from Italian. In (40), the syntactic structure of the sentence is given on top, in terms of the X-bar notation, while the division into phonological phrases is given underneath.

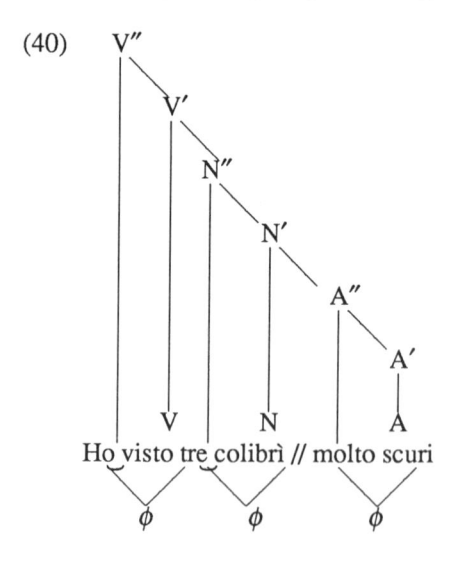

(40)

Ho visto tre colibrì // molto scuri
    φ   φ   φ

'I saw three very dark hummingbirds'

It is clear in (40) that the phonological phrases do not in general correspond to any particular syntactic phrase.

Nespor & Vogel use the structure in (40) to argue for the phonological phrase as the domain of a rule of Italian traditionally called *Raddoppiamento Sintattico*. This rule lengthens a consonant at the beginning of a phonological word if it follows a word-final stressed vowel in the preceding phonological word, provided that the two phonological words are contained within the same phonological phrase. Therefore, the sentence is pronounced *ho [vː]isto tre [kː]olibrì molto scuri*. In (40) the subscripted curve indicates where Raddoppiamento takes place and the double slash (//) indicates where it is inhibited. The *s* of *scuri* is not lengthened because the preceding vowel is unstressed. The *m* of *molto* is not lengthened, despite the preceding stressed vowel, because these two segments are in distinct phonological phrases, as shown.

Nespor & Vogel demonstrate that the phonological phrase is the domain for the operation of two rules in English phonology. One is the phrasal operation of the Rhythm Rule, which they refer to as Iambic Reversal (following Liberman & Prince 1977). In Chapter 4, section 4.7 we adopted Kiparsky's (1979, 424) formulation for word-internal (lexical) application, repeated here in (41).[7]

(41)

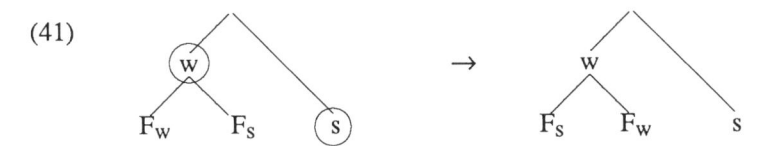

As discussed in Chapter 4, Kiparsky imposes a restriction on (41), which we repeat as (42).

(42) (41) (usually) does not apply when it would create a word-internal metrical structure of the form (i), where the first *s* is nonbranching.

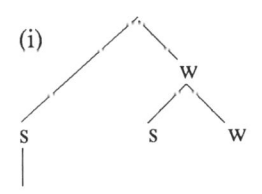

(i)

---

[7] The circled nodes in (41) may be on higher constituents than the ones immediately dominating the feet whose prosodic labelling is switched. For example, in the phrase *fifteen carpenters*, the clitic groups dominating the phonological words are labelled *w* and *s*, not the phonological words themselves.

As we discussed in Chapter 4, section 4.7, examples such as *sensational claim* and *Montana bank* illustrate this constraint on the Rhythm Rule. [Sen]_w [sational]_s and [Mon]_w [tana]_s each consist of two feet, of which the first is weak, thus being potential inputs to the Rhythm Rule when put in a larger phrase whose right member is strong (as is usual in phrases). But the operation of the Rhythm Rule on the phrase *Montana bank* would produce the structure in (i) of (42) within the word *Montana*, and hence the Rhythm Rule does not apply.

Nespor & Vogel show that the Rhythm Rule does not apply to just any sequence of words that happens to have the input structure of (41). For example, the rule applies in (43) but not in (44).

(43) a. More than fífteen cárpenters are working in the house. (<fifteén)
 b. A kángaroo's lífe is full of surprises. (<kangaróo)

(44) a. When she was fiftéen, cárpenters rebuilt the house. (*fífteen)
 b. Kangaróos cárry their young in pouches. (*kángaroos)
 c. John perservéres gládly and diligently. (*pérseveres)
 d. Rabbits reprodúce véry quickly. (*réproduce)

They explain this in terms of the phonological phrase. In (43a) *fifteen carpenters* constitutes a phonological phrase consisting of the head *carpenters* and everything to its left within the maximal projection N″, which includes *fifteen* (and may include more, which is irrelevant to the matter at hand). Kiparsky's restriction has no effect, in this case, and so the Rhythm Rule applies. But, in (44a), *fifteen carpenters* does not constitute a phonological phrase. Each of the two words here constitutes a phonological phrase on its own, and so the Rhythm Rule is blocked. In (43b), *kangaroo's life* constitutes a phonological phrase by reasoning similar to that of *fifteen carpenters* in (44a). But, in (44b), *kangaroos* and *carry* each head their own maximal projection, and cannot be grouped together as a phonological phrase, so the Rhythm Rule is again blocked. Similarly, in (44c, d), the verb constitutes a phonological phrase separate from the adverb phrase that follows. So the Rhythm Rule is blocked here also, for the same reason.

However, there are some cases, superficially similar to (44c, d), where the Rhythm Rule *does* apply, as shown in (45).

(45) a. John pérseveres gládly. (<persevéres)
 b. Rabbits réproduce quíckly. (<reprodúce)

Nespor & Vogel (1986, 173) propose that phonological phrases can optionally be RESTRUCTURED by the rule in (46).

(46) *ϕ Restructuring* (optional)
A nonbranching ϕ which is the first complement of X on its recursive side is joined into the ϕ that contains X.

To see how this works, consider (45a).[8] *Gladly* is the first complement of *perseveres*, the head of V″, and appears on the right of the head, since English is right recursive. *Gladly* constitutes a ϕ on its own, and is nonbranching, since it contains only one word. (Branchingness is computed on prosodic constituents, and this ϕ contains only one C. For the purpose of (46) it does not matter that this C (which contains one F) ultimately branches into two syllables.) Therefore, (46) allows the two ϕs *perseveres gladly* to be combined into a single ϕ, and this provides the environment in which the Rhythm Rule can apply. The same is true of (45b). In the similar sentences (44c, d), the first complement of the head (*persevere* and *reproduce*) is branching, containing (at least) two clitic groups (*gladly and diligently, very quickly*), and so the requirements of (46) are not met. No restructuring of ϕ takes place, and the Rhythm Rule cannot apply.

As a second example, Selkirk (1978) proposes a Monosyllable Rule that reduces monosyllabic words that are not members of the major lexical categories N, A, V. This rule applies only if the monosyllable in question is labelled *w* with respect to a *s* syllable in the same ϕ. Given the labelling of constituents within ϕ in (39III), the monosyllable in question will be labelled *s* if it is final within its ϕ, otherwise it will be labelled *w*. This accounts for Selkirk's examples in (47), where the prosodic labelling is Nespor & Vogel's.

(47) a. [The sluggers]ϕ [boxed]ϕ [in the crowd]ϕ (reduced *in*)
    b. [The cops]ϕ [boxed in]ϕ [the crowd]ϕ (unreduced *in*)

In (47a), the preposition *in* is marked *w* within its ϕ, and so reduced. In (47b), the preposition (or particle) *in* is marked *s* within its ϕ, and so cannot be reduced.

Nespor & Vogel also demonstrate that the phonological phrase is the domain for liaison in French. The examples in (48a) show the application of liaison within the phonological phrase. The examples in (48b) show that liaison does not apply between words that belong to two different phonological phrases, and those in (48c) show that liaison does not apply between the head of a phrase and the first nonbranching complement on its recursive side (the right, in French). As Nespor & Vogel note, (48c) demonstrates that French does not allow restructuring of phonological phrases (examples from Nespor & Vogel 1986, 179). A subscripted curve indicates that liaison takes place; a double slash (//) indicates that it is blocked.

---

[8] Note that, in this definition, the term *complement* is not used in a strictly syntactic sense. In some of the following examples, the complement is syntactically an adjunct.

(48) a. Cette famille a [trois beaux enfants]_φ   [bozɑ̃fɑ̃]
         'This family has three beautiful children'

      Les enfants [sont allés]_φ à l'école   [sɔ̃tale]
         'The children went to school'

      b. Jean a [des livres]_φ // [assez nouveaux]_φ   [livrase]
         'John has some rather new books'

      Nos invités [sont arrivés]_φ // [en retard]_φ   [ariveɑ̃]
         'Our guests arrived late'

      c. [Les maisons]_φ // [italiennes]_φ coûtent beaucoup [mɛzɔ̃italyɛn]
         'Italian houses are expensive'

      Le garçon [les aidait]_φ // [activement]_φ   [ɛdɛaktivmɑ̃]
         'The boy helped them actively'

5.5 The intonation phrase (I)

The intonation phrase was defined by Selkirk (1978, 130) as the domain over which an intonation contour is spread. Nespor & Vogel demonstrate that, in addition, the intonation phrase constitutes the domain of a number of segmental rules in Italian, although they give no examples from English. We will therefore concentrate on the domain of intonation contours in this section. As with the other prosodic categories, the intonation phrase is constructed out of one or more of the immediately subordinate prosodic category, in this case, the phonological phrase. However, certain syntactic constructions obligatorily form intonation phrases on their own. These include "parenthetical expressions, nonrestrictive relative clauses, tag questions, vocatives, expletives, and certain moved elements" (Nespor & Vogel 1986, 188). They give the examples in (49), to which we can add (49g), an appositive.

(49) a. Lions [as you know]_I are dangerous. (parenthetical)
      b. My brother [who absolutely loves animals]_I just bought himself an exotic tropical bird. (nonrestrictive relative)
      c. That's Theodore's cat [isn't it?]_I (tag question)
      d. [Clarence]_I I'd like you to meet Mr Smith. (vocative)
      e. [Good heavens]_I there's a bear in the back yard. (expletive)

f. They're so cute [those Australian koalas]₁ (right dislocation)
g. Duncan and Mary [our next-door neighbours]₁ have a lovely Labrador retriever. (appositive)

Nespor & Vogel suggest that the common element uniting this rather disparate class of items is that they are all external to the root sentence with which they are associated. The concept of root sentence, as defined by Emonds (1976), plays a further role in defining intonation phrases. That is, an intonation phrase can be no longer than a root sentence. Roughly, a root sentence includes a matrix sentence and any subordinate clauses embedded within it; however, conjoined sentences are separate root sentences and so form separate intonation phrases. A contrast first discussed in Downing (1970) illustrates this rather vividly.

(50) a. [Billy thought his father was a merchant]₁ [and his father was a secret agent]₁.
b. [Billy thought his father was a merchant and his mother was a secret agent]₁

In (50a), two root sentences are conjoined, and so they form separate intonation phrases, as indicated by the bracketing. In (50b), however, two subordinate clauses are conjoined within a single root sentence, which forms a single intonation phrase.

It should also be noted that those phrases that obligatorily form *I* do so regardless of where they occur in the sentence. Because of the basic assumptions of the theory, the parts of the sentence outside the obligatory *I* form separate *I*s on one or both sides. This becomes clearer as we examine some of Nespor & Vogel's examples in (51). The phrase *as you know* is a parenthetical, which can occur in various places in the sentence. As a parenthetical, it forms an obligatory *I*. What is left over forms additional *I*s, which are not (necessarily) themselves isomorphic to any syntactic constituent, although they do contain phonological phrases (ɸs).

(51) a. [As you know]₁ [Isabelle is an artist]₁
b. [Isabelle]₁ [as you know]₁ [is an artist]₁
c. [Isabelle is]₁ [as you know]₁ [an artist]₁
d. [Isabelle is an artist]₁ [as you know]₁

Nespor & Vogel speculate that, in right recursive languages such as English, *I*s that are not also isomorphic to syntactic constituents, such as the *I Isabelle is* in (51c), may appear only on the left of an obligatory *I*, here the *I as you know*. This may have to do with where adverbials may be inserted into a syntactic structure. Jackendoff (1972) suggests that parentheticals may only be inserted such that they are dominated by the root S, that is, at the beginning of the sentence, as in (51a), at the end of the sentence, as in (51d), or between major constituents of the sentence. In (51b) the parenthetical occurs after the subject NP, and in (51c) it occurs after the auxiliary verb *is*. These are both major constituents of the sentence. But parentheticals cannot occur between a verb and its direct object, as shown by the ungrammaticality of **Isabelle read, as you know, a book*. The syntactic structure of English is such that only syntactic constituents can appear after adverbs. This may provide a syntactic explanation for this apparent skewness of distribution.

Examples such as (51) lead Nespor & Vogel (1986, 189) to propose the following algorithm for constructing intonation phrases.

(52) *Intonation Phrase Formation*
    I. *I domain*
        An *I* domain may consist of
        a. all the ϕs in a string that is [*sic*] not structurally attached to the sentence tree at the level of s-structure, or
        b. any remaining sequence of adjacent ϕs in a root sentence.
    II. *I construction*
        Join into an n-ary branching *I* all ϕs included in a string delimited by the definition of the domain of *I*.

The relative prominence of ϕs within *I* is not so straightforward as with the lower prosodic categories. Nespor & Vogel suggest the algorithm in (53).

(53) *Intonation Phrase Relative Prominence*
    Within *I*, a node is labelled *s* on the basis of its semantic prominence; all other nodes are labelled *w*.

Nespor & Vogel illustrate this with the sentence in (54). Any one (but only one) of the five *I*s can be labelled *s*; all others are labelled weak.

(54) [[My sister]$_\phi$ [sells]$_\phi$ [fresh fruit]$_\phi$ [at the market]$_\phi$ [on Monday]$_\phi$]$_I$

Like phonological phrases, intonation phrases can be restructured. Unlike ϕ, however, *I* restructuring consists in breaking an *I* up into smaller *I*s, contrasted with ϕ, where restructuring results in longer units. A variety of factors play a role in *I* restructuring, including the length of *I*, speech rate, speech style, and contrastive prominence. The longer an *I* is, the more likely it is to be broken down into smaller *I*s. A related factor is the rate of speech. The faster the speech rate, the less the likelihood of breaking long *I*s into shorter ones. Similarly, the more formal or pedantic the style of speech, the slower it is likely to be and the greater the likelihood of *I* restructuring. Nespor & Vogel speculate that "there is a tendency to establish *I*s of more or less uniform, 'average' length, although at this point we are not able to characterize this ideal length more precisely." (1986, 194)

Semantic and syntactic factors also play a role in *I* restructuring. One semantic factor is that of CONTRASTIVE PROMINENCE, discussed by Bing (1979, 210ff.). A sentence like (55a) is assigned one *I*, since it is dominated by a single root sentence.

(55) a. [Paul called Paula before Carla called Carl]$_I$
 b. [Paul called Paula]$_I$ [before *she*]$_I$ [called *him*]$_I$

But the presence of the pronouns in (55b) forces a specific interpretation in which the pronouns are coreferential to the nouns, so that (55b) cannot be interpreted in the same way as (55a). This interpretation is realized phonologically as extra prominence on the pronouns, which in turn causes the single *I* to be restructured as three smaller *I*s, as indicated in (55b). This is another indication of the independence of the prosodic structure from the syntactic structure, since both sentences in (55) have the identical syntactic structure, but clearly differ prosodically.

One syntactic constraint on restructuring is "a general tendency to avoid restructuring an *I* in any position other than at the end of a noun phrase" (Nespor & Vogel 1986, 197). Thus, the sentence in (54) could be broken into smaller *I*s after *sister, fruit,* or *market,* but it would not be restructured into smaller *I*s such that one ended in *sells*. This can also be seen in embedded possessive constructions, such as (56), where restructuring is possible only to create an *I* ending with *mother*, since a break after any of the other nouns would interrupt the subject NP.

(56) [[my friend's]$_\phi$ [neighbour's]$_\phi$ [aunt's]$_\phi$ [mother]$_\phi$ [knows]$_\phi$ [a famous writer]$_\phi$]$_I$

This NP restriction can also result in restructured *I*s that correspond to no syntactic constituent, providing further evidence for the independence of prosodic from syntactic structure. Nespor & Vogel give the example in (57).

(57) a. [I would never have believed the children of John and Mary to be able to become so ill mannered]$_I$
b. [I would never have believed the children of John and Mary]$_I$ [to be able to become so ill mannered]$_I$

The first *I* in (57b) includes the matrix sentence and the subject of the embedded sentence, but this much is not a syntactic constituent.

Lists and complex embedded structures are another way in which syntax influences *I* restructuring, although this is somewhat problematic. It has long been noticed that lists of similar items have an intonation pattern in which each of the items receives a similar tune. This can be considered a series of *I* phrases in prosodic terms. Consider Nespor & Vogel's examples in (58), showing the division into *I* phrases that seems to reflect the intonation, and which would be created from a prosodic structure where each sentence is a complete *I* by itself.

(58) a. [The big]$_I$ [fat]$_I$ [ugly]$_I$ [nasty beast]$_I$ [scared away the children]$_I$
b. [That mountain road is long]$_I$ [narrow]$_I$ [windy]$_I$ [and bumpy]$_I$
c. [Everyone at the party ate]$_I$ [talked]$_I$ [sang]$_I$ [and danced]$_I$
d. [Ducks]$_I$ [geese]$_I$ [swans]$_I$ [and coots]$_I$ [inhabit this lake]$_I$
e. [They own two cats]$_I$ [three dogs]$_I$ [four parakeets]$_I$ [and a turtle]$_I$

The restructuring in (58a) violates the constraint we proposed to account for (56); that is, it interrupts the NP ending with *beast*.[9] The restructurings in (58b, c) violate the same constraint by creating new *I* boundaries after APs and VPs, not after NPs. The restructurings in (58d, e) do create new *I* boundaries after NPs, but nevertheless break up a compound NP in each case; it is not clear whether this violates the NP constraint. But the common factor in all the examples of (58) is that they are lists. Other examples of lists, which are separated from the matrix sentence to a greater extent, as shown orthographically by the use of a colon, are in (59) (from Nespor & Vogel 1986, 201).

(59) a. [Let's invite]$_I$: [Arnold]$_I$ [Arthur]$_I$ [Archibald]$_I$ [and Zachary]$_I$
b. [We were told to buy the following]$_I$: [milk]$_I$ [eggs]$_I$ [bread]$_I$ [and cheese]$_I$

For these cases, Nespor & Vogel propose List Restructuring (60).

---

[9] In fact, (58a) would initially be divided into ϕs only at the end of *beast, away,* and *children*. Nespor & Vogel suggest that restructuring would be required for (58a), and also for the prehead genitives in (56).

(60) *List Restructuring* (optional)
In a sequence of more than two constituents of the same type, i.e. x_1, $x_2,\ldots x_n$, an intonation break may be inserted before each repetition of the node X.

Finally, Nespor & Vogel discuss cases of the type that we claimed motivated prosodic (as opposed to purely syntactic) constituents in phonology in the first place, such as (1), showing multiple embeddings. The intonation structure of (1) must be that in (61) and cannot be at the points where the major NP boundaries occur as shown in (1).

(61) [This is the cat]$_I$ [that caught the rat]$_I$ [that stole the cheese]$_I$

Nespor & Vogel claim that this case is similar to the list case, since in both cases we have a series of similar items, here embedded, where in lists they are coordinated. But in (61) we have two repetitions of similar items: repetitions of S', where the I boundaries coincide with S' boundaries. However, the same sentence can be represented as having repetitions of NP, as shown in (1). With this structure, there is no way to restructure the intonation phrase into smaller ones. Whereas we accounted for (56) by claiming that *I* boundaries preferably coincide with NP boundaries, for (61) we have to claim that *I* boundaries preferably coincide with the end of an N, providing "evidence of the special role the noun plays in prosody" (Nespor & Vogel 1986, 204).

5.6 The phonological utterance

The final prosodic unit that we will consider is the phonological utterance. Nespor & Vogel define the phonological utterance in terms of the highest node in a syntactic tree X^n. This is often a root sentence, but may be a different syntactic unit, such as a noun phrase. The *U* domain consists of one or more *I*s, and Nespor & Vogel assume that the rightmost *I* of the *U* domain is marked strong, with all other *I*s marked weak in an n-ary branching structure. The relevance of the utterance for phonology is demonstrated by the process of Flapping in North American English. Flapping affects alveolar stops, converting them to the sonorant flap [ɾ] under appropriate conditions. The segmental environment for Flapping can be stated quite generally, under the assumption that Aspiration precedes Flapping. Nespor & Vogel assume that Aspiration makes voiceless stops tense, and formulate Flapping as a rule that applies to untensed alveolar stops, as in (62). We will demonstrate in due course that Flapping has the phonological utterance as its domain, assumed in (62).

(62) *Flapping*
$$\begin{bmatrix} +\text{cor} \\ -\text{strid} \\ -\text{cont} \\ -\text{tense} \end{bmatrix} \rightarrow \mathfrak{r} \;/\; [\ldots [-\text{consonantal}] \underline{\quad} V \ldots]_U$$

This formulation is not without problems; for example, it is not clear that *voiced* stops (*d* in particular) are tensed as a byproduct of Aspiration. However, our main concern here is with the prosodic environment for Flapping. Nespor & Vogel demonstrate that Flapping occurs within words, both simple and complex, and between words in sentences, as in (63).

(63) a. wa[ɾ]er
      b. ri[ɾ]er
      c. whi[ɾ]ish
      d. hea[ɾ]ache
      e. a hundre[ɾ] eggs
      f. whi[ɾ]e owl
      g. My mother bough[ɾ] a parrot
      h. A very dangerous wild ca[ɾ], as you know, escaped from the zoo.
      i. Ichabo[ɾ], our pet crane, usually hides when guests come.
      j. Pa[ɾ], I'd like you to meet Joe.

Examples (63h, i, j) indicate that the domain of flapping is larger than the Intonation phrase, and at least as large as the sentence. But, as Kahn (1980, 102) observed, Flapping can apply across sentence boundaries as well, as in (64) (additional examples from Nespor & Vogel 1986, 237ff).

(64) a. Have a sea[ɾ]. I'll be right back.
      b. It's la[ɾ]e. I'm leaving.
      c. That's a nice ca[ɾ]. Is it yours?
      d. Turn up the hea[ɾ]. I'm freezing.

Nespor & Vogel propose that more than one syntactic unit of the type X^n can be grouped together to form a single phonological utterance. As with the phonological phrase and the intonation phrase, they refer to this process as restructuring. Notice that U restructuring is like ϕ restructuring in that both join two or more original units into one larger unit, unlike *I* restructuring, which breaks a long *I* into two or more shorter units. However, as the examples in (65) show, not every sequence of two sentences can be restructured into a single *U*.

(65) a. *Have a sea[ɾ]. It's warm in here.
 b. *It's la[ɾ]e. I'm Larry.
 c. *That's a nice ca[ɾ]. Is it after eight already?
 d. *Turn up the hea[ɾ]. I'm Frances.

Nespor & Vogel postulate a number of conditions on U restructuring. First they propose two pragmatic conditions, given in (66). These conditions must be met in order for restructuring to take place.

(66) a. The two sentences must be uttered by the same speaker.
 b. The two sentences must be addressed to the same interlocutor(s).

They then propose two phonological conditions, (67). These must also be met in order for restructuring to take place.

(67) a. The two sentences must be relatively short.
 b. There must not be a pause between the two sentences.

They then propose syntactic and semantic conditions. One or the other of these must be met in order for restructuring to take place, but not necessarily both. The syntactic condition is that the interpretation of the second sentence depends on material in the first sentence by ELLIPSIS or ANAPHORA, illustrated in (68a, b) respectively.

(68) a. Martha didn't invite To[ɾ]. I did.
 b. Where's Pa[ɾ]? I need him.

The semantic condition is that the two sentences must be (implicitly) related by one of the three "logico-semantic connectors" *and, therefore,* or *because.* These are illustrated in (69a, b, c) respectively.

(69) a. You invite Charlo[ɾ]. I'll invite Joan.
 b. It's la[ɾ]e. I'm leaving. (= 64h)
 c. Take your coa[ɾ]. It's cold out.

Nespor & Vogel claim that *U* restructuring is possible if either (or both) the syntactic or semantic conditions are met, but the pragmatic and phonological conditions must be met in any case for two sentences to be restructured as a single phonological utterance.

The segmental conditions on flapping are also interesting, especially when an alveolar stop follows a nonvowel. The segmental conditions require that a segment to be flapped be preceded by a [–consonantal] segment and be followed by a vowel. This correctly predicts that both *t* and *d* will be flapped after *r*, in flapping dialects, since *r* is [–consonantal], and that *Carter* will be pronounced the same as *carder* for these speakers.

The picture is a little different after nasals. Nasals are [+consonantal] and *cinder* is never homophonous with *sinner*. However, *winter* can be homophonous with *winner* and *Toronto* can have the pronunciation [təˈrɑnə]. This much can be derived by appealing to rules we introduced in Chapter 1, along with the Flapping rule introduced in this chapter. Consider the derivations of *winter* and *winner* in (70).

(70)   lexical representations   /wɪntər/   /wɪn + ər/
       Nasalization (8a) in Ch. 1   ɪ̃   ɪ̃
       Nasal C Deletion (8b) in Ch. 1 ∅   ———
       Flapping (62)   ɾ   ɾ
       Output   [wɪɾər]   [wɪɾər]
       Nasal Spreading   [wɪ̃ɾ̃ər]   [wɪ̃ɾ̃ər]

The outputs are identical. As formulated in (62), the Flapping rule affects nasals as well as obstruent stops. It is probable that nasality spreads to the flap, as shown in the last line of (70), to produce the final phonetic form.

An example similar to Flapping concerns the linking-*r* and intrusive-*r* that characterize certain "*r*-less"[10] dialects of English. Oversimplifying somewhat, *r* is not pronounced in these dialects at the ends of words in isolation, but is pronounced when a vowel follows, within the word or across word boundaries. As we saw with Flapping, it can also be inserted across sentence boundaries. In these examples, the symbol *r̸* is used to represent orthographic *r* that is not pronounced.

(71)   a. clea*r̸*
       b. clea[r]est
       c. gnaw
       d. gnaw[r]ing
       e. that spider is dangerous   →   ...spide[r] is...
       f. the panda eats bamboo   →   ...panda[r] eats...
       g. It's my mother. I have to go → ...mothe[r] I...
       h. Try that sofa. It's softer →   ...sofa[r] It's...

---

[10] The term is something of a misnomer, since the dialects in question lack *r* only in syllable codas. We retain it as a convenient cover term for these dialects.

Once again, Nespor & Vogel observe that the insertion of *r* does not apply between any pair of sentences, as shown in (72).

(72) a. It's my mother. I have three cats → *...mothe[r] I...
 b. Try that sofa. It's after midnight → *...sofa[r] It's...

Once again, we observe that the domain of *r*-insertion cannot be identified with any syntactic category, even if we allow a sequence of two such categories (sentences) as a possible syntactic environment for phonological rules. However, the Phonological Utterance as described for Flapping will serve as the appropriate environment here as well.

5.7 The ordering of the rules

We take it as an axiom of phonological theory that phonological rules can be ordered. Some ordering is implicit in the lexical model of phonology that we assume here. For example, rules assigned to the cyclic component (i.e., stratum 1) are necessarily ordered before rules assigned to the postcyclic component (stratum 2); and rules of these two lexical components are necessarily ordered before the postlexical rules. Here we will discuss the ordering of rules *within* the postlexical component.

As discussed more extensively in Chapter 6, the rules of the lexical phonology are generally considered to be STRUCTURE PRESERVING, in the sense that they do not create new segments (or segment types) not present in underlying representations. The rules we have been discussing in this chapter are primarily non–structure preserving, and so are assigned to the postlexical component. We will discuss two cases: one involves the various rules we have proposed to account for the allophones of stops in English, and the other involves the interaction of Diphthong Shortening with Flapping.

Given the very general formulation of Flapping in (62), we might expect it to apply to voiceless stops that are glottalized by rule (10) or aspirated by rule (17). In order to avoid this result, Nespor & Vogel assume that Aspiration is ordered before Flapping. Thus, in cases like *attire*, where the /t/ meets the environment for both Aspiration (by virtue of being in foot-initial position), and Flapping (by appearing between vowels within an utterance), Aspiration wins because it applies first. Under the assumption that Aspiration makes stops [+tense], Flapping, as stated in (62), cannot apply, and the right result is obtained. In such a case we say that Aspiration BLEEDS Flapping by destroying the environment in which the latter could apply. Similarly, Nespor & Vogel argue that Flapping is ordered before Glottalization. This is shown by compounds and phrases, such as those in (73), where both rules could apply. (Notice that Aspiration cannot apply here because its environment is not met: the /t/ is not at the beginning of a foot.)

(73) a. night owl   [ɾ]   *[tʔ]
     b. heart ache   [ɾ]   *[tʔ]
     c. wait a minute [ɾ]   *[tʔ]
     d. wait eagerly [ɾ]   *[tʔ]

The (first) /t/ in each example of (73) is in syllable-final position (and follows a [–consonantal] segment) and is thus in the environment for Glottalization, according to (10). But Flapping is observed, not Glottalization. If Flapping is ordered first, it makes the stops in question [+voiced], thereby removing them from the domain of Glottalization. Once again, this is a BLEEDING order of the rules. This establishes the ordering in (74). Following the usual convention, a curved line drawn between two rules indicates that the top rule must be ordered before the bottom one.

(74) Aspiration (17)
      Flapping (62)
      Glottalization (10)

We next consider the ordering of Diphthong Shortening (30) and Flapping (62). For many English speakers, the words *writer* and *rider* both have a flap medially, but are distinguished by the nature of the diphthong preceding the flap—*writer* having a shortened diphthong but *rider* having a normal diphthong. Since Diphthong Shortening applies only before voiceless obstruents, it is clear that Diphthong Shortening must apply before Flapping, which neutralizes both *t* and *d* into a *voiced* flap. Consider the derivations in (75).

(75) a. /rayt + r/ 'writer'   b. /rayd + r/ 'rider'
        rəytr   —   Diphthong Shortening (30)
        rəyɾɾ   rayɾɾ   Flapping (62)
        [rəyɾɾ̬]   [rayɾɾ̬]   output

In the derivation of *rider*, the rule of Diphthong Shortening is not applicable, since the diphthong is not followed by a voiceless obstruent at any point in the derivation. Flapping produces the medial flap, but the order of the rules is irrelevant. In the derivation of *writer*, however, Diphthong Shortening must apply before Flapping, since Flapping produces a voiced segment after the diphthong. The prior application of Flapping would BLEED Diphthong Shortening; however, in the reverse order, the actual order, Diphthong Shortening is not bled because it precedes Flapping. This is known as a COUNTERBLEEDING order. This same ordering of the rules will also work for rider. We assume that a single ordering of the rules is valid for all derivations. This establishes the ordering in (76). We have no evidence of any crucial ordering of Diphthong Shortening with respect to either Aspiration or Glottalization.

(76) $\begin{cases} \text{Diphthong Shortening (30)} \\ \text{Flapping (62)} \end{cases}$

5.8 Conclusion

This chapter has discussed a number of rules of English whose domains are defined in terms of prosodic categories. The prosodic categories are established both lexically and postlexically. Lexically the rules of syllabification and stress at stratum 1 produce syllable structure and foot structure, and phonological words are assigned at stratum 2. Postlexically, after words have been concatenated into sentences, higher prosodic categories are assigned, to which postlexical phonological rules have access. The phonological rules at each lexical stratum and postlexically are ordered. We will encounter more rule ordering in Chapters 6 and 7, where we investigate the lexical rule system in greater detail.

5.9 Exercises

1. The following words illustrate the rules determining stop allophones (Flapping, Glottalization, and Aspiration), Diphthong Shortening, Alveopalatalization, and Sonorant Devoicing. Discuss the way that these rules apply to these words and give a phonetic transcription of each.

    a. potato
    b. atlas
    c. night owl
    d. Nye trait
    d. nitrate
    f. night rate
    g. cowslip
    h. house lip
    i. Islip
    j. ice lip
    k. I slip

2. Indicate how the following sentences will be divided into Intonation phrases.

   a. Isabelle is, as you know, a very talented violinist.
   b. I'd like you to meet Isabelle, Mr Jones.
   c. It's so nice, having some leisure time for a change.
   d. This time, definitely, I'll check the numbers first.

3. Discuss the possibility of flapping across sentence boundaries (i.e., converting the final alveolar stop of the first sentence to a flap) in the following examples. Assume that the pragmatic and phonological conditions are met and concentrate on the semantic condition.

   a. It's all right. I understand.
   b. It's on the right. I don't understand this problem.
   c. Where's Scott? I don't understand this problem.
   d. It's late. I'm getting tired.
   e. It's late. I can keep going, though.
   f. Stop that. It's rude.
   g. Stop that. I'll leave otherwise.
   h. Take your coat. It's cold out.
   i. Take your coat. It's a full moon tonight.

6 Lexical phonology: the cyclic rules

6.1 Principles of lexical phonology

As we saw in Chapter 1, the *SPE* model of phonology, as diagrammed in the T-model (15 of Chapter 1), had all the phonological rules applying to the output of the syntax. A number of subsequent developments challenged this assumption. Even within *SPE*, a major distinction was drawn between the cyclic rules, which reapply to successively larger (morpho-)syntactic structures, and word level rules, which apply only once, to structures of the form ##...##, where ## is a word boundary and ... contains no occurrence of ##; i.e., within minimal words. *SPE* did not discuss phrasal phonology in great detail, the one exception being the stress (intonation) contours of phrases, which they assumed to be part of the cyclic rules. *SPE* assumed that the cyclic and word-level rules could be freely interspersed, although in actual practice they ordered the cyclic rules together. There is little convincing evidence that word-level rules can precede cyclic rules.

In *SPE* theory the traditional domain of morphology was divided between a generative syntax of the *Aspects* type (Chomsky 1965) and the phonology. The lexicon is essentially a list of morphemes, each provided with phonololgical, syntactic, and semantic structure. The syntactic component dealt with these morphemes, in *SPE* also called FORMATIVES, manipulating them in various ways, such as concatenating them into words, reordering them, or providing them with phonological substance. (Recall our discussion in Chapter 1, section 1.2, where an abstract morpheme "past" is converted to the phonological /d/ or integrated into an irregular stem like *sing* to produce *sang*.) Such an abstract morpheme appeared necessary in a theory that assumed no presyntactic manipulation of morphemes. Subsequent investigations into the nature of morphology and the lexicon revealed a more active role for the lexicon. Such studies as Chomsky (1970), Aronoff (1976), Siegel (1974; 1977), and Allen (1978) concluded that the lexicon was the locus of derivational morphology, and for some, inflectional morphology as well. Among other things, they noticed that certain phonological rules, such as Trisyllabic Laxing, operated when certain affixes were attached to stems, but not when other affixes were added that produced superficially similar sequences of sounds. The former set of suffixes was further observed to occur closer to stems than the latter, and the former set of suffixes conditioned stress changes that were not observed with the latter. These correlations did not appear to be accidental.

The result of integrating these ideas, and others from both phonology and morphology, is the theory of lexical phonology, most cogently defended in Kiparsky (1982a; 1982b; 1985) and Mohanan (1986). According to this model, the UNDERIVED LEXICAL ITEMS of a language are subject to a series of lexical phonological rules before morphological operations concatenate them or perform various alterations that affect meaning. The lexicon is organized into a series of STRATA, with the morphology and phonology interacting on each stratum. The output of the last lexical phonological stratum constitutes the LEXICAL ITEMS of the language. It is these that are manipulated by the syntax, the output of which is operated on by a further set of phonological rules, known as the POSTLEXICAL PHONOLOGY.

To put this into more concrete terms, let us consider the organization of the lexicon in English shown in Figure 1 (opposite). We will then discuss the detailed motivation for each component of this system.

The organization in Figure 1 represents the culmination of several attempts to develop a model of a lexical phonology. Since the earliest work in lexical phonology, a major division has been assumed between the lexical rules, which are word bounded and structure preserving, and the postlexical rules, which are neither word bounded nor necessarily structure preserving. In addition, rules of the lexical phonology are assumed to have distinct properties depending on whether they apply at a cyclic level or a noncyclic level. The right and left-pointing arrows in stratum 1 of Figure 1 represent the cyclic nature of this stratum in English. According to this conception, stratum 1 phonological rules apply first before any morphological operations and again after each morphological operation. Stratum 2 is noncyclic in English. On this stratum, affixes are added before any phonological operations, and all phonological rules follow the addition of all affixes at this stratum, as shown by the arrows in Figure 1. We can summarize the properties of rules of different strata in Table 1 (page 158).

CYCLIC RULES 157

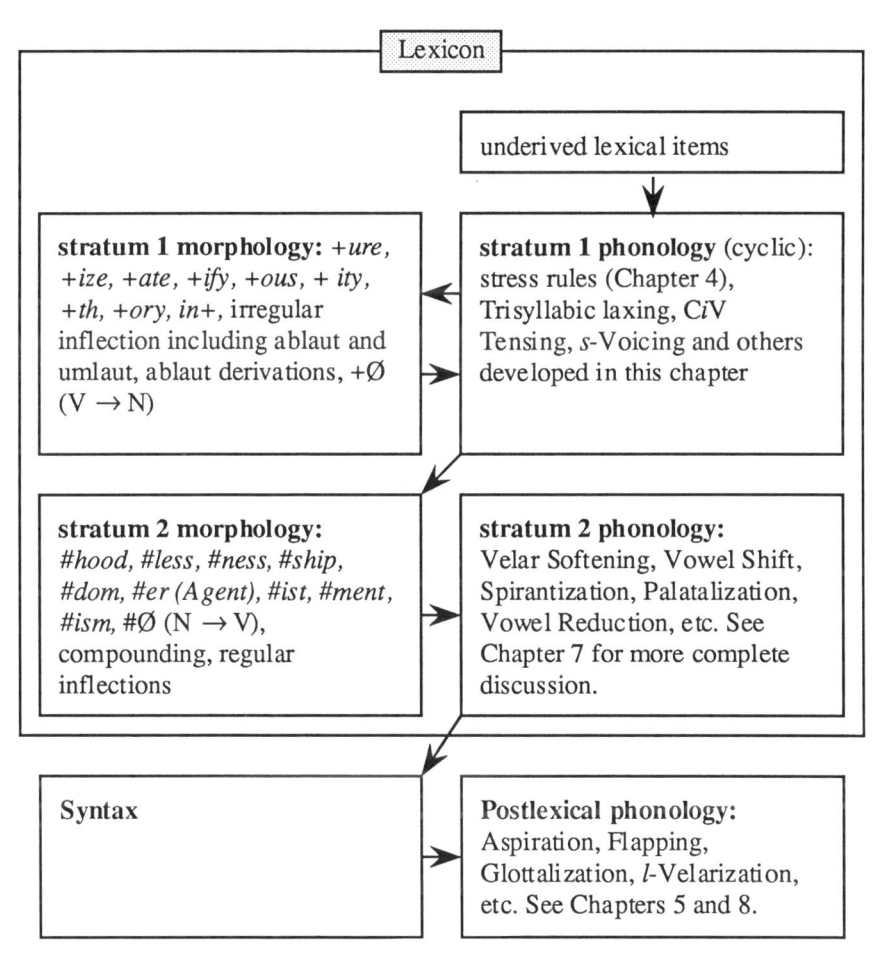

```
┌─────────────────────────── Lexicon ───────────────────────────┐
│                                                                │
│                              ┌────────────────────────────┐   │
│                              │ underived lexical items    │   │
│                              └────────────────┬───────────┘   │
│                                               ▼                │
│  ┌─────────────────────────┐   ┌────────────────────────────┐ │
│  │ **stratum 1 morphology:** +*ure*, │◄──│ **stratum 1 phonology** (cyclic): │ │
│  │ +*ize*, +*ate*, +*ify*, +*ous*, + *ity*, │   │ stress rules (Chapter 4), │ │
│  │ +*th*, +*ory*, *in*+, irregular │   │ Trisyllabic laxing, C*i*V │ │
│  │ inflection including ablaut and │──►│ Tensing, *s*-Voicing and others │ │
│  │ umlaut, ablaut derivations, +Ø │   │ developed in this chapter │ │
│  │ (V → N) │   │ │ │
│  └─────────────────────────┘   └────────────────────────────┘ │
│                                               │                │
│  ┌─────────────────────────┐   ┌────────────────────────────┐ │
│  │ **stratum 2 morphology:** │   │ **stratum 2 phonology:** │ │
│  │ #*hood*, #*less*, #*ness*, #*ship*, │   │ Velar Softening, Vowel Shift, │ │
│  │ #*dom*, #*er (Agent)*, #*ist*, #*ment*, │──►│ Spirantization, Palatalization, │ │
│  │ #*ism*, #Ø (N → V), │   │ Vowel Reduction, etc. See │ │
│  │ compounding, regular │   │ Chapter 7 for more complete │ │
│  │ inflections │   │ discussion. │ │
│  └─────────────────────────┘   └────────────────────────────┘ │
└────────────────────────────────────────────────────────────────┘
   ┌─────────────────────────┐   ┌────────────────────────────┐
   │ Syntax                  │──►│ Postlexical phonology:     │
   │                         │   │ Aspiration, Flapping,      │
   │                         │   │ Glottalization, *l*-Velarization, │
   │                         │   │ etc. See Chapters 5 and 8. │
   └─────────────────────────┘   └────────────────────────────┘
```

Figure 1. The model of lexical phonology.

Lexical rules are necessarily word bounded, since they apply within the lexicon, where words are formed, but not phrases. Postlexical rules can apply to phrases as well as to individual words. Lexical rules can have access to word-internal structure; we shall see in section 6.5 why this should be restricted to structure assigned at the same level. By an extension of this restriction, we conclude that postlexical phonology, like syntax, has no access to word-internal structure. In the earliest forms of lexical phonology, it was assumed that all lexical phonologi-

		cyclic lexical stratum	noncyclic lexical stratum	postlexical stratum
1.	word bounded	yes	yes	no
2.	structures accessed	word-internal structure at same stratum	word-internal structure at same stratum	phrase structure and segmental information only
3.	cyclic	yes	no	no
4.	Strict Cycle Condition	applicable	inapplicable	inapplicable
5.	structure preserving	yes	yes	no
6.	lexical exceptions	possible	possible	none

Table 1. Properties of rules of different strata.

cal rules were cyclic. According to the model presented in Table 1, however, only rules of stratum 1 are cyclic.

The distribution of cyclic and noncyclic strata in lexical phonology is still somewhat controversial. Mohanan & Mohanan (1984), for example, claim that there is no reason to consider any of the four lexical strata that they propose for Malayalam to be cyclic. For English, stratum 1 is indisputably cyclic, while stratum 2 is not. Accordingly, stratum 2 can be referred to as postcyclic. The number of lexical strata for English is also somewhat controversial, with three strata proposed in Kiparsky (1982a; 1982b) and four strata proposed in Halle & Mohanan (1985) and Mohanan (1986). However, evidence for more than two strata in English is unconvincing, and we will stay with the two-stratum model given in Figure 1.

6.2 The interaction of morphology and phonology

6.2.1 An affix sensitive to stress

The model in Figure 1 indicates that some phonological rules apply before some morphological operations on level 1. The evidence for this is somewhat limited, but there is one reasonably convincing case in English. As we discussed in Chapter 4, stress on English words is predictable to a considerable extent. Now, English has a suffix, -al, which is attached to certain verbs to give derived nouns. While the attachment of this suffix is idiosyncratic to some extent, there are phonological conditions on its attachment. Specifically, the verb must have stress on its final syllable and, if it ends in a consonant, that consonant must be [+anterior] or a sonorant. Up to two final consonants are permitted only if the sequence is a sonorant followed by an anterior consonant. We list some of the possibilities in (1).

(1) *Vowel final   Labial final   Alveolar final   Sonorant final   Two consonants*

    deny   retrieve   appraise   procure   rehearse
    try   arrive   propose   disperse
    withdraw survive   dispose   reverse
    renew   remove   acquit   rent
    avow   approve
    betray
    portray

We account for the morphological facts by assuming that each affix is provided with a SUBCATEGORIZATION FRAME, which determines what it can attach to in order to form words. For noun-forming *-al*, we assume that the lexical representation is roughly as in (2).

(2) -al_N / $\begin{bmatrix} +\text{syll} \\ +\text{stress} \end{bmatrix} \left(\begin{bmatrix} -\text{syll} \\ +\text{son} \end{bmatrix} \right) \left(\begin{bmatrix} -\text{syll} \\ +\text{ant} \end{bmatrix} \right) \,]_V \underline{}$

This formula does not imply that every verb that meets its requirements can have *-al* attached to become a noun: we assume that it is an accidental gap that there are no words **derival*, **convinceal*, and **forceal*. But verbs that do not meet the requirements of *-al* attachment in (2) cannot acquire this suffix: the requirement of anteriority is failed by *begrudge, rebuke, impeach,* and *encroach;* the requirement of final stress is failed by *promise, abandon, develop,* and *edit;* and verbs like *accept* and *resist* show that there can be only one obstruent after the stressed vowel. If you try adding *-al* to each of these words, the result has a clear enough meaning in each case, yet it cannot be an English word.

    There is one exception to this generalization: the word *burial*, since *bury* does not have final stress. But final orthographic *y* behaves like a glide in many ways, suggesting that we consider it so in underlying representation, letting it become syllabic by a later rule of the phonology. In Chapter 4, we saw that final orthographic *y* often acts like a nonvowel for the purpose of stress assignment. This is also true of a number of other rules, like Trisyllabic Laxing, discussed in section 6.4, which does not affect *piracy,* although it does affect *divinity.* There are other morphological effects of assuming final orthographic *y* to be an underlying glide. Comparative *-er* normally attaches only to monosyllables, as in *longer*, but it also attaches to final orthographic *y*, as in *prettier, wearier, thirstier, dustier*. Similarly, adjective-forming *-ful* normally attaches only to final stressed nouns, as in *artful*, but it also attaches to penultimately stressed nouns in *y*, as in *fanciful, merciful, beautiful*.[1]

6.2.2 Zero derivation

A second case of the interaction of morphology and phonology occurs in ZERO DERIVATION, sometimes called CONVERSION. This refers to a kind of derivational morphology in which there is no overt affix, but there is a change in category accompanied by a corresponding change in meaning. In English, the major cases involve a noun and a verb of identical phonological form (save for stress, which will be important in this discussion) and closely related meanings. Among disyllabic cases, there are some where stress remains the same for the noun and the verb (3a), whereas, in others, the stress patterns are distinct (3b).

(3)   a.   pattern, poison, ransom, comfort, picture, focus
            b.   torment, conflict, import, export, increase, permit

The question becomes, how can we have verbs like *to páttern* that clearly violate the stress pattern we have observed for verbs, like *cavórt, usúrp*, which also end in clusters and which have final stress?

Besides the stress, there are certain other differences between the pairs in groups (3a) and (3b). Semantically, verbs of the form (3a) mean 'to do something with N' as *to pattern* means 'to do something after a pattern.' On the other hand, the nouns of (3b) mean 'that which Vs' or that which is Ved,' as *an increase* is 'something which increases.'

We can explain this pattern by saying that the noun is basic in (3a), while the verb is basic in (3b). If we assign stress to the basic form, before the morphological conversion, we obtain exactly the right results. In (3a), stress is assigned to the noun, which is the basic form, at stratum 1. If we assume that the zero derivation of noun to verb is a morphological process of stratum 2, the noun's stress carries over to the verb, since no restressing occurs on stratum 2. In (3b), the noun has a remnant of the verb's stress in the form of a secondary stress on the second

---

[1] It is less clear how the sequence *ry* of *bury* fulfils the subcategorization requirements of (2), unless *y* be counted as anterior or some provision be made for a sequence of two sonorants. Another possibility is to consider final *y* to be extrametrical before the stress rules operate. This may be necessary in any case, since otherwise the Sonority Sequencing Generalization (4 of Chapter 3) would necessarily make it syllabic.

syllable. This too is explained by the model under the assumption that stratum 1 is cyclic and that the zero derivation of verb to noun takes place at this stratum. First, we assign verb stress on the final syllable of *increase,* for example. This then enters the stratum 1 morphology, where it can undergo zero derivation to a noun. The principle of the cycle now requires that this form reenter the phonology, where it receives stress according to the noun pattern. This new stress becomes the primary stress, with the final syllable stress reduced to secondary stress. This correctly derives the stress pattern of the words in (3b).

As a further demonstration of the correctness of this approach, Kiparsky notes that the model predicts zero derivations of the form V → N → V, but makes zero derivations N → V → N impossible.[2] This is because the zero derivation of verb to noun takes place on stratum 1 while zero derivation of noun to verb takes place on stratum 2, and stratum 1 feeds stratum 2 but not vice versa. We give some examples in (4) from Kiparsky (1982a, 13).

(4)   a.   protést$_V$ → prótèst$_N$ → prótèst$_V$ 'stage a protest'
         b.   discóunt$_V$ → díscòunt$_N$ → díscòunt$_V$ 'sell at a discount'
         c.   compóund$_V$ → cómpòund$_N$ → cómpòund$_V$ 'join or become joined in a compound'
         d.   digést$_V$ → dígèst$_N$ → dígèst$_V$ 'make a digest'

In each case the verb derived from the noun has a meaning distinct from the verb that the noun was originally derived from. As Kiparsky puts it, "demonstrators may *prótèst* but a child can only *protést.*"

6.3   The order of affixes

We saw in section 6.2 that stratum 1 can feed stratum 2 but not vice versa. This means that overt affixes should behave in the same way. That is, stratum 1 affixes are added to stems before stratum 2 affixes, and so stratum 1 affixes should appear closer to roots than stratum 2 affixes. In general this claim is correct. A standard

---

[2] Kiparsky suggests two possible counterexamples to this claim. One is the derivation *food*$_N$ → *feed*$_V$ → *feed*$_N$ 'food for feeding livestock' and perhaps *brood*$_N$ → *breed*$_V$ → *breed*$_N$ 'genetic type produced by breeding.' As Kiparsky observes, the first step in these derivations must take place on stratum 1, since the resulting verb has irregular (stratum 1) inflection. The second step is evidently our familiar stratum 1 conversion of verb to noun. But the first step is not zero conversion, but an entirely separate process of umlaut at stratum 1, which fronts the stem vowel in the process of converting the noun to the verb. Therefore, these two examples are not counterexamples to the proposed stratal ordering of zero derivation.

example is adjective-forming -*ian* and noun-forming -*ism*. These can appear only in the order -*ian-ism*, as shown in (5).

(5)   a. Mendelianism
        b. Mongolianism
        c. *Mendelismian
        d. *Mongolismian

This is not merely a consequence of the subcategorization frames of these two suffixes. Since -*ism* can attach to both adjectives *(socialism)* and nouns *(heroism)*, while -*ian* can attach only to nouns, (5c, d) might be expected to be possible. But they are not. Siegel (1974) divided English affixes into PRIMARY (our stratum 1) and SECONDARY (our stratum 2) groups. By the logic of the flow of the arrows in Figure 1, primary affixes should occur inside but not outside secondary affixes.

We can derive similar results with other morphological operations listed in Figure 1. For example, we stated that compounding occurs on stratum 2. This implies that compound nouns can become verbs by zero derivation, as in (6a), but that compound verbs cannot become zero-derived nouns, as in (6b) (Kiparsky's examples).

(6)   a. to grandstand, to wallpaper, to snowball, to quarterback
        b. *an air-condition, *a stage-manage

Stratum 2 deverbal suffixes can be added to zero-derived denominal verbs, which are also derived on stratum 2, as shown in (7) (Kiparsky's examples).

(7)   placement, commissionable, riveter, masquerading

And zero-derived deverbal nouns (stratum 1) can get stratum 1 suffixes, as in (8) (Kiparsky's examples).

(8)   contractual, murderous, rebellious

But we predict that zero-derived denominal verbs (stratum 2) cannot receive stratum 1 deverbal suffixes. This is also correct, as shown by the ungrammaticality of (9) (again Kiparsky's examples).

(9)   *gesturation, *figurive, *patternance, *crusadatory, *cementant

Somewhat more difficult is the reverse of the last three cases, adding a zero affix to a form with an overt affix. Here we find that verbs with suffixes never yield zero-derived nouns. By our hypothesis so far, we might expect these to be grammatical if the verb is formed with a stratum 1 suffix, since verb-to-noun zero derivation is also on stratum 1. Contrary to this expectation, the forms in (10) are ungrammatical (Kiparsky's examples).

(10) *a publicize, *a demonstrate, *a clarify

Furthermore we find nouns formed with stratum 1 suffixes yielding zero-derived verbs (11a), but not nouns formed with level 2 suffixes (11b), even though we might expect the latter, since both processes are on level 2 (Kiparsky's examples again).

(11) a. to pressure, to picture, to commission, to proposition, to requisition, to trial, to engineer, to reverence, to reference
    b. *to singer, *to beating, *to freedom, *to promptness, *to championship, *to alcoholism, *to nationalist, *to sisterhood

What (10) and (11b) have in common is that both involve adding a zero affix to something derived with an overt affix on the same stratum. To rule this out Kiparsky proposes the constraint in (12).

(12) *Constraint on zero derivation*
    *] X] Ø]   (X ≠ Ø)

This now gives us a problem in allowing the examples in (11a). Kiparsky assumes a very general procedure of BRACKET ERASURE, stated in (13).

(13) *Bracket Erasure*
    Erase all internal brackets at the end of a stratum

This ensures that morphological and phonological rules have access to word-internal structure only when it has been assigned at the same stratum (property 2 of lexical rules described in Table 1). Thus, the internal brackets assigned to [[press]$_V$ ure]$_N$ on stratum 1 are erased when [pressure]$_N$ enters stratum 2, and (12) is no longer able to prevent the addition of a zero suffix to this form.

6.4 Rule cyclicity

We have already noted in Chapter 4 that the stress rules apply cyclically. We will now extend this claim to all stratum 1 phonological rules in English, including segmental rules. We will further use this to motivate a constraint on cyclic rules known as STRICT CYCLICITY. This has further interesting results for the abstractness of underlying phonological representations.

The first cyclic segmental rule we will examine is known as TRISYLLABIC LAXING. This rule was proposed in *SPE* to account for a number of vowel alternations in English, such as those illustrated in (14). (Some of these forms were introduced in 6 of Chapter 2.) The derivation of the exact quality of the vowels involved in these alternations will be discussed at greater length in Chapter 7.

(14) *Tense vowel (diphthong)*   *Lax vowel*

    a. div*i*ne   [ay]   div*i*nity   [ɪ]
    b. ser*e*ne   [iː]   ser*e*nity   [ɛ]
    c. s*a*ne   [ey]   s*a*nity   [æ]
    d. verb*o*se   [ow]   verb*o*sity   [ɒ]
    e. red*u*ce   [yuw]   red*u*ction   [ə]
    f. prof*ou*nd [aw]   prof*u*ndity [ə]

SPE demonstrates that each of the alternations in (14) can be derived by assuming that both alternants in each row are derived from a single tense underlying vowel, roughly the *tense* version of the vowels that appear in the *lax vowel* column. So, for example, the stressed vowels of *divine* and *divinity* are both derived from an underlying /ī/. We shall return to this demonstration in Chapter 7; for now we can assume this result and concentrate on the laxing rule that derives the phonetic quality of the vowels in the lax vowel column. This rule is Trisyllabic Laxing in *SPE*; Halle & Mohanan (1985) refer to it as Trisyllabic Shortening, but we will retain the term Laxing. The formulation in (15) is a metrical version of the rule.

(15)   *Trisyllabic Laxing*

                    σ   σ_w   σ
                    |
      V → [–tense] / ____

In section 6.6 we will discuss the possibility of collapsing this rule with other laxing rules in English phonology. None of our results in this section will be affected by this move. Trisyllabic Laxing laxes a vowel that is followed by two (or more) syllables in the same domain, as long as the syllable following the vowel in question is not stressed. First we can establish that the domain of Trisyllabic Laxing is stratum 1: it applies when its environment is the result of the addition of stratum 1 suffixes, as illustrated in (14), but not when stratum 2 suffixes are added, as in (16).

(16)   ch*i*ldlessness, h*ee*dlessness, l*e*galism, st*o*icism, p*a*ganism

The requirement that the following vowel not be stressed is shown by examples like those in (17), where the italicized vowel remains tense despite the two following syllables brought about by stratum 1 suffixation.

(17)   a.   qu*o*tátion, fl*o*tátion, gy*rátion, c*i*tátion, m*i*grátion
       b.   f*i*nálity, v*i*tálity, gl*o*bálity, t*o*nálity, t*i*tánic

This restriction on Trisyllabic Laxing has important consequences for the interaction of this rule with the rules of stress, as we will detail in section 6.7.

6.5   The Strict Cycle Condition

We proposed in Chapter 4 that cyclic rules are subject to the Strict Cycle Condition, of which we gave a preliminary formulation in (74) of that chapter. As we stated there, the effect of this condition is to restrict cyclic rules so that they do not change structure except in derived environments. The stress rules of Chapter 4 are permitted to add metrical structure to underived lexical items, but they cannot change underlying stress. Likewise, Trisyllabic Laxing can change the underlying tenseness of the vowel of *sane* when this is affixed with the suffix *-ity,* because this affixation produces a derived environment. However, Trisyllabic Laxing cannot affect the vowel in the first syllable of *nightingale,* even though this vowel meets the structural description of (15). Because *nightingale* is monomorphemic, it does not constitute a derived environment, and so Trisyllabic Laxing cannot apply.

In examples such as *nightingale,* the Strict Cycle Condition has the effect of sharply reducing the abstractness of phonological representations. In *SPE,* words like *nightingale* had to be exempted from Trisyllabic Laxing by manipulating its underlying representation. *SPE* gave the underlying form /nixtingæl/ for *nightingale*. Because the first syllable has a lax vowel, Trisyllabic Laxing can't affect it. Later rules convert the sequence /ix/ to /i:/, from which phonetic [ay] is derived by Vowel Shift and other rules, discussed in Chapter 7. The rules converting /ix/ to /i:/ are used elsewhere in *SPE*, for example in deriving the word *right* from /rixt/, which they motivate on the basis of rules affecting *righteous*, a derivative of *right*. We discuss these rules in Chapter 7 also, where we will suggest a less abstract analysis of *righteous*. Back to *nightingale*, we no longer need an abstract underlying representation with the segment /x/, which is never realized phonetically. With the more concrete underlying representation /nĭtingæl/, the correct phonetic form is produced, since Trisyllabic Laxing is blocked from applying to this form by the Strict Cycle Condition. This has the right effect for all the relevant cases. Cases like *ivory, vacancy, secrecy, potency,* and *piracy* can be exempted from Trisyllabic Laxing by assuming a final underlying glide /y/, which we motivated in Chapter 4 on the basis of stress rules. But there are no such tricks available for words like *stevedore, Averell,* and *Oberon*. However, the Strict Cycle Condition takes care of these as well, since these are monomorphemic words.

A complementary problem is that words like *alibi, sycamore, camera, pelican, enemy, Amazon, Pamela, calendar* have two possible derivations in the *SPE* approach. They can be set up with an underlying lax vowel in the first syllable, in which case no rules apply, or they can have a tense vowel in the underlying representation and get a "free ride" on the rule of Trisyllabic Laxing. This problem too is resolved in a grammar that includes the Strict Cycle Condition. Setting up a tense vowel in *alibi*, etc. is disallowed on the grounds that the vowel in question would be phonetically tense (and diphthongized) since, being in a nonderived environment, it could not be laxed by Trisyllabic Laxing. Thus only one derivation is available for these words, as required.

The formal statement of the Strict Cycle Condition in (18) is from Kiparsky (1985, 89).

(18) *Strict Cycle Condition* (SCC)
   If W is derived from a lexical entry W', where W' is nondistinct from XPAQY and distinct from XPBQY, then a rule A → B/XP__QY cannot apply to W until the word level.

In this definition, a LEXICAL ENTRY is either an underived lexical item from the top box in Figure 1 or an item derived on a previous stratum. An item is said to be DISTINCT from another item if the two items have contradictory specifications for some phonological feature or else contradictory metrical structure; otherwise, they are nondistinct. The WORD LEVEL refers to the last lexical stratum of the lexical phonology, thus, stratum 2 in English in the model of Figure 1. Some rules, like Trisyllabic Laxing, are restricted to stratum 1, and will not get a chance to apply after that stratum. For many other rules we need not stipulate the stratum where the rule applies, since this can be determined by the SCC.

Consider the rule of *n*-Deletion, discussed in more detail in Chapter 7. This rule is responsible for the simplification of the nasal clusters in (19b) but not in (19a) (Kiparsky's examples).

(19) a. n *retained before stratum 1 suffix*
damn + ation
damn + able
hymn + al
hymn + ody
hymn + ology

b. n *deleted elsewhere*

damn # ing
damn # s
damn
hymn
hymn ## index

The rule of *n*-Deletion is given in (20).

(20) n-*Deletion* (postcyclic)
n → Ø / [+nasal] ___]

To see how the Strict Cycle Condition restricts (20) to stratum 2, consider the derivation of *damnation*. On the first cycle we have the lexical item [damn]; this will be W'. W in this case is also [damn], derived from W' by doing nothing, in this case. W' is nondistinct from the structural description of (20) (in fact it *contains* the structural description of the rule) but is distinct from the structural change of the rule (W' contains a sequence of nasals, while the structural change of (20) specifies that there be only one nasal), the SCC is applicable, and (20) cannot apply on cycle 1. On the second cycle, still on level 1, we add *-ation*. W is now [[damn] ation], derived from W' [damn] by the addition of *-ation*. However, W' is still nondistinct from the structural description of (20) and distinct from its structural change (W' is the same as in the last cycle). As a result, (20) cannot apply on cycle 2. When we move on to stratum 2, Bracket Erasure (13) applies, giving [damnation], and (20) is no longer applicable, since it stipulates deletion before a boundary, which has been eliminated by bracket erasure. However, in *damn, damning,* and the other examples in (19b), we still have a boundary at stratum 2, and so (20) can apply to these forms.

Let us give a comparable example from the domain of stress. Consider the derivation of *parental*. On the first cycle we have the noun [parent] which is stressed on its first syllable by familiar rules of Noun Extrametricality and the English Stress Rule. The structure is (21), at this stage.

(21) F
      /\
      s w
      parent

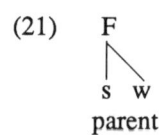

On the second cycle we derive W = *parental* by addition of the adjective suffix *-al*. The lexical item that this is derived from is the W' *parent*, without any metrical structure. It is important to notice that W' is not identified with (21): (21) is not a lexical item, since it is neither an underived lexical item (it has undergone stress rules) nor the output of a stratum (we have still not left stratum 1). Therefore, W' is not distinct from the result of applying stress to the adjective *parental*, a hypothetical form that we can represent as in (22), and stress is allowed to apply.

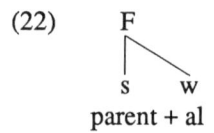

(22) F
      /\
      s w
      parent + al

But (22) is not what we actually derive by applying stress to *parental*. We must continue the cyclic derivation, and apply the rule to (21). Adjective Extrametricality and the English Stress Rule give (23), from which the final form is derived by Prestress Destressing and Stray Syllable Adjunction (24).

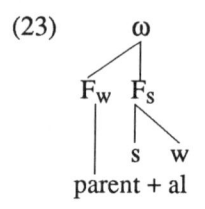

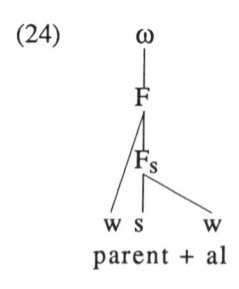

(23)   ω
          /\
        F_w F_s
         | /\
             s w
      parent + al

(24)   ω
           |
           F
          /|
         /F_s
        / /\
       w s w
       parent + al

The derivation just given illustrates another point about the derivation of metrical structure. When a rule assigning metrical structure encounters previously assigned structure, it may destroy just as much structure as is necessary for it to build its own structure. So the application of the English Stress Rule to (21) wiped out the righthand weak branch of the foot already assigned in order to build a new foot with its strong branch in that position, but the strong branch of the original foot remained as a nonbranching foot that later becomes a weak foot by Word Tree Construction (23) and is ultimately destressed.

This point can be illustrated somewhat more vividly with a more complex derivation, such as that for *sensationality,* discussed in Kiparsky (1979). On the first cycle, we derive the stress of *sensation* in the usual way.[3]

(25)

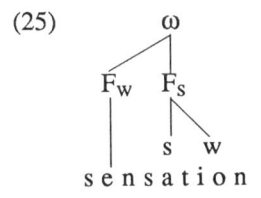

$$\begin{array}{c} \omega \\ F_w \; F_s \\ | \quad | \\ \quad s \; w \\ \text{s e n s a t i o n} \end{array}$$

When we add the adjective suffix *-al* on the second cycle, the structure is minimally distorted to produce (26). In effect, the strong foot of (25) is redrawn with the additional syllable accommodated.

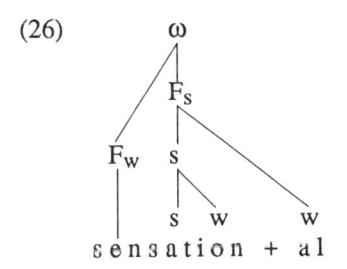

(26)

$$\begin{array}{c} \omega \\ F_s \\ F_w \quad s \\ | \quad | \\ s \; w \; w \\ \text{s e n s a t i o n + a l} \end{array}$$

Finally, we add the suffix *-ity*. Stress rules build a foot on *-ality*. This has the effect of removing *-al* from the foot built on *-ational* in (26). Appropriate adjustments to the foot structure and the final word tree construction produce (27).

---

[3] There is probably an earlier cycle on *sense,* but Kiparsky disregards this and we follow him in this respect, since it has no bearing on the point at hand.

(27)

```
           ω
        ╱     ╲
       w       Fs
      ╱╲      ╱╲
     Fw  Fs  s    ╲
     │  ╱╲  ╱╲    ╲
     s  s w s  w  w
     sensation + al + ity
     3   2         1
```

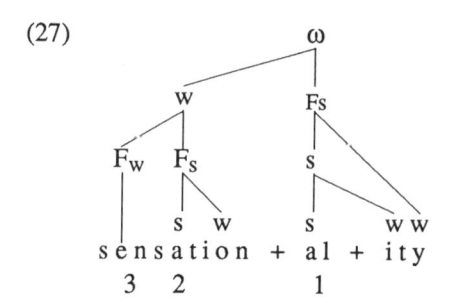

This results in the relative prominence of secondary stresses in the first two syllables shown by the *SPE*-style stress numbers below the relevant syllables. Given the structure in (27), you might expect the Rhythm Rule (69 of Chapter 4) to apply, reversing the relative prominence of the 3 and 2 stresses. However, Kiparsky's condition on the Rhythm Rule (71 of Chapter 4) disallows such application. Once again, this shows how a cyclic derivation of stress produces patterns which reflect the patterns of embedded structures. The stress on *-ation* in *sensationality* is stronger than the stress on *sen* because the same relationship holds in the simpler *sensation*.

6.6 C*i*V Tensing and *s*-Voicing

SPE proposed a rule to make vowels tense when followed by a single consonant, a high vowel or glide and another vowel. This accounts for the alternations in (28), from Rubach (1984a, 39).

(28) a. Canada   b. Canadian
         Panama   Panamanian
         comedy   comedian
         colony   colonial
         Mongol   Mongolia, Mongolian
         Arab   Arabia, Arabian
         courage   courageous
         Jordan   Jordanian
         college   collegian
         harmony   harmonious
         custody   custodian

We have to assume that the words in (28a) have underlying lax vowels in the second syllable. If these vowels were tense, they would be stressed in (28a) by the rules of Chapter 4. Furthermore, there is no rule that laxes vowels in that position. Therefore, there must be a rule that tenses the vowels in (28b). Rubach argues for the formulation of C*i*V Tensing in (29).

(29) C*i*V Tensing

$$\begin{bmatrix} V \\ -high \end{bmatrix} \rightarrow [+tense] / \underline{\quad} C \begin{bmatrix} -cons \\ +high \\ -back \end{bmatrix} \begin{bmatrix} V \\ +low \end{bmatrix}$$

with σ_w above.

Rubach restricts the context vowel to low vowels in order to exclude the suffix *-ion* from the context of the rule. He gives this suffix the underlying form /-yon/, with a mid vowel. This correctly prevents tensing in words such as those in (30).

(30) companion, confession, battalion, procession, medallion, discussion

Some words are idiosyncratic exceptions to C*i*V Tensing, such as those in (31) (Halle & Mohanan 1985, 78).

(31) Italian, Maxwellian, centennial, rebellious, special, gaseous, precious, patio

Notice that the second segment in the environment can be either a vowel *i* (Canadian) or a glide *y* (Lilliputian, although the glide is deleted in this word by a later rule which we examine in Chapter 7, *y*-Deletion).

In structures consisting of a prefix plus a stem, we observe voicing of stem-initial *s* after a vowel (32a) but not after a consonant (32b).

(32) a. resign, design   b. consign
         resume, presume   consume
         resist   consist

Rubach proposes the rule of *s*-Voicing to account for these cases.

(33) *s-Voicing*

$$s \rightarrow [+voice] / \begin{bmatrix} V \\ +tense \end{bmatrix} \underline{\quad} [-cons]$$

S-Voicing applies only after tense vowels, as shown by examples like *fallacy, necessary, necessity, accessory,* and *accessible.* Rubach (1984, 38, fn. 17) argues that the vowel of the prefix *re-* is ultimately destressed and laxed by a special rule.

S-voicing does not apply to a large number of monomorphemic words like *mason, bison, jacinth, mimosa, Isocrates, Medusa.* This is explained by assuming that *s*-Voicing is cyclic, since the Strict Cycle Condition (18) will block its application in such cases, while allowing it to apply in cases like (32a).

We now observe that C*i*V Tensing is ordered before *s*-Voicing. Rubach gives the examples in (34).

(34) a. Cauca*s*us   b. Cauca*s*ian   /æ/
       Malthu*s*   Malthu*s*ian   /ə/
       gymna*s*tics   gymna*s*ium   /æ/

The stress pattern of *Caucasus* shows that it must have an underlying lax vowel in its second syllable. In (34a) we have a lax vowel and a voiceless fricative in the italicized position, while in (34b) we have a tense vowel and a voiced fricative in that position. This results from applying C*i*V Tensing and *s*-Voicing, in that order, to the forms in (34b).

6.7 Interaction of stress rules with cyclic segmental rules

At this point we will summarize the stratum 1 (cyclic) rules we have developed in (35) (opposite), and then provide some examples of their interaction. Recall that Trisyllabic Laxing is blocked if the syllable following the target vowel is stressed (examples in 17). Because of the ordering relations in (35), Trisyllabic Laxing may be blocked by a stress that is present at stratum 1, but which is deleted later in the derivation. Kiparsky (1982a, 43) illustrates this possibility with words like *migratory, vibratory, rotatory, phonatory. Mígratòry* is derived from *mígràte*. When *-ory* is added on the second cycle, it receives a stress by Long Vowel Stressing. Trisyllabic Laxing is potentially applicable to the vowel of the first syllable, but it is blocked by the following stress. Prestress Destressing removes the foot on *-gra-*. Poststress Destressing is not available to remove the foot on *-ory*, since this foot is not adjacent to a strong foot, which is a condition on Poststress Destressing.

Kiparsky (1982a, 43–44) argues that Medial Destressing applies before Trisyllabic Laxing in derivations like *proclamation*. This is derived cyclically as follows. On the first cycle, *proclaim* is assigned two feet, with the second marked strong because it dominates the stem. On the second cycle, the suffix *-ation* is

(35) Rule summary

Stratum 1: Cyclic rules

(Re)syllabification (Chapter 3)
Long Vowel Stressing (35 in Chapter 4)
Extrametricality: Consonant, Noun, Adjective
English Stress Rule (iterative, 29 in Chapter 4)
Sonorant Destressing (65 in Chapter 4)
Word tree Construction (48 in Chapter 4)
Rhythm Rule (69 in Chapter 4)
Medial Destressing (62 in Chapter 4)
Trisyllabic Laxing (15), Cluster Laxing (39), and *-ic* Laxing (41)
C*i*V Tensing (29)
s-Voicing (33)
i-Laxing[4]

Stratum 2: Postcyclic rules (Chapter 7)

Sonorant Syllabification (57 in Chapter 4)
Poststress Destressing (56 in Chapter 4)
Prestress Destressing (54 in Chapter 4)
n-Deletion (20)
Prevocalic Tensing (17 in Chapter 7)
Vowel Shift (4 in Chapter 7)

added. Stress rules provide a foot on *-ation,* marked strong with respect to the preceding stem because it is branching. The resulting structure, seen in (36), is subject to the Rhythm Rule (69 in Chapter 4), which produces (37).

---

[4] Rubach (1984a, 43) formulates this rule as in (i).

(i) ɪ → [−tense] / ___ C₀ y V

This rule is needed to lax ɪ in words like *decision* (cf. *decide*) and *precision* (cf. *precise*), since these vowels cannot undergo Trisyllabic Laxing if the suffix *-ion* has the underlying form /-yon/, which Rubach argues for at length.

(36)
```
           ω
      ┌────┤
      w   │
   ┌──┼──┐│
   Fw F₃ Fs
   │  │  │\
[prōklǽm] ǽt yən
```

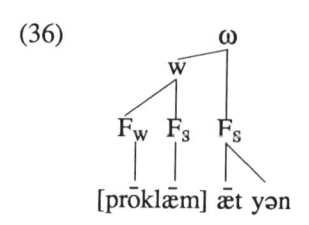

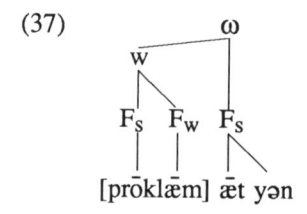

(37)
```
           ω
      ┌────┤
      w   │
   ┌──┼──┐│
   Fs Fw Fs
   │  │  │\
[prōklǽm] ǽt yən
```

At this point, Medial Destressing can remove the medial foot. This could not happen in (36), because the medial foot there is metrically strong. Once the medial foot is removed, Trisyllabic Laxing can lax the vowel of the first syllable. This also could not happen in (36), because there the first syllable is followed by a stressed syllable. Therefore, in this derivation, Medial Destressing precedes and feeds Trisyllabic Laxing. There are many similar forms with a lax prefix vowel, such as *restoration, recitation,* compared to the stem verbs *proclaim, restore, recite,* where the prefix can have a tense vowel when it is not in the environment for Trisyllabic Laxing.

6.8 Other laxing processes

There are two other prominent environments where vowel laxing occurs in English. One is before consonant clusters, as in the examples of (38b) compared to the unlaxed vowels in (38a).

(38) a. interv*e*ne   b. interv*e*ntion
         dec*ei*ve   dec*e*ption
         inscr*i*be   inscr*i*ption
         ded*u*ce   ded*u*ction
         k*ee*p   k*e*pt
         b*i*te   b*i*t[5]

---

[5] We assume that *bit* is derived from /bi:t+t/, with the same (irregular, stratum 1) past tense suffix as in *kept*. The resulting /bitt/ undergoes Degemination (56, section 6.9) after laxing, since geminate consonants are not permitted on stratum 1 in English.

This process is most straightforwardly described by means of a rule of Cluster Laxing that laxes a vowel before two or more consonants, as in (39).

(39)   *Cluster Laxing*
       V → [–tense] / ____ C$_2$

A third environment in which vowels are laxed is before certain suffixes, specifically the adjectival suffix *-ic*.[6]

(40)   a. cone   b. conic
          satire   satiric
          cycle   cyclic
          metre   metric
          state   static

Once again a straightforward rule can account for these alternations, which we give as (41).

(41)   *-ic Laxing*
       V → [–tense] / ____ C -ic

However, the question naturally arises as to why there should be three distinct laxing rules in English phonology. Myers (1987) presents an ingenious attempt to collapse all three rules into one. We will consider his solution, then show why it can't be right, and finally propose an alternative that still allows all three rules to be collapsed.

Myers claims that vowel laxing (shortening in his description) is the result of a natural rule of closed syllable shortening. Most straightforward are the examples in (38b), where the shortened vowel is clearly in a closed syllable. In (38a), we appear to have a closed syllable also, but Myers argues that the word-final consonant in these cases is extrametrical. Therefore, the final syllable is honorarily open, and its vowel can be long. However, in (38b), the consonant cannot be extrametrical, the syllable is closed, and the vowel shortens. But this does not appear to be the case with Trisyllabic Laxing. In *sanity*, for example, laxing has taken place in the first syllable even though it is open. Similar considerations apply in *conic*, an example of shortening before *-ic*. Myers accounts for these

---

[6] *SPE* (180–181) adds *-id* and *-ish* to this list, as in *rapid, radish*, although there is no reason to assign a morpheme boundary before these sequences. They suggest that this might be captured by means of a lexical redundancy rule (p. 181, fn. 16).

cases by claiming that English has a stress-sensitive rule of Resyllabification which has the effect of (42).[7]

(42) CV́.CV̆ → CV́C.V̆

Similar rules have been proposed before, e.g., by Hoard; (1971), Stampe (1972), Selkirk (1982), and Borowsky (1986). These authors appealed to resyllabification to account for the allophones of English stops. In Chapter 5 we saw that the allophones of English stops can be accounted for without such a rule, and in fact we will present evidence that this account makes incorrect predictions about stop allophones in a number of cases. The novelty of Myers's approach is to use Resyllabification to account for a stratum 1 phenomenon, vowel shortening, which has a number of exceptions. This calls into question the claim that shortening is a natural rule. Furthermore, Resyllabification itself is unnatural, in that many people have observed that CV syllables are the most natural syllables in the languages of the world. This is encoded formally in Itô's Onset Principle (cited as 2 in Chapter 3). It seems strange to have a language-specific rule whose purpose is to turn natural syllabifications into unnatural ones, then to have the unnatural syllabifications feed "natural" rules!

Myers mentions stop allophones as a possible source of evidence for the resyllabification analysis. Thus in *atom*, "[t]he /t/ is attracted out of the unstressed final syllable and tacked onto the end of the preceding stressed syllable, where it is transformed into the syllable-final allophone [D]. In *atomic,* on the other hand, the stress pattern does not allow for resyllabification of the /t/, so it is realized as the syllable-initial allophone [t^h]" (1987, 496).[8] Myers observes that this analysis requires Resyllabification to be mirror image as well as cyclic, because resyllabification in *atom* on the first cycle must be undone on the second cycle of *atomic,* to return the /t/ to the syllable it started out in. Myers assumes that the facts of stop allophones can be accounted for entirely in terms of syllable structure. Selkirk (1982) is the most complete account of English stop allophonics in this tradition. Yet Myers's account does not appear to be tenable, given the range of allophonic facts to be accounted for. For example, it cannot account for the alveopalatal allophones discussed in Chapter 5, section 5.2. There we showed that the alveolar stops *t, d* become alveopalatals when followed by *r* in the same syllable. (See rule 23 in Chapter 5 and the data in 24.) Now consider a form such as *metric* in (40b). The shortening of *e* in the first syllable is accounted for by

---

[7] I do not give the rule in Myers's formalism, since he assumes a grid representation for stress. An informal presentation is sufficient for our purposes.

[8] Myers uses [D] to represent the alveolar flap [ɾ].

resyllabification of *t* from the second syllable to the first, on Myers's account, putting the vowel in a closed syllable. But this has the unfortunate effect of bleeding the Alveopalatalization rule. Myers would apparently predict "the syllable-final allophone [D]" here. But *t* is manifestly not flapped here. Selkirk distinguishes between flapped and glottalized allophones of *t* in terms of an ad-hoc feature [release], stating that "after [–cons] and before [–syll] nonrelease is OBL[igatory]." This would predict glottalization here, which is also not observed. In fact, we noted in (9) of Chapter 5 that glottalization is normal for syllable-final stops. Resyllabification seems unable to capture the alveopalatal allophones.

Similar considerations apply with Palatalization, a process that will be discussed in greater detail in Chapter 7. This converts the sequence *ty* to [č] and the sequence *sy* to [š] (also dy to [ǰ] and zy to [ž]) under certain conditions. According to Borowsky (1986, 311), the conditions are that *t* and *y* be heterosyllabic. Contrast the examples in (43a) where palatalization applies with those of (43b) where it does not.

(43) a. na*t*ural
        ac*t*ual
        ac*t*uality
        tinc*t*ure
        spa*c*ial
        offi*c*ial
        perpe*t*ual
     b. *t*une
        *t*uition
        perpe*t*uity

In (43a), on Borowsky's account, the italicized consonant is shifted leftward into the preceding syllable (obligatorily if the syllable is stressed), making it heterosyllabic with the following *y*, which may be either underlying (as in *spacial, official*) or inserted by a rule to be discussed in Chapter 7 (in the other examples of 43a). In (43b), on the other hand, it is not possible for the consonant to be resyllabified, either because it begins a word *(tune, tuition)* or because it begins a stressed syllable *(tune, perpetuity)*. Borowsky claims that Palatalization is blocked when the consonant to be palatalized and the conditioning glide are in the same syllable. But Resyllabification produces some fairly bizarre syllabifications in these cases. Consider *tincture:* Resyllabification produces *tinct.[y]ure*, which seems highly counterintuitive. Furthermore, Resyllabification would once again predict glottalized allophones in these cases. If we consider higher prosodic structure, foot, phonological word, and so forth, we can more easily account for the stop allophones without a rule of Resyllabification. In this case we can say that Palatalization affects coronal obstruents which are followed by *y* and which are *not foot initial*. This characterization of the environment is no more stipulative than Borowsky's requirement that they be heterosyllabic, and it allows us to dispense with Resyllabification.

There is at least one class of cases where our reformulation of palatalization differs in its empirical consequences from Borowsky's rule, and that is where a coronal obstruent followed by *y* occurs between two unstressed syllables, as in (44), where the syllable *tu* is Chomsky adjoined to the following foot.

(44) oppor*t*unistic   [oppor]$_F$ [tu [nistic]$_F$]$_F$

Clearly, the italicized *t* is not palatalized in (44). Resyllabification of *t* would not apply *obligatorily* here, because the syllable before it is unstressed. But Borowsky allows *optional* resyllabification between two unstressed syllables (basically Selkirk's approach also) to account for the optional flapping of *t* in cases like *sanity*. Optional resyllabification of *t* would predict the possibility of palatalizing *t* in (44), which is not an option. In our terms, we would claim that (44) has the foot structure shown to the right in (44), a structure that is produced automatically if it is derived cyclically from [oppor]$_F$ [tune]$_F$, where the structure in (44) represents the least amount of restructuring of the earlier cycle necessary to produce the final results.

The same examples can be used to resolve a different but related problem in those dialects (Borowsky's A dialects, basically North American) that do not allow *y* after coronals in words like those in (45a), as opposed to (45b), where the glide is required in all (standard) dialects.

(45)   a.   news   b.   continue
            avenue   annual
            numerical   volume
            tune
            tuition
            duke
            duration
            continuity
            annuity
            voluminous

Borowsky claims that the A dialects disallow the sequence coronal–*y*–vowel in syllable-initial position. Resyllabification in (45b) puts the coronal consonant in a different syllable than the following *y*, allowing the same sequence across a syllable boundary. Resyllabification in (45a) is impossible for the same reasons as in (43b): the coronal either begins a word or begins a stressed syllable. Therefore, in the A dialects, *y* cannot surface in (45a). Once again, though, an alternative explanation is available by taking the foot into consideration. In the A dialects, *y* is deleted when it follows a foot-initial consonant. Again, cases like (44) provide an interesting test. Speakers of the A dialects uniformly reject the pronunciation [tyu] in (44), suggesting, in our terms, that the italicized *t* is foot initial there, as it is in our structure.

Myers cites additional evidence that he claims provides independent evidence for resyllabification. One concerns the distribution of *h*, which Borowsky claims can appear only in syllable onsets, as in (46a) but not in (46b).

(46)   a.   ve[h]ícular, pro[h]íbit
         b.   vé[Ø]icle, pròfØ]ibítion

Borowsky claims that resyllabification of *h* into the coda of the first syllable in the examples of (46b) prevents its realization. But, with higher prosodic structure available, we can simply say that *h* is restricted to *foot*-initial position. The appearance of *h* in *hilarious* is possible because the initial syllable is also foot initial by Stray Syllable Adjunction. Further support for restricting *h* to foot-initial position comes from the contrast in (47), first noted by Brame (1972, 62).

(47)   a.   [pro]$_F$ [hi[bition]$_F$]$_F$ 'act of prohibiting'
         b.   [prohi]$_F$ [bition]$_F$ 'a period in American history'

Clearly, (47a) is derived from *prohibit,* with the foot structure [pro]$_F$ [hibit]$_F$, and the least amount of distortion to this structure on the second cycle produces (47a), with the syllable *hi* destressed by Medial Destressing. With a less close association to the verb, (47b) presumably has no inner cycle, and so has the structure shown. Therefore, *h* can appear initially in an unstressed syllable as long as that syllable is foot initial, as in (47a), something which the resyllabification analysis can't capture.

Returning to vowel shortening, we have seen that Myers's collapse of all English shortening rules relies crucially on the rule of Resyllabification, which we have shown cannot exist. However, it is relatively easy to reformulate his rule in terms of higher prosodic stucture (Jensen 1991). The rule in (48) laxes a (stressed) vowel that is followed by another mora in the same foot.[9]

(48) *Laxing*

$$\begin{array}{c}\sigma_s\\|\\V\end{array} \to [-\text{tense}] \, / \, [\ldots \underline{} \ldots m \ldots]_F$$

This rule laxes vowels in all the same environments as Myers's rule without appealing to Resyllabification. Furthermore, we do not lose any of the advantages claimed for the resyllabification analysis. So (48) is LOCAL, in the sense that it appeals to only two structurally adjacent elements within a domain, like Myers's rule, but unlike the *SPE* rule (15), which must count off a sequence of three vowels. Second, we can explain the diachronic development (Kiparsky 1968a) in which Cluster Laxing and Trisyllabic Laxing both generalize in the same way in the passage from Old to Middle English by losing a consonant from their environments. Finally, we note that the lexical exceptions that Myers lists in the appendix to his article are exceptions in the present treatment also. These include the forms in (49a), where the italicized vowels are in a shortening context even without Resyllabification, some monomorphemic forms in (49b), and some derived forms in (49c).

(49) a. ch*a*mber, c*ou*ncil, sh*ou*lder, s*ei*smic
      b. d*i*nosaur, tr*i*lobite, v*i*tamin, s*ou*venir, *e*delweiss, d*y*nasty
      c. ph*o*bic, b*a*sic, sc*e*nic, n*i*cety, *o*besity, pr*o*bity, pr*i*macy

There is some dialectal variation here—note the British pronunciation of *vitamin* and *dynasty*. The basic conclusion of this section still holds, which is that the various laxing rules of English phonology can be collapsed into a single rule (48) without the need for a resyllabification rule, which plays havoc with the rules determining stop allophones as presented in Chapter 5. Notice that (49b) is not a problem, since these can be treated the same way as *nightingale:* the Strict Cycle Condition (18) prevents the application of laxing to these forms. A problem arises, though, in cases like *piracy,* which we argued in section 6.5 were exempted from Trisyllabic Laxing by virtue of having a glide *y* as the final segment. Even with this provision, the first vowel of *piracy* is followed by a second mora within

---

[9] This rule appears slightly too general, in that it will also lax the penultimate vowel in the suffix *-ation*. This is also a problem for Myers's account. However, if we assume that the final suffix is extrametrical (by Noun Extrametricality) at the time of Laxing, no laxing will take place in such forms.

its foot, namely *ra*. This is a problem for Myers's analysis also. Evidently, any attempt at a unified account of English vowel laxing will have to find an alternative explanation for these cases.

6.9 The morphology and phonology of English strong verbs

This section gives a brief overview of the strong verbs in English. It is not meant as an exhaustive description. A thorough treatment may be found in Bloch (1947) or in Quirk et al. (1972). We will also not try to describe all possible patterns in terms of generative rules, as has been done by Halle & Mohanan (1985, 104–114). We will rather describe the basic patterns and try to straighten out some of the theoretical issues involved. This analysis is heavily indebted to Halle & Mohanan's discussion, however.

6.9.1 Verbs suffixed at stratum 1

It is perhaps well to begin by distinguishing the strong patterns from the regular paradigm. Regular verbs in English form their past tense by suffixing *-d* at stratum 2, as in *called* from *call*. Some phonology enters the picture in forms like *walked* and *decided*. In *walked*, the suffix *-d* is devoiced by a progressive assimilation rule that we can write as in (50).[10]

(50) *Progressive Assimilation*

$$\begin{bmatrix} C \\ +cor \end{bmatrix} \rightarrow [-voice] / \begin{bmatrix} C \\ -voice \end{bmatrix}] \underline{\qquad}] \text{ (strata 1, 2 and postlexical)}$$

In *decided*, a vowel is inserted by a rule we can write as in (51). This rule is also formulated to insert a vowel before the suffixes mentioned in footnote 10, which is not immediately relevant to the discussion.

(51) *Epenthesis*

$$\emptyset \rightarrow \upsilon / \begin{bmatrix} C \\ +cor \\ \alpha strid \end{bmatrix}] \underline{\qquad} \begin{bmatrix} C \\ +cor \\ +voice \\ \alpha strid \end{bmatrix}] \quad \text{(postlexical)}$$

In a case like *delight*, Epenthesis (51) applies rather than the assimilation rule (50). This implies that the two rules are ordered (51) before (50) in a bleeding (but

---
[10] This rule also devoices the plural suffix *-z*, the possessive suffix *-z* and the reduced version of the third person singular of the verb *to be*. We will not be specifically concerned with this extension here.

TRANSPARENT[11]) order. The important thing to realize is that (50) and (51) are *phonological* rules that have no *direct* bearing on the morphology.

The strong verbs include some which undergo affixation on stratum 1, and which therefore undergo certain stratum 1 phonological processes. For example, the verbs in (52) receive the past-tense suffix -*t* at level 1.

(52)   leave, mean, sleep, sweep, weep, keep, feel, dream, leave, creep

A derivation for *leave,* present and past, appears in (53).

(53) leave /leːv/   left   /leːv/   underlying form
            /leːv/   /leːv+t/   level 1 morphology
            /leːv/   /lɛv+t/   level 1 phonology: Cluster Laxing (39)
                               /lɛft/   voicing assimilation
            /liyv/   level 2 phonology: Vowel Shift

The voicing assimilation seen in *left* is progressive rather than regressive, and cannot be effected by rule (50) as it stands. Halle & Mohanan suggest a MIRROR IMAGE voicing assimilation rule, which we can give as in (54). A mirror image rule operates in both directions, and is indicated by using the percent sign % instead of the environment slash / of standard phonological rules. This rule is a domain span rule, in the terminology of Nespor & Vogel (1986), where the domain is the foot.[12]

(54)   *Voicing Assimilation*
       [−son] → [−voice] % [... ____ [−voice]...]$_F$

       (Strata 1, 2, and postlexical; before Degemination on stratum 1)

The verbs in (55) illustrate the same rules so far discussed plus a new rule of Degemination.

(55)   bite, light, meet, lose

---

[11] This term is defined in Chapter 8, section 8.1.4.
[12] Halle & Mohanan (1985, 105) claim that the domain of this rule is the syllable, but it must be the foot, because obstruents of opposite voicing can appear at syllable boundaries across foot boundaries (e.g., *Aztec*) but not between syllables that belong to the same foot (e.g., *aster*).

The suffixation of -*t* to *bite* /biːt/, for example, produces /biːt+t/, which is subject to Cluster Laxing (39) and Degemination, which we can also formulate as a foot domain span rule, as in (56).[13]

(56) *Degemination*
$C_i \rightarrow \emptyset / [... \underline{\quad} C_i ...]_F$

Degemination derives the correct forms for *bit, lit, and met*. In *lost*, the stem-final *z* is devoiced by voicing assimilation and the low lax vowel of *lost* is derived by a rule of *o*-Lowering, given as (8) in Chapter 7.

6.9.2 Ablaut

Perhaps the most interesting irregular verbs are those that undergo ablaut processes. Halle (1977, 616) regards these as allomorphy rules. Halle & Mohanan (1985, 114) claim that they are phonological rules on stratum 2. I believe that neither of these characterizations is correct. Aronoff (1976) characterizes allomorphy rules as rules that irregularly change the form of a morpheme in a morphological environment, as in converting *permit* to *permiss-* in *permissive*. There is, however, no morphological environment to condition the change of *sing* to *sang*, for example. They also cannot be characterized as strictly phonological rules, since there is no phonological environment that distinguishes *sing* from *sang*.[14] Two possibilities are open to us: either ablaut processes are MORPHOLOGICAL PROCESSES on stratum 1, as given in Figure 1, or they come from a more abstract representation. Let us consider the analysis in terms of morphological processes first.

First, consider the verbs in (57).

---

[13] Halle & Mohanan (1985, 105) claim that this rule, like (54), has the syllable as its domain. However, Degemination occurs across syllable boundaries in cases like *innumerable*. They also assume that Degemination is postlexical; however, it must be restricted to stratum 1, since geminates derived at stratum 2 are retained. Compare *i[n]umerable* with *u[nn]atural*. We have formulated this rule to delete the first rather than the second of two identical consonants in order to maintain the Onset Principle (2) in Chapter 3. No resyllabification will be required after (56) applies.

[14] Halle & Mohanan (1985, 107) claim that such phonological rules are "triggered in forming the past tense and perfect participle of a lexically marked class of verbs." They give no details as to how this triggering is supposed to take place.

(57) a. drink   drank   b. eat   ate
          sit   sat   lie   lay
          begin   began   c. choose chose
          shrink   shrank
          spring   sprang
          swim   swam

The past tense in (57) has a low vowel, transparently in (57a) where we have [æ] phonetically, but also in (52b) where the pre–Vowel Shift vowel is [æː] and in (57c) where the pre–Vowel Shift vowel is [ɔː]. This justifies a rule of Lowering Ablaut (Halle 1977, 616; Halle & Mohanan 1985, 107) for these verbs. If we consider this to be a morphological process, it will be one that simultaneously changes the form and the meaning of an item. In this case, it makes the vowel [+low] and adds the meaning [+past] to the verb, as in (58).

(58) *Lowering Ablaut*
$$X \quad V \quad C_0 \quad]_V$$
$$1 \quad 2 \quad 3 \quad 4 \quad \rightarrow \quad 1 \quad 2 \quad 3 \quad 4$$
$$ [+\text{low}] \quad \quad [+\text{past}]$$

Since, by assumption, Lowering Ablaut applies in stratum 1 morphology, it precedes Vowel Shift, which applies in stratum 2 phonology. Therefore, Lowering Ablaut will feed Vowel Shift in the forms of (57b, c).

The next class of verbs we will consider includes those in (59).

(59) a. cling   clung   c. get   got
          dig   dug   tread   trod
          fling   flung   d. break   broke
          spin   spun   wake   woke
          spring   sprung   e. wear   wore
          stick   stuck   swear   swore
          sting   stung   bear   bore
      b. bind   bound   tear   tore
          find   found
          grind   ground
          wind   wound

The verbs in (59) are all subject to a process which Halle & Mohanan (1985, 108) call BACKING ABLAUT (Cf. Halle 1977, 616). We formulate it as a morphological process in (60).

(60) Backing Ablaut

$$\begin{matrix} X & V & C_0 &] \\ 1 & 2 & 3 & 4 \\ & [\alpha\text{high}] & & \end{matrix} \rightarrow \begin{matrix} 1 & 2 & 3 & 4 \\ & \begin{bmatrix} +\text{back} \\ -\alpha\text{round} \end{bmatrix} & & [+\text{past}] \end{matrix}$$

Backing Ablaut applies in (59) as follows. In (59a) it converts underlying /ɪ/ to [ɨ], which is then subject to ɨ-Lowering (10 in Chapter 7), since all the verb stems in (59) are closed syllables. This yields ə, the correct phonetic vowel. In (59b), it converts underlying /iː/ to [ɨː], which, as a tense vowel, is subject to Vowel Shift and Diphthongization, correctly producing the phonetic diphthong [aʊ̯]. In (59c), underlying /ɛ/ is both backed and rounded to (lax, mid) [ɔ]. This may in turn be lowered to [ɒ], giving the RP form, and it may be further unrounded to [ɑ] in North American English. In (59d) underlying /æː/ is backed and rounded to [ɔ̄ː], which yields [ōː] by Vowel Shift and Diphthongization. The same is true of (59e), where, however, the vowel quality is somewhat affected by the following *r*.

The final group of verbs we will consider here are those in (61).

(61) write   wrote
      rise   rose
      speak   spoke
      freeze   froze

Although we could write another ablaut rule to account for (61), Halle (1977, 616) suggested that, by simply marking them for undergoing both Lowering Ablaut (58) and Backing Ablaut (60), *in that order,* we would get the correct results. This suggestion is followed in Halle & Mohanan (1985), although they discuss a much wider range of strong verbs and propose additional rules to account for them. They also consider the participial forms, which we have not discussed specifically. We will not summarize their entire discussion here; the interested reader is invited to consult their paper for details.

We claim that our ablaut rules should be regarded as morphological processes that both add meaning and change the form of items, as opposed to Halle & Mohanan's view that they are purely phonological rules. Our conclusion is forced by the logic of lexical phonology, which holds that lexical items, including inflected forms, are formed in the lexicon prior to insertion into syntactic structures. In this model, phonological rules are sensitive to phonological structures built up by morphological operations, including constituent structure assigned on the same level. Halle & Mohanan do not specify how the triggering features for past and participle are assigned to the lexical items which undergo various ablaut rules. In this respect, their discussion is more akin to the analysis of *SPE,* which assumed an abstract morpheme 'past' which was changed to /d/ in [[mend]$_V$ past]$_V$ but triggered ablaut in [[sing]$_V$ past]$_V$.

The use of morphological processes can be disputed, however. We have defined a morphological process as one that simultaneously adds meaning and changes the form of items. We presume that forms are specially marked for undergoing particular processes, and that the Elsewhere Condition (49 in Chapter 7) or something like it blocks the regular formation for these specially marked forms. But then we have a problem with forms like those in (61), which are marked to undergo *two* ablaut processes, both of which have the same effect on the meaning but which effect distinct phonological changes. Shouldn't the Elsewhere Condition prevent the application of a second ablaut rule in such a case?

Another problem with morphological processes is that they are written in a TRANSFORMATIONAL format. It has been strongly argued in syntax that transformations are a highly powerful device, which can express many processes that simply do not occur in languages. In morphology, transformations have been used to express reduplications and infixations (Jensen 1990), but the very restrictive nature of reduplications and infixations has suggested performing those operations by a more restrictive device. McCarthy & Prince (1986) have suggested using prosodic categories to account for reduplications and infixations. Essentially, infixation is restricted to an environment before word-final syllables or segments or after word-initial syllables or segments. Reduplication copies syllables, minimal syllables, bimoraic syllables, and sometimes feet, but always identifiable prosodic units. Is it possible that such a solution is available for ablaut (and umlaut) phenomena?

We might, for example, reformulate Lowering Ablaut (58) in terms of an abstract morpheme that consists of a floating phonological feature [+low] and the morphological feature [+past], along with a subcategorization frame that says it can attach to a verb marked with the diacritic [+L(owering) A(blaut)] somewhat in the manner of (62a). The floating feature would have the property of attaching to the nearest V to its left, displacing any contradictory phonological features, while the morphological feature would percolate to the resulting word. This means that ablaut can be expressed as a morpheme not too unlike normal morphemes like the regular morpheme 'past' in English, given as (62b).

(62) a. $\begin{bmatrix} \boxed{[+\text{low}]} \\ [+V, -N, +LA] \underline{\quad} \\ [+\text{past}] \end{bmatrix}$ b. $\begin{bmatrix} -d \\ [+V, -N] \underline{\quad} \\ [+\text{past}] \end{bmatrix}$

The boxed feature [+low] in (62a) indicates that it is floating; the -d of (62b) stands for an ordinary nonfloating feature matrix.

Backing Ablaut is much more difficult to express in this framework, since it not only adds the feature [+back] to the stem vowel of the verb, but it also adds a value of [round] that depends on the value for [high] already assigned to that vowel. No doubt an appropriate formalism could be devised within the autosegmental framework. However it is done, it is clear that some alternative to the overly powerful transformational format is needed. This problem, and the still more difficult morphological question of how to permit two morphemes with the same meaning to affect a single lexical item, must be left to future research.

6.10 Exercises

1. What does each of the following sets of forms indicate about the strata at which the italicized morphological operation(s) take place?

    a. mánage*ment*, héed*lessness*
    b. *to* páttern, *to* póison, *to* ránsom, *to* cómfort, *to* pícture, *to* fócus
    c. protést_V, prótest_N, prótest_V; discóunt_V, díscòunt_N, díscòunt_V *(zero derivation of nouns and verbs)*
    d. Mendel*ianism*, *Mendel*ismian;* Mongol*ianism*, *Mongol*ismian*
    e. rehears*al*, procur*al*, apprais*al*, arriv*al*, deni*al*, *rebuk*al*, *promiss*al*, *accept*al*

2. Explain why the italicized vowel in each of the following words does not undergo Trisyllabic Laxing. There is a different explanation in each case.

    a. n*i*ghtingale
    b. f*ai*thlessness
    c. ob*e*sity
    d. m*i*gratory
    e. v*a*cate
    f. v*a*cancy
    g. qu*o*tation

3. Discuss the problems that the following forms pose for the theory of stratum-ordered morphology presented in this chapter.

   a. patentability
   b. hospitalize
   c. demonize

7 Lexical phonology: the postcyclic rules

7.1 Vowel Shift

7.1.1 Basic cases of Vowel Shift

This chapter explores the postcyclic rule system of English phonology. This section will concentrate on the vowel system, and in particular on the underlying representations of the vowels related by alternations involving Trisyllabic Laxing, as discussed in Chapter 6. Subsequent sections will be concerned with the consonant system and some other vowel processes, including vowel reduction.

In historical studies, Vowel Shift is regarded as the major phonological change that took place in the course of the evolution of early Modern English from Middle English. It was a major contribution of *SPE* to demonstrate that this process must be recognized as a synchronic rule of Modern English as well.[1] This is shown by the alternations that various pairs of vowels enter into. We have already discussed Trisyllabic Laxing, which is responsible for alternations of the type given in (14) of Chapter 6. In Chapter 6 we were not very specific about the exact nature of the rules involved in producing the phonetic forms from the tense and lax varieties of each vowel. Before we discuss these rules, let us introduce some important terminology. We will distinguish between FULL vowels and REDUCED vowels. Full vowels appear in stressed positions, though not necessarily in primary stressed positions; reduced vowels appear in unstressed positions.[2]

---

[1] There are some dissenters to this opinion. For a recent experimental discussion, see Jaeger (1986) and some of the other papers in *Phonology Yearbook* 3.

[2] This somewhat simplified picture is convoluted by the existence of rules that produce tense vowels in unstressed positions, namely before vowels and word finally. We will clarify this in section 7.7.

Full vowels, in addition, can either be long, tense diphthongs, or they can be short, lax monophthongs. Let us illustrate this with a few examples in (1).

(1)   *Full vowels*   *Reduced vowels*
       Long   *Short*
       expl*ai*n   expl*a*natory   expl*a*nation
       harm*o*nious   harm*o*nic   harm*o*ny
       margin*a*lia   margin*a*lity   margin*a*l
       manag*e*rial   manag*e*r

We will refer to the italicized vowels in the first column of (1) as LONG vowels and to those in the second column as SHORT vowels, and to those in the last column as REDUCED vowels. It is important to realize that short vowels are still regarded as full vowels. The reduced vowels in (1) are phonetically [ə]. In section 7.6 we will consider vowel reduction in greater detail and observe that another vowel, [ɪ], besides [ə], can appear as reduced vowels.

We explain the form *explanatory* in terms of Trisyllabic Laxing. The underlying tense vowel of the second syllable is laxed after the suffix *-atory* is added. However, *marginality* and *harmonic* cannot be explained in terms of laxing. If the final vowels[3] of *harmony, marginal, manager* were tense underlyingly, they would be stressed by Long Vowel Stressing. Therefore we assume that the final vowel is lax underlyingly in these words, and that the long vowel in *harmonious, marginalia, managerial* is the result of C*i*V Tensing (29 in Chapter 6).

Thus, we have alternations going both ways. On the one hand, we have underlying tense vowels that undergo laxing in certain environments by the laxing rules of Chapter 6 (Trisyllabic Laxing, Cluster Laxing, and *-ic* Laxing or the generalized *Laxing* (48) in Chapter 6; see the data in (14) of Chapter 6). On the other hand, we have underlying lax vowels that undergo tensing by C*i*V Tensing (29 in Chapter 6; data in (28) of Chapter 6). The alternating segments are not merely tense and lax variants of each other, but differ quite widely phonetically. For example the diphthong [ay] alternates with the lax vowel [ɪ]. It would require a very complex set of rules to convert each of the diphthongs directly to the corresponding lax vowel. It would be highly unexpected to have an equally complex set of rules having exactly the opposite effect.

The ingenious nature of the *SPE* account of these facts consisted in factoring out the laxing and tensing processes from the rules determining the phonetic form of the tense and lax vowels, thereby ensuring that the latter need only be stated once. We have assumed this analysis up to this point, stating Trisyllabic Laxing (15 in Chapter

---

[3] This includes the vowel *o* of *harmony*, if we consider the final *y* to be a glide.

6) and the other laxing rules of section 6.8 as rules that make vowels [−tense], and the tensing rule 29 in Chapter 6) as a rule that makes vowels [+tense]. We therefore need to formulate the rules that determine the phonetic form of the vowels in question, on the basis of appropriately chosen underlying representations for these vowels.

In Chapter 6 we suggested that the alternations between long and short full vowels resulting from Trisyllabic Laxing could be captured by taking a tense version of the vowel that appears in the laxing environment as the underlying form of each of the vowels. This works well as a first approximation to the front vowels that participate in this pattern, so we will consider these in detail first. Then we will extend the analysis to the back vowels, where some minor irregularities blur the picture somewhat. Recall the alternations involving front vowels in (2) (section 6.4), where we have added the underlying vowels.[4]

(2) *Tense vowel (diphthong)*   *Lax vowel*   *Underlying*

  a. div*i*ne   [āy]   div*i*nity   [ɪ]   /i/
  b. ser*e*ne   [iy]   ser*e*nity   [ɛ]   /e/
  c. s*a*ne   [ey]   s*a*nity   [æ]   /æ/

With these underlying forms, it is clear that the lax vowel forms are derived directly by Trisyllabic Laxing.[5] We must now derive the tense diphthongs that appear in the first column of (2). We notice first that the phonetic values for *serene* and *sane* are one step above the corresponding underlying form of the vowel. The phonetic vowel of *divine,* however, is low, where the underlying vowel is high. In a sense, the vowels simply move round a circle, shown schematically in (3).

(3) $\begin{Bmatrix} i \\ e \\ æ \end{Bmatrix}$

Formally, this can be expressed by the two rules in (4). While *SPE*, Halle (1977), and Halle & Mohanan (1985) give this as a single rule, it is easier to see how it works if we state the two subparts separately.[6]

---

[4] As in Chapter 2, we indicate vowel tenseness with a macron where it is not indicated by the phonetic symbol already.

[5] We assume that laxing is automatically accompanied by elimination of the second mora of the vowel.

[6] The notation in (4) is intended to indicate that the vowel is ultimately dominated by a strong syllable, though a mora node presumably intervenes. This expresses our restriction of Vowel Shift to stressed syllables.

(4) *Vowel Shift*

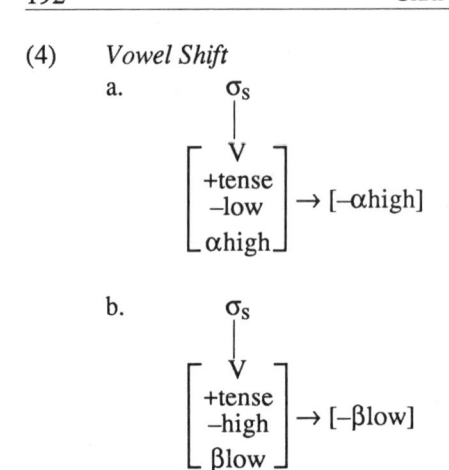

a.
$$\begin{matrix}\sigma_s\\|\\\begin{bmatrix}V\\+\text{tense}\\-\text{low}\\\alpha\text{high}\end{bmatrix}\end{matrix} \rightarrow [-\alpha\text{high}]$$

b.
$$\begin{matrix}\sigma_s\\|\\\begin{bmatrix}V\\+\text{tense}\\-\text{high}\\\beta\text{low}\end{bmatrix}\end{matrix} \rightarrow [-\beta\text{low}]$$

In order to derive the phonetic diphthongs, we need a diphthongization rule, which we give as (5). This rule is formulated to produce front glides after front vowels and back glides after back vowels. We will discuss the back vowels shortly.

(5) *Diphthongization*

$$\emptyset \rightarrow \begin{bmatrix}-\text{cons}\\+\text{high}\\\alpha\text{back}\\\alpha\text{round}\end{bmatrix} / \begin{bmatrix}V\\+\text{tense}\\\alpha\text{back}\end{bmatrix} \underline{\quad}$$

We will now investigate how these rules apply to the underlying forms in (2) to produce the phonetic forms. We give the derivations in (6).[7]

(6)
		/i/	/e/	/ǣ/
	underlying			
	(4a)	e	i	—
	(4b)	ǣ	—	e
	(5)	ǣy	iy	ey
	Backness Adjustment (18)	āy	—	—

---

[7] Note that Vowel Shift, Diphthongization, and the other rules of this chapter, apply to underived forms as well as to derived forms. The Strict Cycle Condition is not applicable to these stratum 2 rules because stratum 2 is noncyclic.

Assuming that the system so far developed is correct, we now extend it to the back vowels, which present a few complications. The most obvious back parallel is represented by (7a). Accounting for (7b) requires a little adjustment in the lax vowel for *lost.*

(7) *Tense vowel (diphthong)* *Lax vowel*   *Underlying*

    a. verbose [ow] verbosity [ɒ] /ō/
    b. lose   [uw] lost   [ɒ] /o/

It is evident that the underlying tense, low, back vowel in (7a) will be raised to mid by (4b) in a way exactly parallel to the low front vowel in (6); likewise, the mid vowel in (7b) will be raised to high by (4a) parallel to the mid front vowel in (6). The complication here is that the lax vowel in *lost* appears as low rather than mid. Previously, we have not encountered any changes in height among the lax vowels. Halle (1977, 619) expresses this as the rule in (8), which Halle & Mohanan (1985, 74 & 84) argue is postlexical.

(8) o-*Lowering* (postlexical)
$$\begin{bmatrix} V \\ +\text{round} \\ -\text{high} \\ -\text{tense} \end{bmatrix} \rightarrow [+\text{low}]$$

We can now investigate the alternations of (9). Here, our reasoning that the underlying forms are tense versions of the vowels that appear in lax versions breaks down somewhat, since the same lax vowel appears in both (9a) and (9b).

(9) *Tense vowel (diphthong)* *Lax vowel*   *Underlying*

    a. profound [aw]   profundity [ə] /ɨ/
    b. reduce   [yuw] reduction   [ə] /ʌ/

We posit the underlying forms in (9) on the basis of the following reasoning. For *profound,* we deduce, on the parallelism of (2a), that its underlying form must contain a [+high] vowel, which will be lowered twice by (4a, b) to produce the phonetic low vowel. Because [a] is back and nonround, the simplest solution is to propose a tense, back, high, nonround vowel for the underlying form. Thus, with the underlying form /ɨ/, nothing needs to be added to our rules to derive the stressed vowel of *profound.* To derive the vowel of *profundity,* we need to add a rule to lower lax ɨ before a consonant within a syllable, which Halle & Mohanan (1985, 91) give as ɨ-Lowering (10).

(10) ɨ-*Lowering*
 ɨ → [–high] / ___ C]_σ

This rule accounts for the fact that the lax versions of the vowels in (9) are identical.

To account for the vowel of *reduce,* two adjustments are needed. Vowel Shift will take tense ʌ to ɨ. This needs to be rounded to [u] by the postlexical rule ɨ-Rounding (11), which applies to both long and short ɨ. Together, ɨ-Lowering and ɨ-Rounding account for the fact that ɨ does not occur phonetically in English utterances.[8]

(11) ɨ-*Rounding* (postlexical)
$$\begin{bmatrix} V \\ +\text{high} \\ +\text{back} \end{bmatrix} \rightarrow [+\text{round}]$$

We must further account for the *y*-glide that appears before the sequence *uw* generated by these rules. As we noted in Chapter 3, section 3.5.1, onsets consisting of a consonant plus *y* are restricted in their distribution: they occur only before the vowel *u*. We suggested there that this *y* is inserted by a rule. We give this rule as *y*-Insertion in (12).

(12) y-*Insertion*
$$\emptyset \rightarrow y / \underline{} \begin{bmatrix} V \\ +\text{high} \\ +\text{back} \\ -\text{round} \end{bmatrix}$$

Although we transcribe *reduce* with [yuw], we note that many North American speakers do not produce a *y* in this position. Halle & Mohanan capture this fact by splitting *y*-Insertion into two dialectally distinct rules: The first part is identical with our (12) and applies in what they term the [dyuwti] dialects, where *y* is pronounced before *uw* (from ʌ) after any consonant, while the second part inserts *y* except after coronals before stressed vowels, to give what they call the [duwti] dialects. We prefer to follow Rubach (1984a, 49) in capturing this dialectal difference by a separate rule which deletes *y* after a foot-initial coronal, given in (13).

---

[8] It can for some speakers, who would have [yɨw] in *reduce,* according to Hoard (1972, 144).

(13)   Dialectal y-Deletion   σ$_s$

$$y \to \emptyset / [_F \begin{bmatrix} C \\ +cor \end{bmatrix}] \underline{\quad} V...$$

An example of the rounding of short, lax *i* is *argue*. The vowel of the last syllable cannot be long or it would be stressed by Long Vowel Stressing. Nevertheless, *y*-insertion applies. If we assume underlying *i*, the rules already given will produce the correct result.

Halle & Mohanan also propose a rule to lengthen *i* when it is stressed, as in *sulphuric* and *credulity*. We know that *sulphur* cannot have an underlying long vowel in its final syllable, because otherwise it would be stressed there. Its underlying form must be /səlfɪr/. However, the stressed vowels of *sulphuric* and *credulity* seem to be the same as in *reduce*. We propose that the rule in question is actually a tensing and lengthening rule, given in (14).

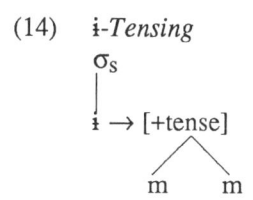

(14)   *i*-Tensing

σ$_s$

i → [+tense]

m   m

We now summarize the derivations for tense back vowels in (15), which gives the derivation of the stressed vowels of *verbose, lose, profound, argue, profundity,* and *reduce* in the respective columns.

(15) underlying   /ō/   /o/   /ɪ̄/   /ɪ/   /ɪ/C   /ʌ/
      (4a)   —   u   ʌ   —   —   ɪ
      (4b)   ō   —   ɑ   —   —   —
      i-Lowering (10) —   —   —   —   ɔC   —
      i-Tensing (14)   —   —   —   ī   —   —
      y-Insertion (12) —   —   —   yɪ   —   yɪ
      (5)   ow   uw   ɑw   yɪw   —   yɪw
      i-Rounding (11) —   —   —   yuw   —   yuw

The fact that *y*-Insertion applies to both tense and lax *i* explains an otherwise curious fact: the vowel *yuw* of *reduce* alternates with ə in *reduction*, but often it remains unaltered in the environment of various laxing rules. Consider *cubic, musical, beautify,* for example. Where *yuw* alternates with ə, we propose an underlying /ə/. Where there is no alternation, we have an underlying lax *i*, which does not undergo Vowel Shift, but does undergo *y*-Insertion, Diphthongization, and *i*-Rounding, so that the results of the two underlying representations are identical, as shown in the fourth and sixth columns of (15).

7.1.2 [oy]

There is one diphthong that we have not yet accounted for: [oy]. *SPE* constructed an ingenious argument that the underlying form of this diphthong is the tense, low, front, round vowel /$\bar{æ}$/. They propose this because independently needed rules convert this to [ɒy] without the need for additional rules. In their version, Vowel Shift is restricted to vowels that agree in backness and roundness. Accordingly, Vowel Shift does not affect /$\bar{æ}$/. Diphthongization supplies it with [y] because it is a front vowel. The final result is achieved by applying Backness Adjustment, introduced at the end of this section in (18).

There is only one flaw to this argument. English has no front round vowels phonetically and no other front round vowels underlyingly. The first objection relates to the abstractness of *SPE* phonology that we discussed in section 1.2 of Chapter 1. The second objection comes from universal grammar. The phonological inventory of a language may contain front rounded vowels. However, when we look at the languages of the world, we find that, if a language has only one front rounded vowel, it is always high [ü]. If a language has two such vowels, they are high [ü] and mid [ö]. No language has a low, front, round vowel without having a mid and high front round vowel also. Assuming that underlying inventories are governed by the same constraints as phonological inventories,[9] it is highly unlikely that the *SPE* underlying representation for [oy] can be correct.

A second objection is that *SPE* may have transcribed the diphthong [oy] incorrectly. According to Hoard (1972, 124) the first part of this diphthong is mid [oy] rather than low [ɒy]. Since Halle & Mohanan allow Vowel Shift to apply to all long vowels, even when they disagree in backness and rounding, they can derive a diphthong [oy] only from an underlying low vowel. Halle & Mohanan would derive the form [öy] from *SPE*'s underlying /$\bar{æ}$/, if this were incorporated into their system. A special rule would then be needed to make the first part of the diphthong back, since Backness Adjustment affects only low vowels. This solution is open to the same objection as *SPE*'s: there would be only one front rounded vowel in the underlying vowel system of English and it would be the low one.

Halle & Mohanan consider two possibilities for the vowel underlying [oy], neither of which has so far been exploited. They are /$\bar{ü}$/ and /$\bar{u}$/. The choice of /$\bar{ü}$/ is more straightforward, since it would undergo Vowel Shift to /$\bar{o}$/.

---

[9] Undoubtedly the lexical level, in the sense of (3b) in Chapter 2, is the appropriate level for determining the phonological inventory.

Diphthongization would produce /ȫy/ and Backness Adjustment (their Diphthong Backing) would produce [ōy], the correct output if you believe that the diphthong begins with a low vowel. This solution entails adding a high front rounded vowel to the system, which is in line with the distribution of front rounded vowels across languages but highly marked in view of the fact that its back counterpart, /u/, would not be an underlying vowel in the system.

The other choice is /u/. Vowel Shift and Diphthongization produce /ɒw/. This must somehow be exempted from Backness Adjustment,[10] and a special rule must be added to front the glide. Halle & Mohanan note that it is not necessary to unround the glide also, since it is generally round phonetically. Halle & Mohanan do not make a clear choice on the matter but Durand (1990, 125), in his review of this material, opts for /u/ as the vowel underlying the diphthong [oy]. We may tentatively adopt this solution for completeness.

It can be noted that Fidelholtz & Browne (1971) made the quite radical suggestion that the underlying representation of [oy] should be /oy/. This is radical because, in the context of *SPE* theory and most subsequent generative phonology, all English diphthongs are derived from underlying simple tense vowels. In Chapter 2, section 2.3.3, we mentioned three sources of evidence that simple vowels underlie diphthongs. One was syllabification. When [oy] is followed by another vowel, the vowel and the glide of [oy] are syllabified together as a unit. This syllabification is easy to understand if [oy] is an underlying simple vowel when syllabification occurs on stratum 1. If [oy] were from an underlying sequence of vowel plus glide in this situation, the glide would be syllabified with the following vowel by the Onset Principle of Chapter 3, section 3.1. Fidelholtz & Browne's underlying /oy/ would have difficulty explaining syllabifications like *Toy.o.ta, voy.age, loy.al*.[11]

7.1.3 Another tensing rule

In Chapter 6, section 6.6 we discussed C*i*V Tensing, which operates on stratum 1. In this subsection we introduce a second general tensing rule, Prevocalic Tensing. As its name suggests, it tenses a vowel before another vowel. We follow *SPE* in ordering this rule before Vowel Shift, in contrast to Halle & Mohanan

---

[10] Halle & Mohanan's Diphthong Backing would not affect this segment, since it only affects front vowels. Our more general rule (18) and this exemption are needed for dialects that have the more general Backness Adjustment as we have formulated it.

[11] Actually, they claim that such syllabifications, though normal, are "quite contrary to the normal pattern of syllabification in English" (1971, 164–5), without revealing what they believe to be "normal patterns of syllabification in English."

   Notice that we cannot allow resyllabification to apply to the derived form [oy], or we will get *To.yo.ta. This is consistent with the general lack of resyllabification on stratum 2.

(1985, 100), who order it later, and collapse it with another tensing rule, Stem-final Tensing. These two rules cannot be collapsed in our system, since Stem-final Tensing is ordered after Vowel Shift. We will postpone discussion of Stem-final Tensing until section 7.7.

Prevocalic Tensing is motivated on the basis of examples like those in (16).

(16) a. v*a*ry, v*a*rious, v*a*riation b. var*i*ety
    notor*i*ous   notor*i*ety
    anx*i*ous   anx*i*ety
    man*i*ac   man*i*acal
    simultan*e*ous   simultan*e*ity

  c. algebr*a*   d. algebr*a*ic
    formul*a*   formul*a*ic

In (16a), the italicized vowels are tense because they precede another vowel (except for *vary*, whose final vowel undergoes Stem-final Tensing, section 7.7). The corresponding vowels are also tense in (16b), but here they have undergone Vowel Shift (except for *simultaneity*) and Diphthongization. In (16c) the italicized vowels are lax and reduced, but the corresponding vowels in (16d) are tense and have undergone Vowel Shift. We therefore propose the rule of Prevocalic Tensing in (17).

(17) *Prevocalic Tensing*
    $\begin{bmatrix} -\text{cons} \\ -\text{back} \end{bmatrix} \rightarrow [+\text{tense}]/\underline{\quad} [-\text{cons}]$

If (17) is ordered before Vowel Shift, the facts of (16) are easily explained. Recall that Vowel Shift (4) applies only to stressed vowels. Therefore, the output of Prevocalic Tensing in (16a) does not undergo Vowel Shift. But the corresponding vowels in (16b) are stressed on stratum 1, and undergo Prevocalic Tensing and Vowel Shift on stratum 2. For (16c, d) we assume an underlying [æ]. This is ineligible to undergo Stem-final Tensing in (16c) (see section 7.7) because it is low, and so it is reduced to [ə]. In (16d), however, it undergoes Prevocalic Tensing and Vowel Shift. For *simultaneity,* we assume an underlying /i/ for the italicized position, but assume that the morpheme *simultane-* is an exception to Vowel Shift.

One final detail needs to be clarified at this point. The result of applying our rules so far to the underlying vowels /i/ and /ĭ/ is [æy] and [ɑw] respectively. However, the former is phonetically [ɑy] (as in *divine*) for most speakers and the latter is [æw] (as in *profound*) for many. To achieve these phonetic outputs, *SPE* (189) suggested a rule which we call Backness Adjustment, and state in (18).

(18)   Backness Adjustment
$$\begin{bmatrix} V \\ +\text{low} \\ \alpha\text{back} \end{bmatrix} \rightarrow [-\alpha\text{back}] / \underline{\qquad} \begin{bmatrix} -\text{cons} \\ -\text{syl} \end{bmatrix}$$

The only phonetically tense vowels that we have not yet treated are the [ā] of *balm* and the [ō] of *baud*. We assume that these are derived from underlying vowels /ɑ/ and /ɔ/ respectively. These are tensed by a rule of *a/o*-Tensing given in Chapter 8, section 8.1.5. In addition the vowel of *baud* is lowered by *o*-Lowering (8). All these rules are postlexical. One final vowel is that of *bomb*. We assume the underlying representation [ɒ], with a rule of ɒ-Unrounding for those dialects where *bomb* has a nonround vowel. This rule is also postlexical, and we return to these rules in Chapter 8.

7.1.4   Summary

To summarize this section, we give a chart of the underlying vowel system of English, following Halle & Mohanan's treatment, substituting symbols where necessary to conform to the notation used here.

	$\begin{bmatrix} -\text{back} \\ -\text{round} \end{bmatrix}$			$\begin{bmatrix} +\text{back} \\ -\text{round} \end{bmatrix}$			$\begin{bmatrix} +\text{back} \\ +\text{round} \end{bmatrix}$		
	[+tense]		[−tense]	[+tense]		[−tense]	[+tense]		[−tense]
$\begin{bmatrix} +\text{high} \\ -\text{low} \end{bmatrix}$	/i/	divine	/ɪ/ bit	/ɨ/	profound	/ɨ/ cube	/u/	boy	/ʊ/ pull
$\begin{bmatrix} -\text{high} \\ -\text{low} \end{bmatrix}$	/e/	serene	/ɛ/ bet	/ʌ/	reduce	/ə/ but	/o/	shoot	/ɔ/ baud
$\begin{bmatrix} -\text{high} \\ +\text{low} \end{bmatrix}$	/æ̃/	sane	/æ/ bat	——		/ɑ/ balm	/ō/	cone	/ɒ/ bomb

Table 1. The English underlying vowel system

7.2   Velar Softening

Another rule that lends some support to Vowel Shift as a synchronic rule of English is Velar Softening. This rule interacts with certain other rules and constraints in interesting ways. Velar Softening is responsible for alternations such as those in (19).

(19) *velar stop*   *coronal strident*
      critic, critical   criticize
      clinic, clinical   clinician
      medicate, medical   medicine
      matrix   matrices
      intellect   intelligent
      fungus, fungal   fungi
      analog, analogous   analogical, analogy
      legal, legality   legislate

The rule of Velar Softening can be formulated as in (20).

(20) *Velar Softening*

$$\begin{Bmatrix} k \rightarrow s \\ g \rightarrow j \end{Bmatrix} / \underline{\hspace{1cm}} \begin{bmatrix} -\text{cons} \\ -\text{low} \\ -\text{back} \end{bmatrix}$$

This rather simple formalization is achieved only if Velar Softening is ordered before Vowel Shift. If ordered after Vowel Shift, Velar Softening would have to be triggered by a set of vowels that is very difficult to capture in terms of distinctive features, namely [ɑy, ɪ, iy, ɛ], or, as Halle (1977, 615) put it, "before any front high vowel, before a lax mid vowel, and before the diphthong [ɑy]." Thus, considerable simplification of the overall grammar is achieved by this ordering.

7.3 Palatalization

In many languages, coronal obstruents are palatalized before high front vowels. In English, in fast speech, palatalization occurs before the high front glide [y], as shown in (21) (Halle & Mohanan's examples 1985, 85).

(21)   a.   miss you   →   [mɪšyə]
       b.   got you   →   [gɒčə]
       c.   did you   →   [dɪǰə]

It is interesting to notice that this process does not take place before the high front vowels in English (some examples are Halle & Mohanan's).

(22) a. miss it   → *[mɪšɪt]
      b. miss Eve   → *[mɪšiv]
      c. got it   → *[gɒčɪt]
      d. got even   → *[gɒčivən]
      e. did it   → *[dǰɪt]
      f. did eat   → *[dǰit]

Palatalization also applies word internally, as the examples in the right column of (23) show.

(23) a. express   expression
      b. supervise   supervision
      c. gas   gaseous
      d. space   spacial
      e. confuse   confusion
      f. office   official
      g. artifice   artificial, artificiality
      h. presidency   presidential

If we assume that the same[12] process is at work here as in (21), it seems that there must be a glide [y] following the alternating coronal obstruents in the right column of (23) at the time that Palatalization applies, and that this glide must be followed by a vowel. In fact, such a glide does not appear phonetically in any of these forms. The evidence for the glide is indirect. This devolves from the fact that Palatalization does not occur if a coronal obstruent is followed by the vowel [i] followed by another vowel, as shown in (24).

(24) invidious   *[ɪn'vɪ̌jiəs]
      Poinsettia *[pɔyn'sɛčiə]
      Kantian   *['kɑnčiən]
      accordion   *[ə'kɔřjiən]

If the vowel following the glide is stressed, there are two possibilities. If the stressed vowel is /u/, Palatalization does not take place, as shown in (25) (from *SPE*, 230).

---

12 In (21) the process is postlexical, since it applies to phrases. We assume that the same rule can appear at different contiguous levels of the grammar, following Halle & Mohanan (1985, 58).

(25) a. endure *[ɪnˈjur]
     b. ensue *[ɪnˈšu]
     c. resume *[rɪˈžum]
     d. perpetuity *[ˌpərpɪˈčuɪtɪ]
     e. tune *[ˈčun]

However for *artificiality* (23g), and similar examples like *consequentiality, essentiality, Christianity,* Palatalization does take place when the following syllable is stressed. We can account for this by appealing to distinct syllabifications for these words. Recall from Chapter 3 that we proposed a constraint that disallows a sequence of a consonant plus /y/ in syllable onsets (26 of Chapter 3). This constraint was proposed to account for the peculiar distribution of superficial CyV initial clusters in English: such an onset occurs only when the vowel is /u/. Therefore, we assumed that underlying the phonetic sequence [yuw] is the underlying vowel /ʌ/, which undergoes Vowel Shift, *y*-Insertion, Diphthongization, and *i*-Rounding to produce [yuw]. In all such sequences, the *y* is inserted and not underlying. There is no constraint against syllabifying Cʌ at stratum 1, and such a sequence is necessarily syllabified with a syllable-initial consonant because of the Onset Principle (2 of Chapter 3). The rule of *y*-Insertion does not change this syllabification, so that, at stratum 2, we get syllable-initial clusters of the form [σCyu...]. If there is an underlying sequence C*y*, the consonant and *y* are necessarily syllabified in different syllables because of the constraint (26) of Chapter 3. Therefore, at the time Palatalization is to apply, *artificiality* and *perpetuity* have distinct syllable structures, as shown in (26). Since these structures are derived at stratum 2, the *y* in *perpetuity* is inserted by *y*-Insertion.

(26) a. arti[σfɪs][σyæ]l + ity
     b. per[σpɛ][σtyu] + ity

Therefore, we can formulate Palatalization as in (27).

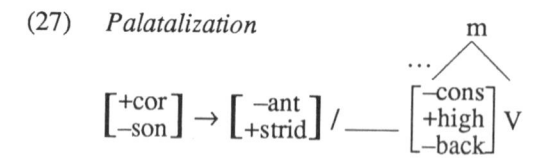

(27) *Palatalization*

$$\begin{bmatrix} +\text{cor} \\ -\text{son} \end{bmatrix} \rightarrow \begin{bmatrix} -\text{ant} \\ +\text{strid} \end{bmatrix} / \underline{\quad} \overset{m}{\overbrace{\begin{bmatrix} -\text{cons} \\ +\text{high} \\ -\text{back} \end{bmatrix} V}}$$

Condition: the consonant to be palatalized is not initial in a foot.

The mora dominating the glide and the following vowel indicates that these two segments must belong to the same mora (although other material may precede in the same mora, as shown by the ellipsis). This permits Palatalization in *perpetual*, since the relevant mora is [tyu], but prevents it in *invidious*, where [di] and the following vowel belong to separate moras. The condition states that the consonant to be palatalized not be foot initial, which blocks Palatalization in *residue* and *perpetuity*. This condition was suggested in section 6.8 of Chapter 6, where we argued against a reformulation of Palatalization in terms of resyllabification.

It should be noted that Palatalization does not fit into any of the categories of prosodic rules developed by Nespor & Vogel and discussed in Chapter 5. That is, it is not a domain span rule, nor a domain limit rule, nor a domain juncture rule. Within words it applies primarily within the domain of the foot, although in cases like *artificiality* the rule applies at the boundary of two feet.

We have noted that Palatalization applies also if an appropriate consonant is followed by a glide *y* that has been inserted by *y*-Insertion (12). This is shown by the right column in (28). Palatalization does not apply in the left column of (28) because of the condition that the consonant in question not be foot initial.

(28)   a.   perpetuity   perpetual
         b.   residue   residual
         c.   constitute   constitutive

This allows us to establish the ordering of *y*-Insertion before Palatalization.

As we mentioned, the *y* that conditions Palatalization never appears as such in phonetic representations in the word internal cases. In most of the examples in (23) the glide is deleted. We can capture this in terms of a rule of *y*-Deletion (29). Unlike Dialectal *y*-Deletion (13), this rule applies in all dialects.

(29)   *y-Deletion* (Domain span: applies within the foot.)

$$y \rightarrow \emptyset / \begin{bmatrix} +\text{cor} \\ -\text{ant} \end{bmatrix} \underline{} V$$

This rule deletes a glide after any alveopalatal consonant when followed by a vowel. However, in one case in (23), *artificiality*, the glide becomes a vowel phonetically. We can account for this case with a rule of *y*-Vocalization that turns *y* into a vowel when a stressed vowel follows. In moraic terms this means moving /y/ from the onset of one syllable to the preceding mora, where it is interpreted as syllabic. We give this rule in (30).

(30)   y-*Vocalization*

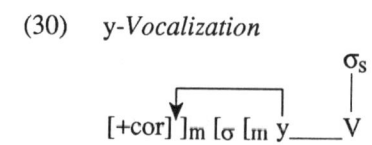

$$[+\text{cor}]_m\ [_\sigma\ [_m\ y\ \underline{\quad}\ \overset{\sigma_s}{V}$$

If y-Vocalization is ordered before y-Deletion, we get vocalization appropriately in *artificiality*. In *artificial,* where the vowel following the glide is unstressed, y is not vocalized, but is deleted by y-Deletion.

This establishes the ordering in (31).

(31)   y-Insertion (12)
        Palatalization (27)
        y-Vocalization (30)
        y-Deletion (29)

We claim that these rules apply on stratum 2. They cannot apply cyclically on stratum 1, because in that case y-Deletion would apply on the *artificial* cycle before the attachment of the suffix *-ity*. It is only with the attachment of *-ity* that the conditions for y-Vocalization are met. This result is ensured by delaying these rules until the postcyclic word level.

Halle & Mohanan, who argue for four lexical strata in English, cite the nonapplication of y-Deletion in compounds as evidence for their claim that compounding is done on their stratum 3, since y-Deletion does not affect compounds. In support of this, they note that *fish university* is pronounced [... šyu ...] not *[... šu ...]. However, there are other ways of achieving this result without proliferating lexical strata. One is simply to restrict y-Deletion to foot-internal application, as we have done. This automatically blocks its application in compounds.

7.3.1 *Spirantization*

In the examples of (23) we had only continuants in the left column, but Palatalization as formulated in (27) applies to all coronal obstruents. In this subsection we investigate its application to noncontinuants. We find two classes of cases. In the first, exemplified in (32a), underlying stops in the left column alternate with palatal fricatives in the right column. In the second, (32b), underlying stops alternate with palatal affricates. Palatalization (27) does not change the value of the feature [continuant] of segments to which it applies; consequently it predicts the cases in (32b) but not those in (32a). We can obtain (32a) if the stem-final *t* is first converted to *s*, by a rule we call Spirantization (33).

(32) a. delete   deletion
          decide   decision
          part   partial
          react   reaction
          Egypt   Egyptian
          exempt   exemption
          extend   extension
      b. beast   bestial
          digest   digestion

(33) *Spirantization*
$$\begin{bmatrix}-\text{son}\\+\text{cor}\end{bmatrix} \rightarrow \begin{bmatrix}+\text{cont}\\+\text{strid}\end{bmatrix} / \left\{\begin{matrix}[+\text{son}]\\[-\text{cont}]\end{matrix}\right\} \underline{\quad} y$$

This rule converts *t, d* to the corresponding fricatives *s, z* when *y* follows. This rule precedes Palatalization, which applies to its output to produce the forms of (32a).

Spirantization does not apply if *y* is inserted by *y*-Insertion (12). This is shown by the examples in (34).

(34) habit   habitual   *[həbtšuəl]
      grade   gradual   *[græžuəl]

This establishes the ordering in (35).

(35) Spirantization (33)
      y-Insertion (12)
      Palatalization (27)

Palatalization applies to the output of Velar Softening, as shown by the examples in (36).

(36) music   musician
      Greek   Grecian
      electric electrician

This establishes the ordering in (37).

(37) Velar Softening (20)
      Palatalization (27)

7.3.2 SPE *on* right *and* righteous

As formulated in (33), Spirantization turns dental stops into the corresponding fricatives when *y* follows as long as the segment preceding the stop is not a fricative. With a fricative in that position, Spirantization is blocked. For example in *question*, the *t* is ineligible for Spirantization because *s* precedes. Instead, the *t* undergoes Palatalization to produce the form [kwɛsčən], not *[kwɛsšən]. In *righteous*, we expect spirantization of the *t*, given an underlying representation /rīt + yəs/. However, Spirantization does not apply. How can we explain this?

SPE proposed an ingenious solution. Their underlying form for *right* is /rɪxt/. The velar fricative blocks Spirantization of *t*, which then undergoes Palatalization and other rules to give the form [rāyčəs]. This analysis explained one other anomaly of *righteous* in their system. Their underlying representation for *righteous* contains a vowel in the position where we have *y:* /rixt + i + ɔs/. We would expect Trisyllabic Laxing to apply to the first syllable if it contained a tense vowel: /rīt + i + ɔs/. Therefore, in the *SPE* system, the abstract underlying form with /x/ solves two problems: the failure of both Trisyllabic Laxing and Spirantization to apply to *righteous*. However, this result comes at the cost of positing an underlying segment that does not appear phonetically in English utterances.

With the argument that the suffixes *-ion, -ious, -ial,* and *-ian* have initial *y* rather than a vowel (Rubach 1984a, 24, 42ff), the argument from the failure of Trisyllabic Laxing disappears. The failure of Spirantization in *righteous* is now the only fact that follows from the posited underlying /x/. In view of the relative abstractness of this solution, we should perhaps seek alternative explanations.

Borowsky (1986, 53ff) suggests a solution in terms of underspecification. Segments that show an alternation between *t* and *s* are unspecified underlyingly for the feature [continuant]. She states Spirantization as a feature filling rule that specifies a segment [+continuant] in the environment of (33); otherwise it is specified [−continuant] by a default rule. The restriction that the rule does not apply after a fricative is explained in terms of a principle of autosegmental phonology that prevents the marking of identical features on adjacent segments.[13] (For example, if two adjacent vowels have the same tone, they must be both linked to the same tone on the tonal tier; they cannot both be individually marked for the same tone.) For *righteous,* she proposes that the final segment of *right* is (irregularly) marked [−continuant], which cannot be changed by Spirantization

---

[13] This principle is known as the Obligatory Contour Principle (OCP). The idea is that it enforces a contour on each autosegmental tier, disallowing a sequence of identical specifications. It was first introduced by Leben (1973) to account for the distribution of tones in Mende illustrated in (10) of Chapter 1.

interpreted as a feature filling rule only. Borowsky's analysis is based on the assumption that Spirantization is a rule of a cyclic stratum which is constrained by the Strict Cycle Condition (section 6.5 of Chapter 6). Since we are assuming that Spirantization is on stratum 2, which is noncyclic, this solution is not available to us. It is clear that much work needs to be done on the role of underspecification. Borowsky suggests that a great many of the effects attributed to strict cyclicity may be derivable from underspecification and a restriction of all lexical rules to a feature filling function. However, it is not clear that all lexical rules can be feature filling only. The rule of Velar Softening, for example, changes a number of features of underlying velar stops and would seem to be very difficult to reanalyze as a feature filling rule.

Alternatively, we might simply suggest that the morpheme *right* is an exception to Spirantization. It may not be possible to decide between these alternatives without making a full study of the range of exceptional cases.

7.4 Types of rule ordering

We can now return more systematically to some terminology that we introduced in Chapter 2 in connection with rule ordering. If two phonological rules are ordered in such a way that the first creates the condition for the second to apply, we say that they are in a FEEDING order. (This terminology is due to Kiparsky 1968a.) We can illustrate this with the derivation of *Grecian* in (38).

(38) start of stratum 2   /grek + yən/
      Velar Softening   /gres + yən/
      (Vowel Shift   /gris + yən/)
      Palatalization   /grišyən/
      y-Deletion   [grišən]

In (38), the prior application of Velar Softening produces the segment /s/, to which Palatalization can apply to produce /š/. That is, Velar Softening FEEDS Palatalization. (Vowel Shift intervenes between the two rules, but it is irrelevant to their interaction; this is why we have put that line in parentheses.) Had Palatalization been ordered before Velar Softening, the former would not have been able to apply, and we would obtain the incorrect form *[grisyən]. This shows that the ordering must be as in (38).

Another relationship that can characterize a pair of ordered rules is a BLEEDING relationship. This occurs when the first rule destroys the environment that would permit the second rule to apply. An example appears in the ordering of *y*-

Vocalization before *y*-Deletion in (31) in the derivation of *artificiality*. As we observed, vocalization of *y* in this form prevents *y*-Deletion from applying (it BLEEDS *y*-Deletion), though *y*-Deletion would apply if it were ordered first, producing the incorrect form *[ɑrtɪftšælɪtɪ]. In fact, *y*-Vocalization and *y*-Deletion in the reverse order would also be in a bleeding relationship. Whichever rule applies first will bleed the other. This is known as a MUTUALLY BLEEDING relationship.

The opposite of feeding order is called COUNTERFEEDING order. This term and COUNTERBLEEDING, to be discussed next, require some care if they are to be understood properly. Counterfeeding order is best introduced by way of example. Consider the derivation of *habitual*, where the relevant rules are given in the order we established in (35).

(39)   start of stratum 2   /hæ'bɪt + ɨ + æl/
       Spirantization   ——
       y-Insertion   /hæ'bɪt + yɨ + æl/
       Palatalization   /hæ'bɪčyɨæl/
       y-Deletion   /hæ'bɪčɨæl/
       other rules   [hə'bɪčuəl]

Spirantization is not applicable to the initial form, because it affects *t* only when *y* follows. The next rule, *y*-Insertion, inserts a *y* in the correct position for Spirantization to take place; however, Spirantization has been passed in the ordering, and so does not take place. Had *y*-Insertion been ordered before Spirantization, the latter rule could have applied. This would have been a feeding order, and would produce the incorrect result *[həbɪšuəl]. Therefore, we must apply the rules in the counterfeeding order given in (39). A counterfeeding order is therefore one where the reverse order would be feeding.

The opposite of a bleeding order is a COUNTERBLEEDING order. Consider Palatalization and *y*-Deletion, which must apply in that order in derivations such as (39). In the reverse order, *y*-Deletion would bleed Palatalization, producing an incorrect *[həbɪtuəl]. This would be a bleeding order. But the actual order is counterbleeding, because the reverse order would be bleeding.

It is important to see that the same order of rules can have different feeding and bleeding relations in different derivations. A simple example is Velar Softening and Vowel Shift, which we have argued must apply in that order. Consider the derivations of *medicate* and *criticize* in (40). In *medicate*, Velar Softening isn't applicable because the velar *k* is followed by a low vowel, and Velar Softening affects velars only when they are followed by nonlow vowels.

(40) Start of stratum 2   /mɛdɪk + æt/   /krɪtɪk + iz/
    Velar Softening   ———   s
    Vowel Shift   e   ǣ
    other rules   ['mɛdɪ,keyt]   ['krɪtɪ,sayz]
                              (counterfeeding)   (counterbleeding)

Vowel Shift subsequently changes the vowel to nonlow *e;* however, Velar Softening is no longer applicable. This is therefore a counterfeeding order: in the reverse order, Vowel Shift would feed Velar Softening. However, in *criticize,* Velar Softening is applicable to the underlying form, changing *k* to *s.* Then Vowel Shift applies, changing the underlying high vowel *i* to a low vowel *æ.* This low vowel would block Velar Softening; however, Velar Softening has been passed and can no longer be blocked. Therefore, this is a counterbleeding order. In the theory of phonology that we are operating with here, there is a single ordering of the rules as part of the grammar. The rules are applicable in this order to all underlying representations. However, feeding and bleeding relations may differ from one derivation to another owing to the varied nature of these underlying representations.

7.5 Other word-level processes

In Chapter 6 we discussed a rule of *n*-Deletion, (20) in that chapter, which we said was restricted to stratum 2 by the Strict Cycle Condition. Recall that this rule accounts for alternations such as *damn* vs *damnation.* Similar alternations can be found with a stem-final sequence of a voiced noncoronal stop and a nasal, in either order, given in (41).

(41) a. sign, signing   signature
        malign, maligning   malignant
     b. bomb, bombing   bombard
        iamb   iambic
     c. long   longer, longest

We can account for these alternations with three more word-level rules. *SPE* and others (Halle & Mohanan 1985) assume underlying forms such as /sign/, /bɒmb/, /lɒng/ for *sign, bomb,* and *long.* This motivates two additional rules. The failure of these rules to apply before stratum 1 suffixes, as in the right column of (41), shows that they cannot apply at stratum 1. Halle & Mohanan (1985, 96) propose Prenasal *g*-Deletion to account for (41a). This rule is of some theoretical interest because, besides deleting the *g* of *sign,* etc., it also lengthens the preceding vowel. Halle & Mohanan build this into their statement of the rule. However, this phenomenon, known as COMPENSATORY LENGTHENING, is quite common in languages of the world: a consonant is lost, and an adjacent vowel is lengthened to compensate for it. Ingria (1980) has proposed that, when an element is deleted from a syllable coda, its metrical structure is retained, to be reassociated with the preceding syllabic nucleus, producing a long segment. This operation, part of what he calls the Empty Node Convention, is reformulated in moraic terms in (42).

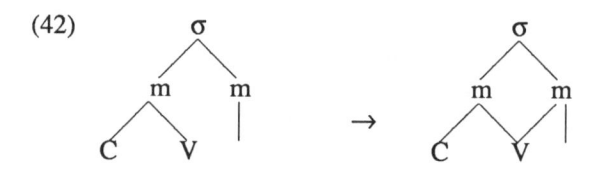

(42)

Accepting this convention, we can formulate Prenasal *g*-Deletion as simply the deletion of *g,* with compensatory lengthening following automatically from (42). We state the rule in (43).

(43)   *Prenasal* g-*Deletion*
        g → Ø / V ___ n]

Prenasal *g*-Deletion deletes the *g* in [sign] and [[sign] ing], since in both these forms the sequence *gn* appears before a boundary at stratum 2. This is because the suffix *-ing* is added at stratum 2. In *signature,* the suffix *-ature* is added at stratum 1, and Bracket Erasure (13 in Chapter 6) erases the internal brackets at the end of stratum 1. Because Prenasal *g*-Deletion is a rule of stratum 2, the boundary is no longer there to condition the rule.

Evidently, Prenasal *g*-Deletion must precede Vowel Shift, because Prenasal *g*-Deletion gives rise to a long tense /iː/ which must be vowel shifted to [ɑy] in words like *sign*. This is a feeding relation. Notice that (42) does not affect any other rules discussed here. Our other deletion rules, *y*-Deletion and Dialectal *y*-Deletion, affect segments in onsets, and so do not trigger compensatory lengthening.

As we mentioned in Chapter 2, the velar nasal ŋ is somewhat marginal in English. While *m* and *n* can clearly be motivated as underlying segments, it is not so for ŋ. *SPE* therefore derives all instances of velar nasals from underlying sequences of *n* plus a velar stop. The voiceless stop *k* is retained after assimilation, while the voiced *g* is deleted under certain conditions. First, we need a rule of nasal assimilation. In terms of autosegmental theory and underspecification, we can propose that nasal consonants are not specified for place features in underlying representations when they are followed by a stop. They receive their value for place by the spreading of the place features of the following stop. We can formulate the rule as in (44). This is a generalization of rule (4a) in Chapter 2.[14]

(44) *Nasal Assimilation*

$$[+\text{nasal}] \rightarrow \begin{bmatrix} \alpha\text{cor} \\ \beta\text{ant} \end{bmatrix} / \underline{\quad} \begin{bmatrix} -\text{son} \\ -\text{cont} \\ \alpha\text{cor} \\ \beta\text{ant} \end{bmatrix}$$

Now we need a rule to delete the final *g* from *long* and the final *b* from *bomb*. In (4b) of Chapter 2 we gave a rule to delete *g* at the end of a morpheme. Halle & Mohanan generalize this to what they call Noncoronal Deletion, which we can express as (45).

(45) *Noncoronal Deletion*

$$\begin{bmatrix} -\text{son} \\ +\text{voice} \\ -\text{cor} \end{bmatrix} \rightarrow \emptyset / [+\text{nasal}] \underline{\quad}]$$

Obviously, Nasal Assimilation (44) must precede Noncoronal Deletion, a counterbleeding relation.

We conclude this section by listing the word-level rules discussed so far in this chapter, along with all the crucial orderings indicated by the usual device of curved lines. This is given in (46), overleaf.

7.6 Vowel Reduction

SPE assumed that all lax unstressed vowels were reduced to schwa [ə], and most subsequent authors on English phonology have followed suit. Halle & Mohanan (1985), for example, do not formulate a rule for vowel reduction, apparently accepting the *SPE* assumption. *SPE* assumed that [ə] was distinct from all other vowels of English and that it was not present in underlying representations. They did not concern themselves with the various contextual and dialectal realizations of reduced vowels. This is, however, an area of English phonology that requires

---

[14] We state this rule in linear terms both for simplicity and to account for the assimilation of the nasal to velar articulation before *h*. An autosegmental rule spreading the place features would not work, because *h* has no place features.

(46) Summary of Stratum 2 (postcyclic) rules

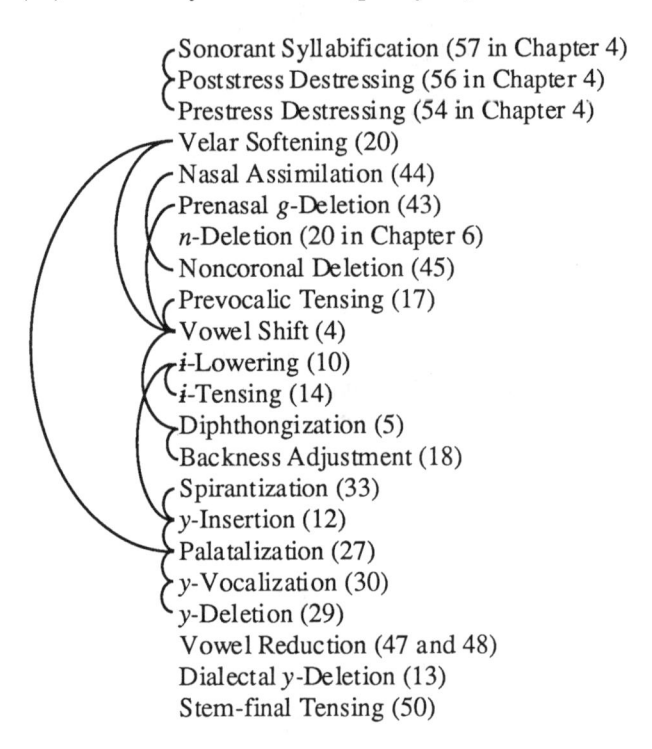

> Sonorant Syllabification (57 in Chapter 4)
> Poststress Destressing (56 in Chapter 4)
> Prestress Destressing (54 in Chapter 4)
> Velar Softening (20)
> Nasal Assimilation (44)
> Prenasal *g*-Deletion (43)
> *n*-Deletion (20 in Chapter 6)
> Noncoronal Deletion (45)
> Prevocalic Tensing (17)
> Vowel Shift (4)
> *i*-Lowering (10)
> *i*-Tensing (14)
> Diphthongization (5)
> Backness Adjustment (18)
> Spirantization (33)
> *y*-Insertion (12)
> Palatalization (27)
> *y*-Vocalization (30)
> *y*-Deletion (29)
> Vowel Reduction (47 and 48)
> Dialectal *y*-Deletion (13)
> Stem-final Tensing (50)

further study.

In Chapter 2 we argued that [ə] is an underlying vowel of English, because it patterns with the other lax (or checked) vowels in cases like *but*, where a final consonant is necessary to make an acceptable English word. We have also assumed tacitly that there are at least two reduction vowels in English, at least in certain varieties. Wells (1982, 167) notes that *Lenin* and *Lennon* form a minimal pair in RP, being pronounced respectively ['lɛnɪn] and ['lɛnən], and that *rabbit* ['ræbɪt] does not rhyme with *abbot* ['æbət] in this dialect. Also, our discussion of systematic phonemics in section 2.4 transcribed the unstressed vowels of *telegraphic* as [ɪ], not [ə], although the penultimate syllable of *telegraphy* has [ə]. These transcriptions were based on *Collins English Dictionary* (1979), which represents these reduction vowels systematically. For any dialect that has these two reduction vowels, the *SPE* treatment is inadequate.

Certain instances of unstressed [ɪ] may be due to assimilation. *SPE*'s example of *courage* and *courageous* may serve as a case in point. Taking these two forms together, we can construct an underlying representation /kəræỹ/, in the manner suggested in section 2.4. Although *SPE* gives the phonetic form ['kʌrəj̃] for *courage*, Collins gives it as ['kʌrɪj̃]. We may assume that this instance of unstressed [ɪ] is the result of assimilation to the following palatal consonant. To see why, we should compare this form to other forms where underlying [æː] comes to be reduced, such as *proclamation*. Taking this together with *proclaim*, we can construct the underlying form /proklæːm/. In this case underlying [æː] does reduce to [ə] when unstressed in *proclamation*. Here there is no palatal consonant for the reduced vowel to assimilate to. The situation is the same with *explain* [ɪkˈspleyn] and *explanation* [ˌɛkspləˈneyšən], with the underlying form /ɛksplæːn/.[15] All this suggests that we need three rules for vowel reduction: one assimilation rule and two context-free rules. We give the assimilation rule in (47).

(47) *Vowel Reduction and Assimilation*

$$\sigma_w \atop \begin{bmatrix} V \\ -\text{tense} \end{bmatrix} \rightarrow \iota / \underline{} \begin{bmatrix} C \\ +\text{cor} \\ -\text{ant} \end{bmatrix}$$

The context-free rules say that a vowel which is nonback and nonlow reduces to [ɪ]; otherwise all vowels reduce to [ə]. We formulate these two rules in (48).

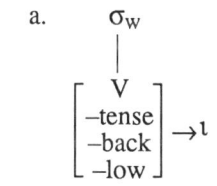

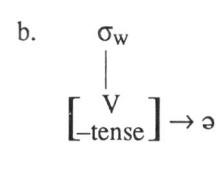

(48) *Vowel Reduction*
 a. $\sigma_w \atop \begin{bmatrix} V \\ -\text{tense} \\ -\text{back} \\ -\text{low} \end{bmatrix} \rightarrow \iota$
 b. $\sigma_w \atop \begin{bmatrix} V \\ -\text{tense} \end{bmatrix} \rightarrow \text{ə}$

---

[15] *Explain* and *proclaim* also require a special laxing rule that does the work of *SPE*'s Auxiliary Reduction Rule I. This rule applies at stratum 1, after the destressing rules. We give this special rule in (i). We also assume that the vowel loses a mora by Structure Preservation, since only tense vowels can be bimoraic at stratum 1.

(i) $\sigma_w \atop V \rightarrow [-\text{tense}] / \underline{}$

We do not have to specify any further features in (48b), because this rule will simply apply to all unstressed vowels that have not undergone (48a). The ordering of (48a) before (48b) in ensured by the ELSEWHERE CONDITION of Kiparsky (1973), which Kiparsky (1982a, 8) restates as (49).

(49) *Elsewhere Condition*
    Rules A, B in the same component apply disjunctively to a form Φ if and only if
    (i) The structural description of A (the special rule) properly includes the structural description of B (the general rule).
    (ii) The result of applying A to Φ is distinct from the result of applying B to Φ.
    In that case, A is applied first, and if it takes effect, then B is not applied.

7.7 Stem-final Tensing

The last rule we will discuss in this chapter is somewhat controversial—the rule of Stem-final Tensing. The statement of the rule is simple enough. We give Halle & Mohanan's statement in (50).

(50) *Stem-final Tensing*
$$\begin{bmatrix} V \\ -\text{low} \end{bmatrix} \rightarrow [+\text{tense}] \,/\, \underline{\quad} \,]$$

This rule tenses a nonlow vowel at the end of a constituent. It is this rule that is mainly responsible for the appearance of unreduced vowels in unstressed positions at the ends of words. This rule must follow Vowel Shift, since the resulting vowels are not shifted. It must furthermore precede Vowel Reduction (47) and (48) in order to bleed it in the relevant cases. Because of this ordering, the resulting tense vowels are not stressed, because stress is assigned at level 1. According to *SPE*, this rule is responsible for the tense vowels at the end of the nouns in (51).

(51) | | *light penult* | *long vowel in penult* | *consonant-final penult* |
|---|---|---|---|
| a. | buffalo | albino | commando |
| b. | broccoli | macaroni | chianti |
| c. | kinkajou | kikuyu | jujitsu |

The stress facts in (51) are exactly parallel to those of (31) of Chapter 4. Were the final vowels underlyingly tense in (51), we would expect them to be stressed (and vowel shifted); however, they are not.

The words of (51) are divided according to their final vowel. Since (50) tenses only nonlow vowels, we have no examples in (51) of æ or a. One unexplained gap is that there are no words ending in unstressed ɛ that would be tensed to e by (50). *SPE* makes use of this gap in explaining certain superficial exceptions to stress (such as *ellipse*) by giving them a final underlying ɛ that is deleted after the stress rules. This is to ensure that stress falls on the second syllable, rather than on the first, as would be expected from an underlying representation /elɪps/. We do not follow this, since we have discussed other ways of accounting for exceptional stress in section 4.8 of Chapter 4. In the case of *ellipse,* we would say that this word is an exception to Consonant Extrametricality. In any case, we should note that some dialects have a more restricted version of (50) that applies to back vowels only. Such a dialect is RP, in which final ɪ is not tensed. So RP has [sɪtɪ] for *city* while North American English, which formed the basis of *SPE*, has [sɪɾi]. (The focus here is on the final vowel, not the flap.)

The controversy we alluded to arises in Halle & Mohanan's treatment of final ɪ. They observe that this vowel is tensed in four environments: word finally, before inflection, stem finally in compounds, and before most level 2 suffixes. Therefore, we have the forms in (52), all with phonetic [i] at the end of the first stem.

(52) a. city
      b. cities
      c. city hall
      d. happiness

There is some variation in the application of this rule before level 2 suffixes. For example, there is generally no tensing before *-ful* and *-ly* in *beautiful, happily,* although some speakers do have tensing in *beautiful*. Halle & Mohanan claim to have found a dialect in which there is tensing in (52a, b, c) but not in (52d). In this (unidentified) dialect, their dialect C, they claim that rule (50) applies at their stratum 3, at which point bracket erasure has deleted the bracket that forms part of the environment for Tensing in (50), so that Tensing does not apply in *happiness* in this dialect. In their model, compounding applies on stratum 3 and inflection on stratum 4, so that these morphological operations follow Tensing (50). However, this proliferation of strata is by no means necessary to account for the facts of tensing. In fact, these additional strata result in a considerable complication of Halle & Mohanan's grammar, since they require a loop from stratum 3 to stratum 2 to allow compounds (e.g. [[air] [condition]) to provide the input to level 2 affixation (e.g., [[re [air] [condition]]]. This complication does not arise in our two-stratum model, in which compounding and regular inflection are included in stratum 2 with stratum 2 affixation.

Nonlow vowels other than [ɩ] seem to undergo Tensing (50) fairly regularly: we have *widowhood, ?hinduhood*, with tense vowels before the suffix *-hood*. It may be objected that the difference between tense and lax [o] in English is difficult to perceive, or even that the lax version of [o], [ɔ], does not exist in English (although this symbol is often used to represent the tense or lax low vowel that is more properly symbolized by [ɒ]). Furthermore examples of tensed stem-final [u] are difficult to construct; no such examples are in common use. As already noted, stem-final [ɛ] does not appear phonetically in English. The problem for tensing therefore seems to be restricted to stems ending in [ɩ]. The appearance of tensing also seems to depend heavily on the nature of the suffix: *babyhood* seems to require tense [i] at the end of the stem. Halle & Mohanan would seem to have difficulties with such forms if this is true of their dialect C. More research is clearly needed on the problem.

7.8 Exercises

1. The derivation of each word on the left demonstrates the ordering of the two rules on the right. Give the underlying form of the italicized portion of each word and show how the rules must be ordered by showing that the correct result is derived in the correct order but not in the opposite order. Classify the order as feeding, bleeding, counterfeeding, or counterbleeding.

    a. medi*ca*te   Velar Softening (20)
                              Vowel Shift (4)

    b. electri*ci*an   Velar Softening
                              Palatalization (27)

    c. artifi*ci*ality   *y*-Vocalization (30)
                              y-Deletion (29)

    d. ri*ng*   Nasal Assimilation (44)
                              Noncoronal Deletion (45)

    e. criti*ci*ze   Velar Softening
                              Vowel Shift

2. What is the underlying form of the italicized vowel in each of the following words? What rules does the vowel undergo in each case to give the phonetic form? Be sure to get the rules in the correct order.

   a. i. s*a*ne   ii. s*a*nity
   b. i. prof*ou*nd ii. prof*u*ndity
   c. i. red*u*ce   ii. red*u*ction
   d. i. c*o*ne   ii. c*o*nic
   e. i. c*u*be   ii. c*u*bic
   f. i. sulph*u*r   ii. sulph*u*ric
   g. i. m*a*n*i*ac ii. m*a*n*i*acal

3. Give a complete derivation of the following words, starting with the underived morphemes and applying all the relevant rules, both morphological and phonological. Be sure to get the rules in the correct order.

   a. invitation
   b. artificiality
   c. conceive
   d. resist
   e. wrote
   f. solidify

4. Explain why the italicized portion of each word on the right does not undergo the corresponding rule on the left. If the form does not meet the structural description of the rule, state precisely why.

   a. Trisyllabic Laxing (15 of Chapter 6)   cl*ea*rance

   b. Spirantization (33)   dige*sti*on

   c. Trisyllabic Laxing   t*ī*tánic

   d. Prenasal g-Deletion (43)   sig*n*ature

   e. Spirantization   habi*tu*al

   f. Palatalization (27)   en*d*ure

8 Postlexical phonology and conclusion

In this final chapter we will first consider aspects of the postlexical phonology, some of which have been discussed at various points in previous chapters. We will then discuss some examples that are problematic in our approach, and discuss some alternative proposals. Finally we will summarize the most important conclusions we have reached on English phonology in the lexical, metrical, and prosodic frameworks.

8.1 Postlexical phonology

As we discussed in Chapter 6, lexical rules are structure preserving. We defined this to mean that lexical rules do not introduce segments or segment types that do not form part of underlying representations. This idea needs some amplification here, since there is some controversy surrounding it. In particular, Borowsky (1986) argues that Structure Preservation constrains stratum 1 of the lexicon but not stratum 2. Her argument centres on the velar nasal. In Chapter 6 we claimed that the velar nasal is derived from an underlying alveolar (or unspecified) nasal by the stratum 2 rule of Nasal Assimilation (NA, rule 44 in Chapter 7). The following voiced velar consonant that the nasal assimilates to is sometimes deleted by Noncoronal Deletion (rule 45 in Chapter 7). This analysis follows Halle & Mohanan (1985) and ultimately *SPE*. In this analysis, the velar nasal is not an underlying segment of English, but is derived wherever it occurs by NA. Borowsky therefore claims that NA is not structure preserving, since the velar nasal is not underlying. From this she concludes that Structure Preservation turns off after stratum 1.

It seems to me that it is possible to reach a more interesting conclusion in this case. To see the question more clearly, contrast the velar nasal with the labiodental nasal [ɱ] that can appear before /f/, as in *emphasis, emphatic*. First observe that assimilation to a labiodental nasal is optional; a bilabial nasal is always possible in these environments. Second, whatever feature it is that distinguishes bilabials from labiodentals in English, it is not distinctive. There are bilabial stops but no labiodental stops; there are labiodental fricatives but no bilabial fricatives, and the labiodental nasal occurs only before a labiodental fricative. The velar nasal, by contrast, can occur where no velar consonant follows phonetically, as in *sing*. This means that the velar nasal can occur lexically but that the assimilation of [m] to [ɱ] can occur only postlexically. This latter process is not structure preserving. In contrast, the feature that distinguishes velars from other points of articulation is distinctive, since it is contrastive in stops, as in *pin, tin, kin*. This suggests a somewhat different formulation of Structure Preservation, which I give in (1).

(1)   *Structure Preservation (revised version)*
      Lexicon: Stratum 1: strict version: no nonphonemes may be produced by a rule.
                    Stratum 2: weaker version: no nondistinctive features may be introduced.
                    Postlexical: no structure preservation

With this formulation, we can consider that Structure Preservation holds of the entire lexicon, but in a weaker version at stratum 2 than at stratum 1. This is superior to Borowsky's claim that structure preservation does not hold at all at stratum 2. Her claim would allow labiodental nasals, aspiration, and other clearly allophonic processes to occur on stratum 2, which is undesirable.

8.1.1 Stop allophones

Considerations of Structure Preservation allow us to designate the rules that determine the allophones of the English stops, developed in Chapter 5, as postlexical. The rule that glottalizes English voiceless stops, rule (10) in Chapter 5, adds the feature [+constricted glottis] to those stops. The feature [±constricted glottis] does not serve to distinguish segments in English, so that this rule must be postlexical, since it is not structure preserving even in the weaker sense of stratum 2 in (1). Similarly, the rule of Aspiration, (17) in Chapter 5, adds the feature [+spread glottis], which does not serve to distinguish segments. This rule too must be postlexical.

The case of Alveopalatalization, rule (23) in Chapter 5, is less clear cut. As stated there, Alveopalatalization makes coronal stops nonanterior. But [±anterior] clearly is a distinctive feature of English consonants, as shown in Table 2 of Chapter 2. In particular, it is the only featural difference between [s] and [š] and between [z] and [ž]. In the case of the noncontinuants, [t] and [č] are distinguished by two features: [t] is nonstrident and anterior while [č] is strident and nonanterior. Alveopalatalization does not merge [t] with [č]; rather, it produces a segment which is nonstrident and nonanterior, which we might write as [t] This is reminiscent of the situation with the velar nasal, which is defined in terms of independently needed features. However, we assigned the rule of Nasal Assimilation to the lexical component, stratum 2, on the basis of its ordering properties (cf. the chart of rule orderings in 46 of Chapter 7). Intuitively, this seems right, because of its quasiphonemic status: it contrasts with other nasals in phonetic representations, as in *sin* vs *sing*. There is no argument for ordering Alveopalatalization before any lexical rule, and phonetically alveopalatal stops occur only in the environment that produces them; namely, with a following *r*. This strongly suggests postlexical status for Alveopalatalization.

The rule of Flapping, (62) in Chapter 5, is assigned to the postlexical component for a different reason. We did not formulate the rule in terms of features, but it could certainly be argued that Flapping adds [+sonorant] (and [+voice]) to an alveolar stop, and these are both distinctive features of English. For example, [sonorant] is the only feature which distinguishes [b] from [m] in the chart in Table 2 in Chapter 2. But Flapping is formulated to apply within the phonological utterance, which can be across words and even across sentences, as we showed in Chapter 5. Since lexical rules apply only within words, and not in larger syntactic constructions, Flapping cannot be a lexical rule.

8.1.2 *l-Velarization*

Beside the stops, we discussed a number of other allophonic rules in Chapter 5, which we now consider postlexical. One is *l*-Velarization, of which we gave several formulations, since it seems to depend on the dialect under consideration (section 5.2). In the dialect considered by Halle & Mohanan (1985, 65), [l] may be light at the end of the first member of a compound but dark in the same words within a phrase. They give the examples in (2).

(2) a. a whale edition   vs the whale and the shark
    b. the seal office   vs the seal offered a donut
        [l]   [ł]

They explain this in terms of a rule of *l*-Resyllabification that shifts *l* to the onset of a following vowel-initial word within compounds and before inflectional *-ing* as in *dealing*. They use this as part of their argument for four lexical strata in English.

This conclusion is questionable, however. First, *l*-Resyllabification is the *only* rule that Halle & Mohanan assign to stratum 4, making the motivation for this stratum rather tenuous. Second, there is good reason to doubt the existence of resyllabification rules in English. For example, in Chapter 6, section 6.8, we have argued against resyllabification as an explanation for vowel laxing and stop allophony in English. Given this, it is doubtful that there is a segment-specific resyllabification rule to account for light and dark [l].

Questioning Halle & Mohanan's division between compounds and phrases, Szpyra (1989, 197) claims that the domain of *l*-Resyllabification is the phonological phrase. According to her, the prosodic analyses of the forms in (2) are as in (3), based on the definition of phonological phrase given by Nespor & Vogel (1986, 168) which we cited as (39) in Chapter 5.

(3) a. (a whale edition)$_\phi$ (the whale)$_\phi$ (and the shark)$_\phi$
    b. (the seal office)$_\phi$ (the seal)$_\phi$ (offered)$_\phi$ (a donut)$_\phi$

This analysis accounts for the same facts as Halle & Mohanan's, without positing a lexicon of more than two strata. (In fact, Szpyra argues against any stratal distinction in the lexicon, a claim we will examine in section 8.2.) But given the availability of prosodic categories, we can dispense with *l*-Resyllabification altogether. In the dialect described by Halle & Mohanan, *l* is light before a vowel within the same phonological phrase, otherwise dark.

Gimson's (1962, 195ff) description of RP is at odds with Halle & Mohanan's description in a number of respects. He gives a number of cases where phrases have light *l*, as in (4).

(4) a. feel it   b. all over   c. fall out

Furthermore, syllabic *l* is normally dark, even before a vowel in a compound, as in (5).

(5) a. special edition   b. little Ann

While the distribution of clear and dark *l* needs further study, especially over various dialects, it seems clear that Halle & Mohanan's data do not justify a rule of *l*-Resyllabification or more than two lexical strata. The rule of *l*-Velarization is postlexical, since the phonological phrase, in terms of which we have reformulated the rule, is not available lexically. This rule is probably postlexical in all dialects, although the conditions for the rule vary from one dialect to another.

8.1.3 Sonorant Devoicing

In (20) of Chapter 5 we gave a rule of Sonorant Devoicing which devoices a sonorant which follows a voiceless consonant within the same syllable. Intuitively, we feel that this should be a postlexical rule, since voice is not distinctive for sonorants in English. But our argument in section 8.1 that Nasal Assimilation could be lexical even though velar nasals are not underlying segments of English raises some doubts about this point. This is because voiceless sonorants are, after all, defined in terms of features that define underlying segments, and in the case of the velar nasal this was enough to allow the rule to be assigned to stratum 2 of the lexicon. For Sonorant Devoicing, we can appeal to language universals. It seems that the feature [±voice] is never distinctive for sonorants in any language. Therefore, it would be surprising to find a rule like Sonorant Devoicing in the lexicon of any language. On universal grounds, then, we assign Sonorant Devoicing to the postlexical component.

8.1.4 Diphthong Shortening

The final rule that we introduced earlier and now will consider postlexical is Diphthong Shortening, given as (30) in Chapter 5. We took the name Diphthong Shortening from Nespor & Vogel, but we formulated it as a rule that makes vowels nonlow and nontense when followed by a glide and a voiceless consonant within the phonological word. Since both [±low] and [±tense] are distinctive features of vowels in our analysis, the question again arises whether this rule could be lexical.

We have observed a number of cases where a postlexical rule produces segments that occur only in the specific environments that produce them. One was the assimilation that produces the labiodental nasal (section 8.1). Another was the alveopalatalization of alveolar stops (section 8.1.1). Others were Flapping and Sonorant Devoicing. In contrast to this, many of the lexical rules we have examined produce segments that occur phonetically in environments other than those that condition them. An example is Palatalization, stated in (27) of Chapter 7. Among other effects, this rule produces [š] from [s] if the glide *y* follows. In the derivation of a word like *artificial,* the conditioning *y* is deleted by *y*-Deletion, (29) of Chapter 7.

Before the development of lexical phonology, Kiparsky (1973) proposed a principle of rule ordering that depends on the notions of TRANSPARENCY and OPACITY. Kiparsky defines opacity as in (6).

(6)   …a process P of the form A → B / C___D [is] OPAQUE to the extent that there are phonetic forms in the language having either (i) or (ii)

    (i)   A in the environment C___D
    (iia) B DERIVED BY THE PROCESS P in the environment 'other than C___D'
    (iib) B NOT DERIVED BY THE PROCESS P (i.e., underlying or derived by another process) in the environment C___D

Transparency is defined as the opposite of opacity. Kiparsky proposes that rules are ordered in such a way as to maximize their transparency. This replaces his earlier proposal (Kiparsky 1968a) that rules are ordered in such a way as to maximize feeding and counterbleeding orders (see the discussion of feeding and counterbleeding orders in Chapter 7, section 7.4). The rules discussed above that produce segments that appear only in their conditioning environment are all transparent by this definition. We can revise Kiparsky's proposal by claiming that rules that are completely transparent are postlexical.

8.1.5 Other rules

There are some other rules that Halle & Mohanan consider to be postlexical. One is *i*-Rounding, which we gave as (11) of Chapter 7. They give no particular reason why it should be postlexical; its only obligatory ordering is after Vowel Shift. Since it is structure preserving, it could be lexical, although it might just as well be postlexical. There are some other vowel adjustments that Halle & Mohanan assign to the postlexical component. One is *a/o*-Tensing, which accounts for the phonetic tenseness of the stressed vowels in *balm, father, rajah, baud,* and *Catawba*. This must clearly follow Vowel Shift in order not to feed it. We follow their formulation, but add the stress requirement in (7).

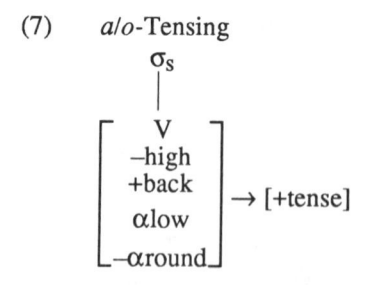

(7)   *a/o*-Tensing

$$\begin{bmatrix} V \\ -\text{high} \\ +\text{back} \\ \alpha\text{low} \\ -\alpha\text{round} \end{bmatrix} \rightarrow [+\text{tense}]$$

with σ_s linked above.

Another postlexical rule in Halle & Mohanan is ɒ-Unrounding, given in (8).[1]

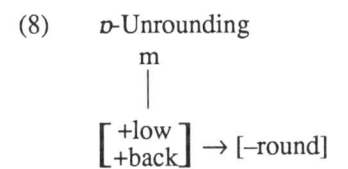

(8)   ɒ-Unrounding

$$\begin{bmatrix} +\text{low} \\ +\text{back} \end{bmatrix} \rightarrow [-\text{round}]$$

(with association line to m)

This rule applies in (most) North American dialects but not in RP. It unrounds the underlying /ɒ/ of *bomb* and *conic,* for example. The low quality of the underlying vowel of *conic* is shown by *cone,* derived by Vowel Shift from [kɒ̄n]. Halle & Mohanan order *a/o*-Tensing before ɒ-Unrounding in order to maintain a phonetic contrast between words like *balm* and *bomb,* as shown by the derivations in (9).

(9)   balm   bomb   baud
      a   ɒ   o   Output of the lexicon
      ā   —   ō   *a/o*-Tensing (7)
      —   a   —   ɒ-Unrounding (8)
      —   —   ɔ̄   *o*-Lowering (8 in Chapter 7)

Halle & Mohanan also assume a rule of æ-Tensing, which tenses æ in stressed syllables before certain consonants. They take their data from Trager (1930), who states that lax [æ] appears before final voiceless stops and *l,* while tense [ǣ] appears before other word-final consonants.[2] The examples are all monosyllabic. The facts are actually much more complicated. Bailey (1973), following Labov (1971), shows that the consonants involved form a hierarchy, not necessarily phonetically motivated, such that, if tensing takes place before the consonants in any column of Table 1 (overleaf), it also takes place before all the consonants in the column(s) to the left. In this table, a plus sign indicates the categorial operation of the rule; that is, it always applies in the given environment. A minus sign indicates the categorial nonoperation of the rule; that is, it never applies in the given environment. The symbol × indicates variable operation of the rule. Variable operation of a rule implies either that it sometimes applies and sometimes doesn't, or that it applies in some words with the given environment and not in

---

[1] Their term is ɔ-Unrounding. I have changed the symbol to conform to the notation adopted in this book.

[2] Trager's description of his own speech (native of Newark, New Jersey) is somewhat more complicated than Halle & Mohanan imply, as we will see shortly.

Sound environments differentiated according to the following consonant:

Locales		m,n (a)	f, θ, s (b)	d (c)	b (d)	š (e)	g (f)	v, z (g)	p, t, k (h)	l (i)
0	*	−	−	−	−	−	−	−	−	−
1	*	×	−	−	−	−	−	−	−	−
2	Birdsboro	+	×	−	−	−	−	−	−	−
3	Philadelphia	+	+	×	−	−	−	−	−	−
4	Mammoth Junction	+	+	+	×	−	−	−	−	−
5	Ringoes	+	+	+	+	×	−	−	−	−
6	Jackson	+	+	+	+	+	×	−	−	−
7	New York City	+	+	+	+	+	+	×	−	−
8	*	+	+	+	+	+	+	+	×	−
9	*	+	+	+	+	+	+	+	+	×
10	Buffalo	+	+	+	+	+	+	+	+	+

Table 1

others. For example, in Philadelphia, variable operation before *d* means that tense [æ:] appears in words like *mad* but not in words like *glad, sad, lad.* Halle & Mohanan appear to be describing the dialect of New York City.

There are some linguistically defined locales that have not been identified. These are indicated by asterisks in the locale column of Table 1. Bailey makes the assumption that these locales must exist, and will eventually be found.

Another complication is the number of syllables: some speakers have tense [æ:] in *ham* but lax [æ] in *hammer,* for example, while other speakers have tense [æ:] in both. Trager states that, for his own dialect, the distribution of tense and lax [æ] depends on the structure of the word, as summarized in (10).

(10) /___ C_1#   æ/___{p, t, k, č, ŋ, l}; otherwise [æ:]
      /___ C_2V   æ:/___{m, n, f, š}; otherwise [æ]
      /___ CV   æ except before š or in inflectional forms that have æ: in the simple form, with some uncertainty before š: *Fashion* has [æ:] but *passion* often has [æ].

All these variables preclude our giving a precise formulation of this rule, but we note that it is postlexical, perhaps because it is so variable. Like *a/o*-Tensing, æ-Tensing must in any case follow Vowel Shift, since otherwise it would feed it. This is assured by assigning these rules to the postlexical stratum.

8.1.6 Summary

The following is a summary of the conditions under which a rule should be considered postlexical.

> A rule is postlexical if it introduces lexically nondistinctive features (e.g., Aspiration).
> A rule is postlexical if it refers to phrasal categories, i.e., the prosodic categories phonological phrase and higher (the clitic group is undecided at the moment).
> A rule is postlexical if it is completely transparent.

Notice that a rule can be postlexical even if it does not meet any of these criteria. Consider the interaction of Diphthong Shortening and Flapping, discussed at the end of section 5.7. The rule of Diphthong Shortening is not completely transparent. In the form *writer,* Diphthong Shortening has applied even though *phonetically* it is followed by a voiced consonant, a flap. Nevertheless, we have argued that both these rules are postlexical. The rule of Flapping does appear to be completely transparent, however.

To complete this section, we provide an ordered list of the postlexical rules discussed in this book.

(11)   *Postlexical rules*

>   Diphthong Shortening (30 of Chapter 5)
>   Aspiration (17 of Chapter 5)
>   Flapping (62 of Chapter 5)
>   Glottalization (10 of Chapter 5)
>   Sonorant Devoicing (20 of Chapter 5)
>   Velar Fronting (22 of Chapter 5)
>   Alveopalatalization (23 of Chapter 5)
>   *a/o*-Tensing (7)
>   *ɒ*-Unrounding (8)
>   *o*-Lowering (8 of Chapter 7)
>   *i*-Rounding (11 of Chapter 7)
>   æ-Tensing (10 and Table 1)
>   Vowel Nasalization (8a in Chapter 1)
>   Nasal Consonant Deletion (8b in Chapter 1)

8.2 Some other approaches

In this section we consider some problems with the lexical model of English phonology, which we have presented in this book, and offer some possible solutions.

Szpyra (1989) has noted a number of cases where the generalizations of lexical phonology and morphology break down. She gives the examples in (12) where a stratum 1 affix apears to be attached outside a stratum 2 affix, contrary to the predictions of the model.

(12) a. [[[patent] able$_{II}$] ity$_I$]
 b. [[[govern]ment$_{II}$] al$_I$]
 c. [[[standard] ize$_{II}$] ation$_I$]

The stratal status of some of these suffixes is open to debate. In Chapter 6 we assumed that -*ize* was a stratum 1 suffix. Szpyra disputes this by examining the stress facts. For example in *standardization,* we might expect secondary stress on the second syllable rather than on the first if -*ize* were on stratum 1. Szpyra refers to affixes like this as "dual class suffixes," implying that they have properties of both stratum 1 and stratum 2 affixes. For example, (13) shows that -*ize* can be both stress neutral (13a) and stress determining (13b).

(13) a. stress-neutral -*ize* b. stress-determining -*ize*

      skéleton skéletonize   díalogue diálogize
      álphabet álphabetize   sýnonym synónymize
      hóspital hóspitalize   nítrogen nitrógenize

A second problem with lexical phonology appears in "bracketing paradoxes," where the morphological bracketing is at odds with the semantic structure. The examples in (14) are typical.

(14)   *morphological structure*   *semantic structure*

    a. [[un$_{II}$ [grammatical]] ity$_I$] [un$_{II}$ [[grammatical] ity$_I$]]
    b. [un$_{II}$ [[happy] er$_{II}$]]   [[un$_{II}$ [happy]] er$_{II}$]
    c. [[transformational]   [[[transformational]
       [[grammar] ian]]   [grammar]] ian]

In *unhappier,* the comparative suffix *-er* is added first, since this suffix is limited to monosyllabic and disyllabic adjectives. But the meaning is 'more unhappy' rather than 'not happier.' In *transformational grammarian, -ian* is added first, since it is a stratum 1 suffix (see the discussion in section 6.3), while the compound is formed on stratum 2. But a *transformational grammarian* is not 'a grammarian who is transformational,' but rather 'a practitioner of transformational grammar.' In these cases the morphological structure is at odds with the semantic structure.

Efforts to resolve bracketing paradoxes within lexical phonology have been made by Kiparsky (1983), Pesetsky (1985), and Mohanann (1986). Kiparsky proposed that morphological brackets could be irregularly retained in certain cases, rather than being erased at the end of each stratum by BRACKET ERASURE (see discussion in section 6.3 of Chapter 6). Then the morphology at the next stratum could *insert* a formative in between existing brackets, rather than just concatenate elements. This directly produces the right form of (13c) by inserting [transformational] between the two left brackets of [[grammar] ian].

Pesetsky's solution is even more ingenious. He allows the morphological component to produce the left-hand structures of (13), as required by the lexical model. He then applies a transformation to the structure, raising the affix, e.g., *-ian* in (13c) and attaching it to the right of the structure by Chomsky Adjunction. Chomsky Adjunction is the means we used in Chapter 4, section 4.2.1, to achieve Stray Syllable adjunction while insuring that all syllables are part of feet. In the case of *transformational grammarian,* Pesetsky's raising rule moves *-ian* from direct attachment to *grammar* and attaches it to the compound. This operation takes place in Logical Form, so that the correct semantic interpretation is ensured.

While both Kiparsky's and Pesetsky's solutions provide the correct forms for the bracketing paradoxes, they appear ad hoc in being proposed just to solve this one problem without adding any new insight to the theory. Mohanan (1986, 60, fn. 10) proposes that semantic structures are entirely independent of phonological and morphological structures, and are encoded in terms of a predicate calculus notation, such that, e.g., *kill* has a semantic representation that includes the elements *cause* and *die* while *linguist* has a semantic representation that includes the elements *do* and *linguistics*. He points out that *kill* is not derived morphologically from *die* and that *linguist* is not derived from *linguistics*. Mohanan assumes that postlexical semantic operations have access to such semantic structures, whether they are derived or underived, so that *beautiful* in *she is a beautiful dancer* can modify either the dancer or the dance, and *transformational* can modify *grammar* in *transformational grammarian*. These examples show that the semantic interpretation of lexical items has to be separated from their morphology, however lexical semantics is ultimately to be accounted for.

The other two problems with lexical phonology are more serious. The only way to deal with affixes that are attached in the wrong order, illustrated in (11), would be to install a loop leading back from stratum 2 into stratum 1. This would seriously compromise the whole idea of stratum ordering, and we have argued against Halle & Mohanan's introduction of the loop on this basis (see section 7.3 of Chapter 7). Similarly, cases where an affix illustrates phonological properties of both stratum 1 and stratum 2, illustrated in (12), could be dealt with by assuming that -*ize* exists on both levels, again seriously compromising the theory.

Szpyra observes another problem with words in -*ize:* Trisyllabic Laxing is inoperable in words with this suffix, even though the conditions for the rule are met, as the examples in (15) show.

(15)   vāpourize   nāsalize
        pōlarize   ītemize
        pēnalize   fīnalize
        schēmatize   vēlarize
        vītalize   lēgalize

The facts in (13a) and (15) suggest that -*ize* is phonologically a stratum 2 suffix, although (12b) suggests that it is phonologically stratum 1. *Morphologically,* however, it seems to be uniformly stratum 1, as we suggested earlier. This is shown by the uniformity with which verbs in -*ize* have nominalizations in -*ation,* without exception.

(16)   legal-iz-ation
        velar-iz-ation
        nasal-iz-ation
        palatal-iz-ation
        hospital-iz-ation

Furthermore, -*ize* can attach outside stratum 1 affixes but never outside stratum 2 affixes.

(17)   centr-al$_I$-ize   *grate-ful$_{II}$-ize
        republic-an$_I$-ize   *worth-less$_{II}$-ize
        poet-ic$_I$-ize   *Jew-ish$_{II}$-ize

Also, -*ize* can attach to nonword stems. This is possible for stratum 1 affixes but never for stratum 2 affixes.

(18) minim-ize (minim-al)
      mechan-ize (mechan-ism, mechan-ic)
      recogn-ize (recogn-ition)

Some of Szpyra's other criticisms of lexical phonology are less convincing. For example, she claims that the penultimate vowel is laxed (shortened) before *-ize*, although it is not a Trisyllabic Laxing environment.

(19) satīre   satĭrize
      divīne   divĭnize
      mobīle   mobĭlize

However, this is not Laxing but destressing[3] followed by a special laxing rule that ultimately results in a reduced vowel (Chapter 7, section 7.6). All the examples in (19) and others like them that Szpyra gives contain the diphthong [ɑy], which is derived from underlying /iː/ and which reduces to [ɪ] in appropriate environments. Some cases where destressing and laxing do not occur involve these same vowels (20a), but most involve vowels immediately preceding another vowel, where they are tensed by Prevocalic Tensing (20b).

(20) a. stȳle   stȳlize
      b. herō   herōize
          echō   echōize
          zerō   zerōize

While *-ize* is the most problematic suffix from this point of view, Szpyra identifies some other problem areas. We will not review these in any great detail, because we wish to present her solution, which makes use of the phonological word. Essentially, her claim is that stratum 2 suffixes form phonological words on their own. In this she follows Aronoff & Sridhar (1983) and Booij (1985). For example, words with stratum 1 affixes will be represented as single phonological words, as in (21), while words with stratum 2 affixes will be represented as more than one phonological word, as in (22).[4]

---

[3] Possibly a generalization of Sonorant Destressing (65 in Chapter 4) or of Medial Destressing (62 in Chapter 4).

[4] Szpyra uses parentheses to set off prosodic constituents, as opposed to square brackets to represent morphological constituents. We follow this convention in this section.

(21) a. (pur + ity)$_\omega$
 b. (music + ian)$_\omega$
 c. (hindr + ance)$_\omega$

(22) a. (un)$_\omega$ (natural)$_\omega$
 b. (bomb)$_\omega$ (ing)$_\omega$
 c. (hinder)$_\omega$ (er)$_\omega$

This requires reformulating a number of stratum 2 (word level) rules to include a phonological word boundary as part of their environments. This is not difficult, since several stratum 2 suffixes refer to the word boundary. For example, Noncoronal Deletion (45 in Chapter 7) can be reformulated as in (23).

(23) *Noncoronal Deletion*
$$\begin{bmatrix} -son \\ +voiced \\ -cor \end{bmatrix} \rightarrow \emptyset \: / \: [+nasal] \underline{\quad} \:)_\omega$$

Thus most stratum 2 rules will be reformulated as domain limit rules, in the terminology of Nespor & Vogel (1986). Stratum 1 rules will be reformulated as domain span rules, applying only within phonological words. Thus, Degemination (56 of Chapter 6) will apply within the phonological word in *innocuous*, for example, but not across phonological words in (21a), where the prefix forms a separate phonological word.

Problematic suffixes can now be handled in the following manner. The suffix *-ize* is considered morphologically stratum 1 (class I) since a stress-determining suffix, such as *-ation*, can be attached to it. This is true whether *-ize* itself is stress determining, as in (13b), or stress neutral, as in (13a). Stress-determining *-ize* will be included with the phonological word that precedes it, as in *synonymize*, while stress-neutral *-ize* will, by a special readjustment, be converted to a phonological word on its own. This is shown in (24).

(24) a. (sýnonym)$_\omega$ (synónymize)$_\omega$ (stress-determining *-ize*)
 b. (hóspital)$_\omega$ (hóspital)$_\omega$ (ize)$_\omega$ (stress-neutral *-ize*)

Szpyra suggests that, in the unmarked case, *-ize* is rebracketed as a separate phonological word, since it functions phonologically as a stratum 2 suffix in the majority of cases. Words where *-ize* functions as stratum 1 phonologically are to be marked as not undergoing this rebracketing. It is a nontrivial technical matter to mark *words* as exceptions to rules in lexical phonology, but this is an issue that we cannot pursue here.

When a stratum 1 suffix is added to a word in *-ize,* one of two things can happen. If *-ize* is part of the preceding phonological word, the entire word becomes a single phonological word, as in (25a). However, if *-ize* is a separate phonological word, it joins with the following suffix to form a single phonological word. This is shown in (25b).

(25) a. (synonym + ize + ation)$_\omega$
     b. (hospital)$_\omega$ (ize + ation)$_\omega$

Szpyra extends this analysis to the other cases that appear problematic within the lexical phonology framework. We can mention just one here, the case of full versus reduced vowels in compounds, discussed in Allen (1978). The examples in (26) are typical.

(26) *reduced vowels*   *full vowel*

mainland	[-lənd]	wasteland	[-lænd]
Iceland	[-lənd]	Toyland	[-lænd]
woodland	[-lənd]	farm land	[-lænd]
fireman	[-mən]	tax man	[-mæn]
chairman	[-mən]	bird man	[-mæn]

Szpyra suggests an analysis in which the reduced forms constitute single phonological words (27a), while the full-vowel forms constitute two phonological words (27b).

(27) a. (mainland)$_\omega$
     b. (waste)$_\omega$ (land)$_\omega$

It should be noted that Vowel Reduction, while a stratum 2 rule, is not reformulated as a domain limit rule in Szpyra's framework. Evidently, the destressing rules will have to be reformulated in terms of the phonological word for Szpyra's solution to work. Vowel Reduction will have the form we gave it in section 7.6 of Chapter 7, where it applies without reference to prosodic categories.

One general problem that arises in Szpyra's analysis involves the Strict Layer Hypothesis, which we cited as (3) in Chapter 5. While we did not accept this principle in its entirety, we did accept the general condition according to which feet consist of syllables, phonological words consist of feet, and so on up the prosodic hierarchy. The only exception we allowed was to permit feet to nest, as a result of Chomsky adjunction. The problem with Szpyra's analysis is the existence of phonological words that contain no feet, such as -ing in (22b) and -er in (22c). These stressless syllables are presumably incorporated into the foot that dominates the stem in each case. Because there is only a single foot, there can only be a single phonological word in these cases. This means that the prosodic version of Noncoronal Deletion (23) could not delete the final *b* of *bomb*, because it is not final in a phonological word. The only way to have it final in a phonological word is to assume that the syllable of the inflectional suffix does not belong to any foot, and that it is Chomsky adjoined directly to the phonological word dominating *bomb*, along the lines of (28).

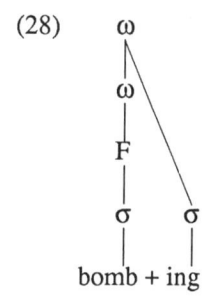

(28)   ω
       /\
      ω \
      | \
      F   \
      | \
      σ   σ
      | |
      bomb + ing

This presents a rather severe violation of the Strict Layer Hypothesis, although it can perhaps technically be made to work. In (27), both the final *b* of *bomb* and the final *g* of *-ing* are final in a phonological word, and so would correctly undergo Noncoronal Deletion (23).

A similar problem arises in the analysis of regular inflectional suffixes, which we argued are on stratum 2. Szpyra suggests that the underlying form of the regular past tense suffix contains a vowel, i.e., it is /ɪd/. When this suffix is attached to a verb stem such as *plead*, the result is analogous to (22b, c). However, this inflectional suffix, like *-ing* in (22b), cannot be a phonological word because it contains no stress, i.e., no foot. Again, a structure like that in (28) may be appropriate in this case. Szpyra uses this underlying form for the regular suffix to distinguish it from the irregular suffix, to which she gives the underlying forms /d/ (as in *bled*) and /t/ (as in *wept*). Recall from Chapter 6 that we distinguished the latter by attaching them at stratum 1, where no vowel insertion takes place, while the regular form was attached at stratum 2, where vowel insertion does take place. Szpyra's underlying forms allow her to account for the distinction between regular and irregular inflection without appealing to stratum ordering, but with a major violation of the prosodic hierarchy.

A consequence of allowing each (phonologically) stratum 2 suffix to start a new phonological word in prosodic structure is that complex words of this type have the same prosodic structure as phrases. Aronoff & Sridhar (1983, 9) note that a word like judge#*ment*+*al,* prosodically (judge)$_\omega$ (mental)$_\omega$, has the same prosodic structure as the phrase *Judge Mendel,* while the word *compartment* +*al* +*ize* + *ation,* prosodically (compart)$_\omega$ (mental)$_\omega$ (ization)$_\omega$, has the same prosodic structure as the phrase *combat mental elation*. Again, we have to observe that this is true only for suffixes and sequences of suffixes that bear a single stress. If *heeded* had two phonological words, as in Szpyra's analysis, it ought to be prosodically equivalent to *heed Ned,* which it isn't. A related problem is in words with sequences of stratum 2 affixes, such as *restlessness,* which is not the prosodic equivalent of a phrase such as *rest your case*. Szpyra, following Aronoff & Sridhar, considers these affixes to be clitics. However, this is again problematic in view of the prosodic hierarchy, according to which phonological words are joined into clitic groups. This implies that the suffixes *-less* and *-ness* are, at some point, phonological words, which can hardly be justified. It is true that certain bisyllabic affixes carry stress, as *-worthy* in *praiseworthy* or *counter-* in *counterargument*. This may have to be explained in an ad-hoc manner by giving such affixes a cycle of their own so that stress can be assigned to them. In any case, the fact that such affixes are stressed reduces the plausibility of calling them clitics.

This section has been somewhat inconclusive. We have discussed some problems with the theory of lexical phonology that has been assumed for most of this book, and some suggestions of other approaches to these issues. But the other approaches also appear to have problems. One can only conclude that further research is needed to resolve these issues.

8.3 General conclusion

This book has considered a number of issues in English phonology within the framework of generative phonology, and more specifically metrical, prosodic, and lexical phonology. The main organizing principle of these theories is the prosodic hierarchy, composed of prosodic units from the smallest, the mora, to the largest, the phonological utterance. The lowest levels of the prosodic hierarchy are assigned to words as part of the phonology of stratum 1, in particular, rules of syllabification (including assignment of moras) and rules of stress assignment. The rules of stress assignment organize the syllables into feet, such that each foot contains one and only one stressed syllable. This prosodic organization has an effect on segmental organization in that many segmental rules depend on stress for their operation. The output of the lexicon consists of words which form the input to the syntax. Here the lexical model differs from the standard T-model (footnote 9 of Chapter 1). We assume that the phonological component is partly in the lexicon, where lexical rules operate. Lexical rules are either morphological (involved in word formation), or phonological (operating on underived and derived lexical items to produce the phonological shape that is manipulated by the syntax). One consequence of the lexical model is that words emerge from the syntax fully inflected. This is because irregular inflection is part of stratum 1 in English, while regular inflection is part of stratum 2. Nevertheless, all past tense verb forms, for example, whether irregular or regular, behave the same way in the syntax and semantics. This has some consequences for the theory of syntax as well. It means that the syntax does not manipulate inflectional markers in any way; it can only interpret lexically assigned inflections. We assume that this is done by checking morphological features representing inflectional categories (e.g., [+past]) rather than by manipulating inflectional markers as such.

We have not used a grid representation for stress. In Liberman & Prince's (1977) original formulation of metrical theory, grids were parasitic on trees, and were introduced principally to account for rhythmic patterns (such as the Rhythm Rule of English, section 4.7 of Chapter 4). However, we follow Kiparsky 1979 in formulating the Rhythm Rule entirely in terms of the tree, obviating the need for grids entirely.[5] One conceptual problem with using grids is that it destroys the uniformity of the prosodic hierarchy in metrical structures. The grid is a formalism unrelated to the constituent structure inherent in all other metrical units, making it impossible to represent utterances in terms of a continuous hierarchy of units.

Although we introduced autosegmental phonology in Chapter 1, we did not find much application for this theory in English. We assume that autosegmental formalism is available for languages with tone and harmony systems, where autosegmental theory is most useful.

Our investigation has confirmed the role that rule ordering plays in phonology. When accounting for a substantial body of linguistic data, a fairly complex set of rules emerges, which applies in the most general fashion if the rules are assigned an order. It seems that it is always possible to find a single ordering of a set of rules, even though the interactions of those rules may differ in distinct derivations. For example, we found that Velar Softening is ordered before Vowel

---

[5] For some discussion of the issues involved in trees vs grids, see Hogg & McCully (1987, chapters 4, 5, and 6).

Shift, but that this order is counterfeeding in the case of *medicate* but counterbleeding in the case of *criticize*.

Our analysis makes considerable use of the mora and the syllable. Stress-dependent rules make use of the strong syllable (which dominates a stressed vowel) and the weak syllable (which dominates an unstressed vowel). The syllable is the domain of two prosodic rules in English, Glottalization (10 of Chapter 5) and *l*-Velarization (14 of Chapter 5). In some dialects, however, *l*-Velarization depends on the foot or the maximal foot. Higher prosodic units condition other phonological processes. These processes are not cyclic; that is, they do not operate on smaller prosodic units before moving on to higher prosodic units. In one case we ordered a rule whose domain is the phonological utterance (Flapping, 62 of Chapter 5) before Glottalization (10 of Chapter 5), a rule whose domain is the syllable.

Our discussion of lexical phonology in Chapters 6 and 7 confirms the two-stratum model of Kiparsky (1985) over the four-stratum model of Halle & Mohanan (1985). The evidence for more than two lexical strata in English in Halle & Mohanan's article is very weak. They have only two rules on their stratum 3, both restricted to a single dialect, and only one rule on stratum 4, *l*-Resyllabification. This last rule is eliminated by developing a prosodic analysis of *l*-Velarization, as we did in section 5.2 of Chapter 5. While Stem-final Tensing remains problematic (see section 7.7 of Chapter 7), it seems unlikely that the number of lexical strata could depend on such dialectally elusive facts. The elimination of strata 3 and 4 further allows us to eliminate the loop, a move which strengthens the theory as a whole.

Another controversial point is the possibility of resyllabification into a marked syllable structure, advocated by Myers (1987). Given that phonological rules may apply within prosodic categories, such as the foot and higher prosodic units, there is no need for resyllabification into a marked structure. However, we have assumed that part of the cyclic component is a set of rules of syllabification which cyclically resyllabify into an unmarked structure in which the onset is maximized. For example, *fra.ter.nize* is resyllabified on the second cycle of the derivation of *fra.ter.ni.za.tion*. Related to the problem of resyllabification is the possibility of ambisyllabification advocated by Kahn (1976), Borowsky, Itô, & Mester (1984), and Hogg & McCully (1987), discussed in section 3.4.2 of Chapter 3. Ambisyllabicity creates problems for the proper bracketing of syllabic structures, and it seems to be dispensable when phonological rules can refer to higher prosodic structures. Our analysis of stop allophones in sections 5.2 and 5.6 of Chapter 5 confirms Kiparsky's (1979) reanalysis of these processes without ambisyllabicity.

Finally, while the evidence for lexical phonology is quite strong, there are certain problems with the theory, noted in particular by Aronoff & Sridhar (1983) and by Szpyra (1989). It is evident that more work needs to be done in order to find solutions to some of these problems. However, it seems that the interplay of metrical, prosodic, and lexical phonology provides powerful tools for analyzing the phonological component of a grammar of English. Lexical phonology has been applied to a number of languages other than English, such as Polish (Rubach 1984b), Malayalam (Mohanan 1986) and Dakota (Shaw 1980). Nespor & Vogel discuss the application of prosodic phonology to a number of languages other than English, such as Italian, French, Spanish, Japanese, and a number of others. Hayes (1980) and Halle & Vergnaud (1987) develop metrical analyses of the stress systems of a number of languages, with some difference of focus owing to the difference between tree and grid representations. These three theories therefore hold considerable promise for the analysis of a number of languages. While we are far from a complete phonological analysis of any language, I hope that this in-depth study of English will provide a basis for future work on English and other languages in these frameworks.

References

Algeo, John (1993) *Problems in the Origins and Development of the English Language* (Fourth Edition), Harcourt, Brace, Jovanovich, New York.
Allen, Margaret Reece (1978) *Morphological Investigations,* Ph.D. dissertation, University of Connecticut.
Allen, W. Sidney (1973) *Accent and Rhythm,* Cambridge University Press, Cambridge, U.K.
Anderson, John M. & Colin J. Ewen (1987) *Principles of Dependency Phonology,* Cambridge University Press, Cambridge, U.K.
Archangeli, Diana (1984) *Underspecification in Yawelmani Phonology and Morphology,* Ph.D. dissertation, MIT.
Aronoff, Mark (1976) *Word Formation in Generative Grammar,* MIT Press, Cambridge, MA.
Aronoff, Mark & S.N. Sridhar (1983) "Morphological levels in English and Kannada or Atarizing Reagan," *Papers from the Parasession on the Interplay of Phonology, Morphology, and Syntax,* Chicago Linguistics Society, 3–16.
Bailey, Charles-James N. (1973) "The patterning of language variation," Richard W. Bailey & Jay L. Robinson (eds.) *Varieties of Present-Day English,* Macmillan, New York.
Bailey, Charles-James N. (1978) "Gradience in English syllabization and a revised concept of unmarked syllabization," Indiana University Linguistics Club.
Bauer, Laurie, John M. Dienhart, Hans H. Harvigson, & Leif Kvistgaard Jakobsen (1980) *American English Pronunciation,* Gyldendal, Copenhagen.
Bell, Alan & Joan Bybee Hooper (1978) "Issues and evidence in syllabic phonology," Alan Bell & Joan Bybee Hooper (eds.) *Syllables and Segments,* North-Holland, Amsterdam.
Bing, Janet (1979) *Aspects of English Prosody,* Ph.D dissertation, University of Massachusetts, Amherst (IULC, 1980).

Bloch, Bernard (1947) "English verb inflection," *Language* 23, 399–418.
Bloomfield, Leonard (1933) *Language,* Holt, Rinehart, and Winston, New York.
Bloomfield, Leonard (1939) "Menomini morphophonemics," *Travaux du cercle linguistique de Prague* 8, 105–115.
Booij, Geert E. (1985) "The interaction of phonology and morphology in prosodic phonology," Edmund Gussman (ed.) *Phono-morphology: Studies in the Interaction of Phonology and Morphology,* Redakcja Wydawnictw Katolickiego Uniwersytetu Lubelskiego, Lublin, 23–34.
Borowsky, Toni Jean (1986) *Topics in the Lexical Phonology of English,* Ph.D. dissertation, University of Massachusetts, Amherst.
Borowsky, Toni Jean (1989) "Structure preservation and the syllable coda in English," *Natural Language & Linguistic Theory* 7, 145–166.
Borowsky, Toni Jean, Junko Itô, & Ralf-Armin Mester (1984) "The formal representation of ambisyllabicity: evidence from Danish," *Proceedings of NELS 14,* University of Massachusetts, Amherst, 34–48.
Brame, Michael K. (1972) "The segmental cycle," Michael K. Brame (ed.) *Contributions to Generative Phonology,* University of Texas Press, Austin.
Brooks, Marie Zagorska (1965) "On Polish affricates," *Word* 29, 207–210.
Chomsky, Noam (1964) *Current Issues in Linguistic Theory,* Mouton, The Hague.
Chomsky, Noam (1965) *Aspects of the Theory of Syntax,* MIT Press, Cambridge, MA.
Chomsky, Noam (1970) "Remarks on nominalization," R.A. Jacobs and Peter S. Rosenbaum (eds.), *Readings in English Transformational Grammar,* Ginn, Waltham, MA, 184–221.
Chomsky, Noam (1981) *Lectures on Government and Binding,* Foris, Dordrecht.
Chomsky, Noam & Morris Halle (1968) *The Sound Pattern of English,* Harper & Row, New York.
Clements, George N. (1985) "The geometry of phonological features," *Phonology Yearbook* 2, 225–252.
Clements, George N. & Samuel Jay Keyser (1983) *CV Phonology: a Generative Theory of the Syllable,* MIT Press, Cambridge, MA.
Collins Dictionary of the English Language (1979), Collins, London.
Cowan, Nelson, Martin D.S. Braine, & Lewis A. Leavitt (1985) "The phonological and metaphonological representation of speech: evidence from fluent backward talkers," *Journal of Memory and Language* 24, 679–698.
Davis, Stuart (1988) "Syllable onsets as a factor in stress rules," *Phonology* 5, 1–19.
Diamond, Robert E. (1970) *Old English Grammar and Reader,* Wayne State University Press, Detroit, MI.

Downing, Bruce Theodore (1970) *Syntactic Structure and Phonological Phrasing in English,* Ph.D. dissertation, University of Texas, Austin.

Durand, Jacques (1990) *Generative and Nonlinear Phonology,* Longman, London.

Emonds, Joseph E. (1776) *A Transformational Approach to English Synatax: Root, Structure Preserving, and Local Transformations,* Academic Press, New York.

Fidelholtz, James L. and E. Wayles Browne (1971) "Oy, oy, oy," Roger W. Shuy and Charles-James N. Bailey (eds.) *Towards Tomorrow's Linguistics,* Georgetown University Press, Washington, D.C. 159–184.

Fudge, Erik (1984) *English Word Stress,* George Allen & Unwin, London.

Furby, Christine E. (1974) *Garawa Phonology,* Pacific Linguistics, series A, No. 37, 1–11, Australian National University, Canberra.

Gimson, A.C. (1962) *An Introduction to the Pronunciation of English,* Edward Arnold, London.

Goldsmith, John (1976) *Autosegmental Phonology,* Ph.D. dissertation, MIT.

Goldsmith, John (1990) *Autosegmental and Metrical Phonology,* Blackwell, Oxford.

Halle, Morris (1977) "Tenseness, vowel shift, and the phonology of back vowels in modern English," *Linguistic Inquiry* 8, 611–625.

Halle, Morris & K.P. Mohanan (1985). "Segmental phonology of Modern English," *Linguistic Inquiry* 16, 57–116.

Halle, Morris & Kenneth N. Stevens (1971) "A note on laryngeal features," *Quarterly Progress Reports* 101, 198–213, Research Laboratory of Electronics, MIT.

Halle, Morris and Jean-Roger Vergnaud (1987) *An Essay on Stress,* MIT Press, Cambridge, MA.

Harris, James W. (1983) *Syllable Structure and Stress in Spanish: A Nonlinear Analysis,* MIT Press, Cambridge, MA.

Harris, Zellig S. (1951) *Structural Linguistics,* University of Chicago Press, Chicago.

Hayes, Bruce (1980) *A Metrical Theory of Stress Rules,* Ph.D. dissertation, MIT (reproduced by Indiana University Linguistics Club, 1981).

Hayes, Bruce (1982) "Extrametricality and English stress," *Linguistic Inquiry* 13, 227–276.

Hayes, Bruce (1986) "Inalterability in CV phonology," *Language* 62, 321–351.

Hayes, Bruce (1989) "The prosodic hierarchy in meter," Paul Kiparsky & Gilbert Youmans (eds.) *Phonetics and Phonology Volume 1: Rhythm and Meter,* Academic Press, New York, 201–260.

Hoard, James E. (1971) "Aspiration, tenseness, and syllabication in English," *Language* 47, 133–140.
Hoard, James E. (1972) "Naturalness conditions in phonology, with particular reference to English vowels," Michael K. Brame (ed.) *Contributions to Generative Phonology,* University of Texas Press, Austin, 123–154.
Hockett, Charles F. (1942) "A system of descriptive phonology," *Language* 18, 3–21.
Hockett, Charles F. (1958) *A Course in Modern Linguistics,* Macmillan, New York.
Hogg, Richard M. & C.B. McCully (1987) *Metrical Phonology: a Coursebook,* Cambridge University Press, Cambridge, U.K.
Hooper, Joan Bybee (1972) "The syllable in phonological theory," *Language* 48, 525–540.
Hooper, Joan Bybee (1976) *An Introduction to Natural Generative Phonology,* Academic Press, New York.
Hyman, Larry M. (1985) *A Theory of Phonological Weight,* Foris, Dordrecht.
Ingria, Robert (1980) "Compensatory lengthening as a metrical phenomonon," *Linguistic Inquiry* 11, 465–495.
Itô, Junko (1986) *Syllable Theory in Prosodic Phonology,* Ph.D. dissertation, University of Massachusetts, Amherst.
Itô, Junko (1989) "A prosodic theory of epenthesis," *Natural Language and Linguistic Theory* 7, 217–259.
Jackendoff, Ray S. (1972) *Semantic Interpretation in Generative Grammar,* MIT Press, Cambridge, MA.
Jaeger, Jeri J. (1986) "On the acquisition of abstract representations for English vowels," *Phonology Yearbook* 3, 71–97.
Jakobson, Roman, Gunnar Fant, & Morris Halle (1963) *Preliminaries to Speech Analysis: The Distinctive Features and their Correlates,* MIT Press, Cambridge, MA.
Jakobson, Roman & Morris Halle (1956) *Fundamentals of Language,* Mouton, The Hague.
Jensen, John T. (1990) "Resyllabification vs prosodic structure in English vowel shortening," *Proceedings of NELS 21,* 173–185.
Jensen, John T. (1991) "Vowel laxing and vowel reduction in English," Paper read at the annual meeting of the Canadian Linguistic Association, May, 1992, *Toronto Working Papers in Linguistics 133–144.*
Kahn, Daniel (1976), *Syllable-based Generalizations in English Phonology,* Ph.D. dissertation, MIT.

Kahn, Daniel (1980) "Syllable structure specifications in phonological rules," Mark Aronoff and Mary-Louise Kean (eds.) *Juncture,* Anma Libri, Saratoga, CA, 91–105.
Kenstowicz, Michael J. & Charles W. Kisseberth (1979) *Generative Phonology: Description and Theory,* Academic Press, New York.
Kim, Suksan (1990) "A nonlinear analysis of reduplicating preterites in Germanic," *Linguistic Analysis* 20, 104–118.
Kiparsky, Paul (1968a) "Linguistic universals and linguistic change," Emmon Bach & Robert T. Harms (eds.) *Universals in Linguistic Theory,* Holt, Rinehart, & Winston, New York.
Kiparsky, Paul (1968b) "How abstract is phonology?" Paul Kiparsky (ed.) *Explanation in Phonology,* Foris, Dordrecht, 119–163.
Kiparsky, Paul (1973) "Abstractness, opacity, and global rules," O. Fujimura (ed.) *Three Dimensions of Linguistic Theory,* TEC, Tokyo, 57–86. Also in Andreas Koutsoudas (ed.) *The Application and Ordering of Grammatical Rules, Mouton,* The Hague, 160–186.
Kiparsky, Paul (1979) "Metrical structure assignment is cyclic," *Linguistic Inquiry* 10, 421–441.
Kiparsky, Paul (1982a) "Lexical morphology and phonology," I.S. Yang (ed.) *Linguistics in the Morning Calm,* Hanshin, Seoul, 3–91.
Kiparsky, Paul (1982b) "From cyclic phonology to lexical phonology," in Harry van der Hulst and Norval Smith (eds) *Tht Structure of Phonological representations (Part I),* Foris, Dordrecht, 131–175.
Kiparsky, Paul (1983) "Word formation and the lexicon," in Frances A. Ingeman (ed.) *Proceedings of the 1982 Mid-America Linguistics Conference,* University of Kansas, Lawrence.
Kiparsky, Paul (1984) "Underspecification," unpublished paper, Stanford University.
Kiparsky, Paul (1985) "Some consequences of lexical phonology," *Phonology Yearbook* 2, 85 138.
Klavans, Judith L. (1982) *Some Problems in a Theory of Clitics,* Ph.D. dissertation, University College, London. IULC.
Klavans, Judith L. (1985) "The independence of syntax and phonology in cliticization," *Language* 61, 95–120.
Kreidler, Charles W. (1989) *The Pronunciation of English,* Basil Blackwell, Oxford.
Labov, William (1971) "Methodology," William Orr Dingwall (ed.) *A Survey of Linguistic Science,* Linguistics Program, University of Maryland, College Park, 412–491.

LaCharité, Darlene (1992) *The Internal Structure of Affricates*, Ph.D. dissertation, University of Ottawa.

Ladefoged, Peter (1971) *Preliminaries to Linguistic Phonetics*, University of Chicago Press.

Ladefoged, Peter (1972) *A Course in Phonetics* (second edition), Harcourt, Brace, Jovanovich, New York.

Leben, William (1973) *Suprasegmental Phonology*, Ph.D. dissertation, MIT.

Leben, William (1982) "Metrical or autosegmental?" Harry van der Hulst and Norval Smith (eds.) *The Structure of Phonological Representations (Part I)*, Foris, Dordrecht, 177–190.

Levin, Juliette (1985) *A Metrical Theory of Syllabicity*, Ph.D dissertation, MIT.

Liberman, Mark & Alan Prince (1977) "On stress and linguistic rhythm," *Linguistic Inquiry* 8, 249–336.

Lightner, Theodore M. (1972) *Problems in the Theory of Phonology*, Linguistic Research, Edmonton.

MacKay, Ian R.A. (1987) *Phonetics: The Science of Speech Production*, Pro-Ed, Austin, Texas.

Malécot, André (1960) "Vowel nasality as a distinctive feature in American English," *Language* 36, 222–9.

Marsack, C.C. (1962) *Teach Yourself Samoan*, The English Universities Press Ltd, London.

McCarthy, John J. (1981) "A prosodic theory of nonconcatenative morphology," *Linguistic Inquiry* 12, 373–418.

McCarthy, John J. & Alan S. Prince (1986) *Prosodic Morphology*, unpublished, to appear, MIT Press, Cambridge, MA.

McCarthy, John J. & Alan S. Prince (1990) "Foot and word in prosodic morphology: the Arabic broken plural," *Natural Language and Linguistic Theory* 8, 209–283.

McCawley, James D. (1968) *The Phonological Component of a Grammar of Japanese*, Mouton, The Hague.

Mohanan, Karuvannur Puthanveettil (1986) *The Theory of Lexical Phonology*, Reidel, Dordrecht.

Mohanan, Karuvannur Puthanveettil & Tara Mohanan (1984) "Lexical phonology of the consonant system in Malayalam," *Linguistic Inquiry* 15, 575–602.

Myers, Scott (1987) "Vowel shortening in English," *Natural Language and Linguistic Theory* 5, 485–518.

Nespor, Marina & Irene Vogel (1986) *Prosodic Phonology*, Foris, Dordrecht.

Osborn, Henry A., Jr (1966) "Warao I: phonology and morphophonemics," *International Journal of American Linguistics* 32, 108–23.

Pesetsky, David (1985) "Morphology and logical form," *Linguistic Inquiry* 16, 193–246.
Pike, Kenneth L. (1947) "Grammatical prerequisites to phonemic analysis," *Word* 3, 155–172.
Pilch, Herbert (1976) *Empirical Linguistics,* Francke, München.
Postal, Paul M. (1968) *Aspects of Phonological Theory,* Harper & Row, New York.
Prince, Alan S. (1980) "A metrical theory for Estonian quantity," *Linguistic Inquiry* 11, 511–562.
Prince, Alan S. (1983) "Relating to the grid," *Linguistic Inquiry* 14, 19–100.
Pulgram, Ernst (1970) *Syllable, Word, Nexus, Cursus,* Mouton, The Hague.
Pulleyblank, Douglas (1990) *Introduction to Nonlinear Phonology,* manuscript, University of Ottawa.
Quirk, Randolph, Sidney Greenbaum, Geoffrey Leech, & Jan Svartvik (1972) *A Grammar of Contemporary English,* Seminar Press, New York.
Ross, John R. (1972) "A reanalysis of English word stress (Part I)," Michael K. Brame (ed.) *Contributions to Generative Phonology,* University of Texas Press, Austin.
Rubach, Jerzy (1984a) "Segmental rules of English and cyclic phonology," *Language* 60, 21–54.
Rubach, Jerzy (1984b) *Cyclic and Lexical Phonology: The Structure of Polish,* Foris, Dordrecht
Sagey, Elizabeth Caroline (1986) *The Representation of Features and Relations in Nonlinear Phonology,* Ph.D. dissertation, MIT.
Schane, Sanford A. (1968a) "On the nonuniqueness of phonological representations," *Language* 44, 709–716.
Schane, Sanford A. (1968b) *Generative Phonology,* Prentice-Hall, New York.
Schane, Sanford A. (1968c) *French Phonology and Morphology,* MIT Press, Cambridge, MA.
Selkirk, Elisabeth O. (1972) *The Phrase Phonology of English and French,* Ph.D. dissertation, MIT, published (1980) by Garland, New York.
Selkirk, Elisabeth O. (1978) "On prosodic structure and its relation to syntactic structure," Fretheim (ed., 1981) *Nordic Prosody II,* TAPIR, Trondheim, 11–140.
Selkirk, Elisabeth O. (1980a) "Prosodic domains in phonology: Sanskrit revisited," Mark Aronoff & Mary-Louise Kean (eds.) *Juncture,* Anma Libri, Saratoga, California, 107–129.
Selkirk, Elisabeth O. (1980b) "The role of prosodic categories in English word stress," *Linguistic Inquiry* 11, 563–605.

Selkirk, Elisabeth O. (1982) "The syllable," Harry van der Hulst & Norval Smith (eds.) *The Structure of Phonological Representations (Part II)*, Foris, Dordrecht, 337–383.

Selkirk, Elisabeth O. (1984a) *Phonology and Syntax: the Relation between Sound and Structure*, MIT Press, Cambridge, MA.

Selkirk, Elisabeth O. (1984b) "On the major class features and syllable theory," Mark Aronoff & Richard T. Oehrle (eds.) *Language Sound Structure*, MIT Press, Cambridge, MA, 107–136.

Shaw, Patricia A. (1980) *Theoretical Issues in Dakota Phonology and Morphology*, Garland, New York.

Siegel, Dorothy C. (1974) *Topics in English Morphology*, Ph.D. dissertation, MIT.

Siegel, Dorothy C. (1977) "The adjacency condition and the theory of morphology," *Proceedings of NELS* 8, 189–197.

Stampe, David (1972) *How I Spent My Summer Vacation*, Ph.D. dissertation, University of Chicago.

Szpyra, Jolanta (1989) *The Phonology-Morphology Interface: Cycles, Levels, and Words*, Routledge, London.

Trager, George L. (1930) "The pronunciation of 'short A' in American English," *American Speech* 5, 396–400.

Trager, George L. (1972) *Language and Languages*, Chandler, San Francisco.

Tryon, Darrell T. (1970) *An Introduction to Maranungku, Northern Australia* (Pacific Linguistics Monographs, Series B, No. 15), Australian National University, Canberra.

Vennemann, Theo (1974) "Words and syllables in natural generative grammar," *Papers from the Parasession on Natural Phonology*, Chicago Linguistics Society, 346–374.

Vennemann, Theo (1988) *Preference Laws for Syllable Structure and the Explanation of Sound Change*, Mouton de Gruyter, Berlin.

Vogel, Irene (1989) Review of Hogg & McCully (1987), *Journal of Linguistics* 25, 221–225.

Wang, William S.-Y. (1967) "Phonological features of tone," *International Journal of American Linguistics* 33, 93–105.

Wells, J.C. (1982) *Accents of English 1: Introduction*, Cambridge University Press, Cambridge, UK.

Withgott, Mary Margaret (1982) *Segmental Evidence for Phonological Constituents*, Ph.D. dissertation, University of Texas, Austin.

Index

A

ɒ-Unrounding   225
a/o-Tensing   224
ablaut   20, 183
absolute neutralization   41
abstractness   7, 41
Adjective Extrametricality   95
æ-Tensing   225
Allen, Margaret   156, 233
Allen, W. Sidney   55
allomorphs   40
allomorphy rules   183
allophone   2
allophonic rules   26
Alternation Condition   41
Alveopalatalization   131, 177, 220
anaphora   149
Archangeli, Diana   19
Aronoff, Mark   156, 183, 231, 235
Aspiration   129, 151, 220
assimilation   212
association   12
autosegmental phonology   11, 236

B

Backing Ablaut   184
Backness Adjustment   199
Bailey, Charles-James N.   22, 58, 225
Bell, Alan   47
Bing, Janet   145
bleeding order   152, 181, 207

Bloch, Bernard   181
Bloomfield, Leonard   7, 26, 56
Booij, Geert   231
Borowsky, Toni
   J.   20, 33, 60, 70, 71, 72, 73,
   176, 206, 219, 237
Bracket Erasure   163, 167, 229
Brame, Michael K.   179
Brooks, Marie Zagorska   30
Browne, E. Wayles   197

C

Chomsky Adjunction   85, 124, 229
Chomsky, Noam   1, 3, 5, 6, 17, 26, 40,
   122, 155, 156
CiV Tensing   190
class node   14
Clements, George N.   13, 14, 59
clitic group   132, 134
Cluster Laxing   175, 180, 183
complementary distribution   2
Compound Stress rule   98
Consonant Extrametricality   92
conversion   160
counterbleeding order   5, 153, 208
counterfeeding order   208
cyclicity   111

D

Dakota   238
Danish   32
Degemination   183, 232

degenerate foot 80
Demotic Greek 132
destressing rules 102
Dialectal *y*-Deletion 195
Diphthong Shortening 5, 25, 126, 131, 132, 134, 152, 223, 227
Diphthongization 192
diphthongs 77
distinctness 166
domain juncture 125
domain juncture rule 18
domain limit 125
domain limit rule 18
domain span 125
domain span rule 18
Downing, Bruce Theodore 143
Durand, Jacques 197

E

Eastern Cheremis 87
ellipsis 149
Elsewhere Condition 186, 214
Emonds, Joseph 143
English Stress Rule 93
Epenthesis 181
Estonian 90
exceptions 115

F

Fant, Gunnar 30
feeding order 207
Fidelholtz, James L. 197
Finnish 13, 42
Flapping 5, 25, 147, 150, 151, 221, 223, 227, 237
foot 16, 125
formative 8
free variation 2
French 34, 238
Fudge, Erik C. 119
full vowels 77, 189

G

Garawa 119
general phonology 1
German 4
Gimson, A.C. 222
Glottalization 126, 152, 220, 237
Goldsmith, John A. 11

H

Halle, Morris 1, 30, 31, 34, 36, 38, 80, 127, 158, 164, 171, 181, 183, 191, 219, 221, 224, 237, 238
Harris, James W. 20
Harris, Zellig S. 3, 5
Hayes, Bruce 71, 73, 78, 79, 117, 124, 134, 238
Hoard, James E. 36, 58, 176, 194, 196
Hockett, Charles F. 3, 56
Hogg, Richard M. 60, 237
Hooper, Joan B. 42, 47, 58
Hungarian 13, 133
Hyman, Larry M. 63

I

i-Lowering 194
i-Rounding 194, 224
i-Tensing 195
Iambic Reversal 139
-*ic* Laxing 175
Ingria, Robert 210
International Phonetic Association 29
intonation phrase 142
Intonation Phrase Formation 144
Italian 135, 238
Itô, Junko 60, 63, 237

J

Jackendoff, Ray 144
Jaeger, Jeri J. 9
Jakobson, Roman 30
Japanese 9, 19, 78, 138, 238

J

Jensen, John T.   85, 179, 186
Jingpho   32

K

Kahn, Daniel   56, 59, 91, 92, 125, 128, 237
Kenstowicz, Michael J.   56
Keyser, Samuel Jay   14, 59
Khalkha Mongolian   87
Kiparsky, Paul   17, 20, 41, 86, 93, 97, 104, 108, 112, 114, 125, 130, 139, 156, 161, 166, 169, 172, 207, 214, 223, 229, 236, 237
Kisseberth, Charles W.   56
Klavans, Judith L.   136
Korean   32, 78
Kreidler, Charles W.   78

L

l-Velarization   128, 221, 237
Labov, William   225
LaCharité, Darlene   15
Ladefoged, Peter   2, 78
Latin   89, 132
Latvian   80
Laxing   180
Leben, William R.   11, 77
lect   22
levels of representation   25
Levin, Juliette   14
lexical alphabet   40
lexical entry   166
lexical items   156
lexical phonology   11, 20, 27, 155, 157
lexical representations   27
lexicalization   42
Liberman, Mark   16, 82, 89, 91, 96, 139, 236
Lightner, Theodore M.   56
linear phonology   7
List Restructuring   147
long retraction   97
Long Vowel Stressing   95, 190
Lowering Ablaut   184

M

MacKay, Ian R.A.   37, 42, 77
Malayalam   40, 238
Malécot, André   6
Maranungku   81
maximally binary foot   80
McCarthy, John J.   14, 63, 186
McCawley, James D.   26, 62
McCully, C.B.   60, 237
Medial Destressing   107, 172
Mende   11
Mester, Ralf-Armin   60, 237
metrical grid   83
metrical phonology   11, 15
Middle English   180
Modern Greek   135
Mohanan, K.P.   26, 29, 34, 36, 38, 102, 127, 156, 158, 164, 171, 181, 183, 191, 219, 221, 224, 229, 237, 238
Mohanan, Tara   158
Mongolian   13
Monosyllable Rule   141
morphological processes   183
morphological rule   20
morphophonemic rules   26
mutually bleeding order   208
Myers, Scott   175, 237

N

n-Deletion   167, 209
Nasal Assimilation   211, 219, 221, 223
Nasal Consonant Deletion   6, 150
Nasal Spreading   150
Nasalization   6, 150
Naturalness Condition   8
Nespor, Marina   5, 18, 23, 86, 122, 203, 222, 238
neutralization   3
Noncoronal Deletion   211, 219, 232, 234
nondistinctive features   31
nonlinear phonology   11
Noun Extrametricality   94

O

o-Lowering 193
Old English 54, 180
opacity 223
overlapping allophones 4

P

Palatalization 177, 200, 202, 206, 223
Pāṇini 1, 7
panlectal grammar 22
parameter 78
Pesetsky, David 229
phoneme 2
phonetic implementation 26
phonological cycle 10
phonological phrase 18, 137
Phonological Phrase Formation 137
Phonological Phrase Restructuring 141
phonological utterance 18, 147
phonological word 81, 132
Pike, Kenneth L. 7
Polish 238
polylectal grammar 22
Postal, Paul 8
postlexical phonology 20, 27, 156
postlexical rules 227
Poststress Destressing 104, 172
Prenasal g-Deletion 210
Prestress Destressing 102, 104, 172
Prevocalic Tensing 198, 231
primary affixes 162
Prince, Alan S. 16, 63, 82, 89, 90, 91, 96, 139, 186, 236
prosodic constituents 121
prosodic hierarchy 123
Prosodic Licensing 63, 85, 123
prosodic phonology 11, 17, 122
pseudodifferentiation 3, 5, 6
Pulgram, Ernst 55
Pulleyblank, Douglas 12

Q

quantity insensitive system 79
quantity sensitive system 86
Quirk, Randolph 181

R

Raddoppiamento Sintattico 139
readjustment rules 8, 121
reduced vowels 77, 189
resyllabification 176
Rhythm Rule 112, 139, 236
Ross, John R. 117
Rubach, Jerzy 170, 173, 194, 206, 238
rule ordering 151, 207, 236

S

Sagey, Elizabeth Caroline 13
Sanskrit 1
Schane, Sanford A. 56
secondary affixes 162
Selkirk, Elisabeth O. 16, 18, 60, 91, 123, 125, 135, 141, 142, 176
sentence stress 77
Shaw, George Bernard 43, 44
Shaw, Patricia A. 238
Siegel, Dorothy 156
Simplicity Metric 56
skeleton 14
Sonorant Destressing 108
Sonorant Devoicing 130, 223
Sonorant Syllabification 105
Sonority Sequencing Generalization 160
Spanish 19, 20, 42, 238
Spirantization 205, 206
spreading 12, 13
Sridhar, S.N. 231, 235
Stampe, David 58, 176
Stem-final Tensing 118, 214, 237
Stevens, Kenneth N. 31
stop allophones 220
stratum 20
Stray Syllable Adjunction 85
stress retraction 96
stress subordination convention 10
Strict Cycle Condition 20, 114, 165, 166, 180, 207
strict cyclicity 164
Strict Layer Hypothesis 123, 233
strong retraction 96

Structure Preserva-
   tion   20, 106, 151, 219, 220
subcategorization frame   159
systematic phonemic level   26
systematic phonetic level   26
Szpyra, Jolanta   222, 228

T

T-model of grammar   17, 20
taxonomic phonemic level   26
taxonomic phonemics   1
Telegu   19, 20
Thai   2
tier   12
timing elements   14
Trager, George L.   225
transformational format   186
transparency   223
transparent order   182
Trisyllabic
   Laxing   41, 116, 164, 180, 189, 191, 230
Turkish   13, 132

U

unbounded foot   80
underlying alphabet   40
underlying representation   26
underspecification   13, 20
underspecification theory   11, 18

V

Velar Fronting   131
Velar Softening   199, 207, 236

Vennemann, Theo   42
Vergnaud, Jean-Roger   80, 238
Vietnamese   34
Vogel,
   Irene   5, 18, 23, 61, 86, 122, 203, 222, 238
Voicing Assimilation   182
vowel harmony   13
Vowel Reduction   134, 211, 213, 233
Vowel Reduction and Assimilation   213
Vowel Shift   189, 192, 236

W

Warao   84
Warlpiri   40
weak retraction   96
Wells, J.C.   29, 128, 212
Winnebago   89
Withgott, Mary Margaret   106, 127, 129
word level   166
word stress   77
Word Tree Construction   98, 101

Y

y-Deletion   203
y-Insertion   194
y-Vocalization   204
Yawelmani   19
Yoruba   12, 13

Z

zero derivation   160
ω domain   133

In the CURRENT ISSUES IN LINGUISTIC THEORY (CILT) series (Series Editor: E.F. Konrad Koerner) the following volumes have been published thus far, and will be published during 1994:

1. KOERNER, E.F. Konrad (ed.): *The Transformational-Generative Paradigm and Modern Linguistic Theory.* Amsterdam, 1975.
2. WEIDERT, Alfons: *Componential Analysis of Lushai Phonology.* Amsterdam, 1975.
3. MAHER, J. Peter: *Papers on Language Theory and History I: Creation and Tradition in Language.* Foreword by Raimo Anttila. Amsterdam, 1977.
4. HOPPER, Paul J. (ed.): *Studies in Descriptive and Historical Linguistics: Festschrift for Winfred P. Lehmann.* Amsterdam, 1977. Out of print.
5. ITKONEN, Esa: *Grammatical Theory and Metascience: A critical investigation into the methodological and philosophical foundations of 'autonomous' linguistics.* Amsterdam, 1978.
6. ANTTILA, Raimo: *Historical and Comparative Linguistics.* Amsterdam/Philadelphia, 1989.
7. MEISEL, Jürgen M. & Martin D. PAM (eds): *Linear Order and Generative Theory.* Amsterdam, 1979.
8. WILBUR, Terence H.: *Prolegomena to a Grammar of Basque.* Amsterdam, 1979.
9. HOLLIEN, Harry & Patricia (eds): *Current Issues in the Phonetic Sciences, Proceedings of the IPS-77 Congress, Miami Beach, Fla., 17-19 December 1977.* Amsterdam, 1979. 2 vols.
10. PRIDEAUX, Gary (ed.): *Perspectives in Experimental Linguistics. Papers from the University of Alberta Conference on Experimental Linguistics, Edmonton, 13-14 Oct. 1978.* Amsterdam, 1979.
11. BROGYANYI, Bela (ed.): *Studies in Diachronic, Synchronic, and Typological Linguistics: Festschrift for Oswald Szemerényi on the Occasion of his 65th Birthday.* Amsterdam, 1980.
12. FISIAK, Jacek (ed.): *Theoretical Issues in Contrastive Linguistics.* Amsterdam, 1980.
13. MAHER, J. Peter with coll. of Allan R. Bomhard & E.F. Konrad Koerner (ed.): *Papers from the Third International Conference on Historical Linguistics, Hamburg, August 22-26, 1977.* Amsterdam, 1982.
14. TRAUGOTT, Elizabeth C., Rebecca LaBRUM, Susan SHEPHERD (eds): *Papers from the Fourth International Conference on Historical Linguistics, Stanford, March 26-30, 1980.* Amsterdam, 1980.
15. ANDERSON, John (ed.): *Language Form and Linguistic Variation. Papers dedicated to Angus McIntosh.* Amsterdam, 1982.
16. ARBEITMAN, Yoël & Allan R. BOMHARD (eds): *Bono Homini Donum: Essays in Historical Linguistics, in Memory of J. Alexander Kerns.* Amsterdam, 1981.
17. LIEB, Hans-Heinrich: *Integrational Linguistics.* 6 volumes. Amsterdam, 1984-1986. Vol. I available; Vol. 2-6 n.y.p.
18. IZZO, Herbert J. (ed.): *Italic and Romance. Linguistic Studies in Honor of Ernst Pulgram.* Amsterdam, 1980.
19. RAMAT, Paolo et al. (eds): *Linguistic Reconstruction and Indo-European Syntax. Proceedings of the Coll. of the 'Indogermanische Gesellschaft' Univ. of Pavia, 6-7 Sept. 1979.* Amsterdam, 1980.
20. NORRICK, Neal R.: *Semiotic Principles in Semantic Theory.* Amsterdam, 1981.
21. AHLQVIST, Anders (ed.): *Papers from the Fifth International Conference on Historical Linguistics, Galway, April 6-10, 1981.* Amsterdam, 1982.
22. UNTERMANN, Jürgen & Bela BROGYANYI (eds): *Das Germanische und die Rekonstruktion der Indogermanische Grundsprache.* Akten, Proceedings from the Colloquium of the Indogermanische Gesellschaft, Freiburg, 26-27 February 1981. Amsterdam, 1984.
23. DANIELSEN, Niels: *Papers in Theoretical Linguistics.* Edited by Per Baerentzen. Amsterdam/Philadelphia, 1992.
24. LEHMANN, Winfred P. & Yakov MALKIEL (eds): *Perspectives on Historical Linguistics. Papers from a conference held at the meeting of the Language Theory Division, Modern Language Ass., San Francisco, 27-30 December 1979.* Amsterdam, 1982.
25. ANDERSEN, Paul Kent: *Word Order Typology and Comparative Constructions.* Amsterdam, 1983.

26. BALDI, Philip (ed.) *Papers from the XIIth Linguistic Symposium on Romance Languages, University Park, April 1-3, 1982.* Amsterdam, 1984.
27. BOMHARD, Alan: *Toward Proto-Nostratic.* Amsterdam, 1984.
28. BYNON, James: *Current Progress in Afroasiatic Linguistics: Papers of the Third International Hamito-Semitic Congress, London, 1978.* Amsterdam, 1984.
29. PAPROTTÉ, Wolf & René DIRVEN (eds): *The Ubiquity of Metaphor: Metaphor in Language and Thought.* Amsterdam, 1985.
30. HALL, Robert A., Jr.: *Proto-Romance Morphology.* Amsterdam, 1984.
31. GUILLAUME, Gustave: *Foundations for a Science of Language.* Translated and with an introd. by Walter Hirtle and John Hewson. Amsterdam, 1984.
32. COPELAND, James E. (ed.): *New Directions in Linguistics and Semiotics.* Houston/Amsterdam, 1984. No rights for US/Can. *Customers from USA and Canada: please order from Rice University.*
33. VERSTEEGH, Kees: *Pidginization and Creolization: The Case of Arabic.* Amsterdam, 1984.
34. FISIAK, Jacek (ed.): *Papers from the VIth International Conference on Historical Linguistics, Poznan, 22-26 August 1983.* Amsterdam, 1985.
35. COLLINGE, N.E.: *The Laws of Indo-European.* Amsterdam, 1985.
36. KING, Larry D. & Catherine A. MALEY (eds): *Selected Papers from the XIIIth Linguistics Symposium on Romance Languages.* Amsterdam, 1985.
37. GRIFFEN, T.D.: *Aspects of Dynamic Phonology.* Amsterdam, 1985.
38. BROGYANYI, Bela & Thomas KRÖMMELBEIN (eds): *Germanic Dialects: Linguistic and Philological Investigations.* Amsterdam, 1986.
39. BENSON, James D., Michael J. CUMMINGS & William S. GREAVES (eds): *Linguistics in a Systemic Perspective.* Amsterdam, 1988.
40. FRIES, Peter Howard and Nancy (eds): *Toward an Understanding of Language: Charles C. Fries in Perspective.* Amsterdam, 1985.
41. EATON, Roger, et al. (eds): *Papers from the 4th International Conference on English Historical Linguistics.* Amsterdam, 1985.
42. MAKKAI, Adam & Alan K. MELBY (eds): *Linguistics and Philosophy. Essays in honor of Rulon S. Wells.* Amsterdam, 1985.
43. AKAMATSU, Tsutomu: *The Theory of Neutralization and the Archiphoneme in Functional Phonology.* Amsterdam, 1988.
44. JUNGRAITHMAYR, Herrmann & Walter W. MUELLER (eds): *Proceedings of the 4th International Hamito-Semitic Congress.* Amsterdam, 1987.
45. KOOPMAN, W.F., F.C. VAN DER LEEK, O. FISCHER & R. EATON (eds): *Explanation and Linguistic Change.* Amsterdam, 1987.
46. PRIDEAUX, Gary D., and William J. BAKER: *Strategies and Structures: The Processing of Relative Clauses.* Amsterdam, 1986.
47. LEHMANN, Winfred P.: *Language Typology 1985. Papers from the Linguistic Typology Symposium, Moscow, 9-13 Dec. 1985.* Amsterdam, 1986.
48. RAMAT, Anna Giacalone (ed.): *Proceedings of the VII International Conference on Historical Linguistics, Pavia 9-13 September 1985.* Amsterdam, 1987.
49. WAUGH, Linda R. & Stephen RUDY (eds): *New Vistas in Grammar: Invariance and Variation.* Amsterdam/Philadelphia, 1991.
50. RUDZKA-OSTYN, Brygida (ed.): *Topics in Cognitive Linguistics.* Amsterdam/Philadelphia, 1988.
51. CHATTERJEE, Ranjit: *Aspect and Meaning in Slavic and Indic.* Amsterdam/Philadelphia, 1988.
52. FASOLD, Ralph & Deborah SCHIFFRIN (eds): *Language Change and Variation.* Amsterdam/Philadelphia, 1989.
53. SANKOFF, David (ed.): *Diversity and Diachrony.* Amsterdam, 1986.
54. WEIDERT, Alfons: *Tibeto-Burman Tonology. A Comparative Analysis.* Amsterdam, 1987.
55. HALL, Robert A. Jr.: *Linguistics and Pseudo-Linguistics.* Amsterdam, 1987.

56. HOCKETT, Charles F.: *Refurbishing our Foundations. Elementary Linguistics from an Advanced Point of View*. Amsterdam, 1987.
57. BUBENIK, Vít: *Hellenistic and Roman Greece as a Sociolinguistic Area*. Amsterdam/Philadelphia, 1989.
58. ARBEITMAN, Yoël L.: *FUCUS. A Semitic/Afrasian Gathering in Remembrance of Albert Ehrman*. Amsterdam/Philadelphia, 1988.
59. VOORST, Jan van: *Event Structure*. Amsterdam/Philadelphia, 1988.
60. KIRSCHNER, Carl and Janet DECESARIS (eds): *Studies in Romance Linguistics*. Amsterdam/Philadelphia, 1989.
61. CORRIGAN, Roberta, Fred ECKMAN and Michael NOONAN (eds): *Linguistic Categorization*. Amsterdam/Philadelphia, 1989.
62. FRAJZYNGIER, Zygmunt (ed.): *Current Progress in Chadic Linguistics*. Amsterdam/Philadelphia, 1989.
63. EID, Mushira (ed.): *Perspectives on Arabic Linguistics I. Papers from the First Annual Symposium on Arabic Linguistics*. Amsterdam/Philadelphia, 1990.
64. BROGYANYI, Bela (ed.): *Prehistory, History, and Historiography of Language, Speech, and Linguistic Theory*. Amsterdam/Philadelphia, 1992.
65. ADAMSON, Sylvia, Vivien A. LAW, Nigel VINCENT and Susan WRIGHT (eds): *Papers from the 5th International Conference of English Historical Linguistics*. Amsterdam/Philadelphia, 1990.
66. ANDERSEN, Henning and Konrad KOERNER (eds): *Historical Linguistics 1987. Papers from the 8th International Conference on Historical Linguistics, Lille, August 30-September 4, 1987*. Amsterdam/Philadelphia, 1990.
67. LEHMANN, Winfred (ed.): *Language Typology 1987. Systematic Balance in Language. Papers from the Linguistic Typology Symposium, Berkeley, 1-3 December 1987*. Amsterdam/Philadelphia, 1990.
68. BALL, Martin, James FIFE, Erich POPPE and Jenny ROWLAND (eds): *Celtic Linguistics / Ieithyddiaeth Geltaidd. Readings in the Brythonic Languages. Festschrift for T. Arwyn Watkins*. Amsterdam/Philadelphia, 1990.
69. WANNER, Dieter and Douglas A. KIBBEE (eds): *New Analyses in Romance Linguistics. Papers from the XVIII Linguistic Symposium on Romance Languages, Urbana-Champaign, April 7-9, 1988*. Amsterdam/Philadelphia, 1991.
70. JENSEN, John T.: *Morphology. Word Structure in Generative Grammar*. Amsterdam/Philadelphia, 1990.
71. O'GRADY, WILLIAM: *Categories and Case. The sentence structure of Korean*. Amsterdam/Philadelphia, 1991.
72. EID, Mushira and John McCARTHY (eds): *Perspectives on Arabic Linguistics II Papers from the Second Annual Symposium on Arabic Linguistics*. Amsterdam/Philadelphia, 1990.
73. STAMENOV, Maxim (ed.): *Current Advances in Semantic Theory*. Amsterdam/Philadelphia, 1992.
74. LAEUFER, Christiane and Terrell A. MORGAN (eds): *Theoretical Analyses in Romance Linguistics*. Amsterdam/Philadelphia, 1992.
75. DROSTE, Flip G. and John E. JOSEPH (eds): *Linguistic Theory and Grammatical Description*. Amsterdam/Philadelphia, 1991.
76. WICKENS, Mark A.: *Grammatical Number in English Nouns*. Amsterdam/Philadelphia, 1992.
77. BOLTZ, William G. and Michael C. SHAPIRO (eds): *Studies in the Historical Phonology of Asian Languages*. Amsterdam/Philadelphia, 1991.
78. KAC, Michael B.: *Grammars and Grammaticality*. Amsterdam/Philadelphia, 1992.
79. ANTONSEN, Elmer H. and Hans Henrich HOCK (eds): *STÆFCRÆFT: Studies in Germanic Linguistics*. Amsterdam/Philadelphia, 1991.
80. COMRIE, Bernard and Mushira EID (eds): *Perspectives on Arabic Linguistics III*. Amsterdam/Philadelphia, 1991.

81. LEHMANN, Winfred P. & H.J. HEWITT (eds): *Language Typology 1988. Typological Models in Reconstruction.* Amsterdam/Philadelphia, 1991.
82. VAN VALIN, Robert D. (ed.): *Advances in Role and Reference Grammar.* Amsterdam/Philadelphia, 1993.
83. FIFE, James & Erich POPPE (eds): *Studies in Brythonic Word Order.* Amsterdam/Philadelphia, 1991.
84. DAVIS, Garry W. & Gregory K. IVERSON (eds): *Explanation in Historical Linguistics.* Amsterdam/Philadelphia, 1992.
85. BROSELOW, Ellen, Mushira EID & John McCARTHY (eds): *Perspectives on Arabic Linguistics IV.* Amsterdam/Philadelphia, 1992.
86. KESS, Joseph L.: *Psycholinguistics. Psychology, Linguistics, and the Study of Natural Language.* Amsterdam/Philadelphia, 1992.
87. BROGYANYI, Bela & Reiner LIPP (eds): *Historical Philology: Greek, Latin, and Romance Papers in Honor of Oswald Szemerényi II.* Amsterdam/Philadelphia, 1992.
88. SHIELDS, Kenneth.: *A History of Indo-European Verb Morphology.* Amsterdam/Philadelphia, 1992.
89. BURRIDGE, Kate: *Syntactic Change in Germanic. A study of some aspects of language change in Germanic with particular reference to Middle Dutch.* Amsterdam/Philadelphia, 1992.
90. KING, Larry D.: *The Semantic Structure of Spanish. Meaning and grammatical form.* Amsterdam/Philadelphia, 1992.
91. HIRSCHBÜHLER, Paul and Konrad KOERNER (eds): *Romance Languages and Modern Linguistic Theory. Selected papers from the XX Linguistic Symposium on Romance Languages.* Amsterdam/Philadelphia, 1992.
92. POYATOS, Fernando: *Paralanguage: A linguistic and interdisciplinary approach to interactive speech and sounds.* Amsterdam/Philadelphia, 1993.
93. LIPPI-GREEN, Rosina (ed.): *Recent Developments in Germanic Linguistics.* Amsterdam/Philadelphia, 1992.
94. HAGÈGE, Claude: *The Language Builder. An essay on the human signature in linguistic morphogenesis.* Amsterdam/Philadelphia, 1993.
95. MILLER, D. Gary: *Complex Verb Formation.* Amsterdam/Philadelphia, 1993.
96. LIEB, Hans-Heinrich (ed.): *Prospects for a New Structuralism.* Amsterdam/Philadelphia, 1992.
97. BROGYANYI, Bela and Reiner LIPP (eds): *Comparative-Historical Linguistics: Indo-European and Finno-Ugric. Papers in honor of Oswald Szemerényi III.* Amsterdam/Philadelphia, 1993.
98. EID, Mushira and Gregory K. IVERSON: *Principles and Prediction. The analysis of natural language.* Amsterdam/Philadelphia, 1993.
99. JENSEN, John T.: *English Phonology.* Amsterdam/Philadelphia, 1993.
100. MUFWENE, Salikoko S. and Lioba MOSHI (eds). *Topics in African Linguistics.* Amsterdam/Philadelphia, 1993.
101. EID, Mushira and Clive HOLES (eds): *Perspectives on Arabic Linguistics V. Papers from the Fifth Annual Symposium on Arabic Linguistics.* Amsterdam/Philadelphia, 1993.
102. GARGOV, George and Petko STAYNOV (eds): *Explorations in Language and Cognition.* Amsterdam/Philadelphia, 1993.
103. ASHBY, William J., Marianne MITHUN, Giorgio PERISSINOTTO and Eduardo RAPOSO (eds): *Linguistic Perspectives on the Romance Languages.* Amsterdam/Philadelphia, 1993.
104. KURZOVÁ, Helena: *From Indo-European to Latin. The evolution of a morphosyntactic type.* Amsterdam/Philadelphia, 1993.
105. HUALDE, José Ignacio and Jon ORTIZ DE URBINA (eds): *Generative Studies in Basque Linguistics.* Amsterdam/Philadelphia, 1993.
106. AERTSEN, Henk and Robert J. JEFFERS (eds): *Historical Linguistics 1989. Papers from the 9th International Conference on Historical Linguistics, New Brunswick, 14-18 August 1989.* Amsterdam/Philadelphia, 1993.

107. VAN MARLE, Jaap (ed.): *Historical Linguistics 1991. Papers from the 10th International Conference on Historical Linguistics, Amsterdam, August 12-16, 1991.* Amsterdam/Philadelphia, 1993.
108. LIEB, Hans-Heinrich: *Linguistic Variables. Towards a unified theory of linguistic variation.* Amsterdam/Philadelphia, 1993.
109. PAGLIUCA, William (ed.): *Perspectives on Grammaticalization.* Amsterdam/Philadelphia, n.y.p.
110. SIMONE, Raffaele (ed.): *Iconicity in Language.* Amsterdam/Philadelphia, n.y.p.